Haynes for HOME DIY

Electrical Appliance Manual

3rd Edition

DIY repair and maintenance of a wide range of domestic electrical appliances

First edition published in 1991
Reprinted 1991
2nd Edition 1995
Reprinted 1996
Reprinted 1997
Reprinted 1998 (twice)
Reprinted 1999
3rd Edition 2000

Published by:
Haynes Publishing Group Sparkford, Nr Yeovil, Somerset BA22 7JJ

Haynes Publications Inc. 861 Lawrence Drive, Newbury Park, California 91320, USA

British Library Cataloguing in Publication Data
Dixon, Graham
The home electrical appliance manual.
1. Households. Equipment. Maintenance
I. Title 683.80288

ISBN 1 85960 800 0

Library of Congress catalog card number 91 -71115

Printed in Great Britain by
J. H. Haynes & Co. Ltd

Contents

Contents

Introduction

Each year sees an increase in the number and variety of small electrical appliances. Some are for convenience; some are luxuries and others for saving labour. Indoor and outdoor electrical appliances of various shapes and sizes are to be found in every home. From the humble kettle to video recorder, the electric drill to the lawn strimmer, they all have one thing in common – at some time they will fail to function correctly. It is usually at this point that you realise what a necessity this appliance is and how you have come to depend on it. Often it is the lack of care and maintenance that is responsible for failure in both old and new equipment.

Mass production and volume sales result in the cost of many smaller appliances being relatively low. One may be forgiven for concluding that, in some instances, repair would be neither practical nor worthwhile. This may be due to the lack of spare parts for small appliances or difficulty in obtaining them. Gone are many of the smaller shops who were willing to repair the smaller items, and those that remain are forced to charge realistic labour charges that can make the repair uneconomical to the customer.

The penalty paid in disposing of a complete item, when only a simple fault or previous poor maintenance is to blame, not only hurts one's pocket, but is more far-reaching, given that much of each appliance is made from non-renewable sources, and the disposal of many items or their contents can be dangerous. It would seem that with better care of a product and the extension of its

working life by repair of a simple fault, the benefits are at least three-fold.

1 Money saved by repairing rather than renewal.

2 Environmental benefit – making better use of ultimately restricted resources. We cannot 'un-invent' such items to save resources but we can all do our bit in making sure they are used efficiently with as little waste as possible.

3 The satisfaction of successful repair.

It is with these points in mind that this book has been written. The main aim is to help you to understand how many of our household items work, which in turn will help you to understand how and why faults occur, how to prevent faults from occurring, how to repair faults and thus, ultimately, to prolong the working life of your appliances. By reading the book you will become more aware of safety around the home due to a better understanding of your electrical equipment and its limitations. Regular checks for faults, which can be rectified prior to failure or accident, greatly increase the safety of your appliances. You will also gain more efficient use of your items through understanding their correct operation.

Safety in the use of and servicing/repair of items is paramount and in no way should it be compromised. All the checking, servicing and repairs highlighted in this book are carried out with the appliance completely isolated from its electrical supply. Under no circumstances should any machine be worked on in a live state, ie still connected to the mains supply.

Such practices are dangerous, not only to yourself but others around you, and are totally unnecessary. All checking and testing in the book can be carried out using battery-powered test equipment.

The manual has been thoughtfully designed to help you understand the function and operation of the internal components of various appliances. Flowcharts, diagrams and step-by-step photographic sequences have been used to attain a logical pattern to fault finding. This enables the reader to follow a sequence of events in theory (using the flowcharts), in practice (using the photographic sequences) and in detail (using the diagrams). Such an approach will help you find the fault and give you the know-how and confidence to repair it. An important aspect is the regular checking and maintenance of your appliances, which will be covered in the individual sections. The information within this book covers an extremely wide variety of popular home electrical products but unfortunately not all appliances could be included. However, the way in which the principle functions such as heating, motors, thermostats etc., are split into sections allows the reader to apply the information to most if not all home electrical appliances.

I hope you will use this manual to assist you in the Do-it-Yourself repair of your appliances. Hopefully your faults will be few and far between, but remember prevention is better than cure and regular checks and servicing of your appliances can prevent many bigger problems arising in the future.

Chapter 1
A General safety guide

Electricity at all voltages is to be respected. Those who do not observe the basic rules of electricity are not only a danger to themselves but to those around them. Electrical accidents should be regarded as avoidable. Most are due to plain carelessness and the failure to follow basic rules of electricity even when they are already known.

There are in the region of sixteen million homes in Britain supplied with electricity, each home having on average twenty five electrical appliances. With such a volume of items, it may be a surprise to find that fatalities due to electrical accidents are less than eighty per year. Although this is a small percentage figure in terms of population and only represents 1 per cent of the 8,000 deaths resulting from accidents in the home, the figure is still too high.

The three most common causes of shock or fires from electrical appliances are:

1 Faulty wiring of the appliances, ie frayed or damaged flex or cable, incorrect fuse, poor socket, poor/damaged plug, incorrectly wired plug, etc.
2 Misuse of the appliance. The combination of water and electricity greatly increases the possibility of injury.
3 Continuing to use an electrical appliance knowing it to be unsafe, for example with a cracked casing, faulty plug, damaged cable, faulty on/off switch, etc.

By being aware of the need for safety, several of the above faults can be avoided. Others can be eliminated by regular inspection and immediate correction of faults, failure or wear. As for misuse, this may be due to a purely foolhardy approach or genuine ignorance of danger. This can be overcome by understanding and, above all, acting upon the guidelines in this book. If at anytime you feel you lack the ability to do a particular job yourself, then it is best not to try. You can still carry out the diagnosis of the problem thus ensuring that any work carried out

by a repair company is correct. This alone can sometimes save much time and expense.

DO'S

● Thoroughly read all the information in this book prior to putting it into practice.
● Isolate any appliance before repair or inspection commences.
● Correctly fit the mains plug (see *Plugs and sockets*), ensuring the connections are in the correct position, tight and the cord clamp fitted on the outer insulation of the cable.
● Check that the socket used is in good condition and has a sound earth path (see *Basics – electrical*).
● Take time to consider the problem at hand and allow enough time to complete the job without rushing.
● Follow a methodical approach to the stripdown of the item and make notes. This helps greatly with reassembly.
● Double-check everything.
● Ask or seek help if in doubt.
● Ensure that only the correct rated fuse is used. It is dangerous to exceed the required rating. Even if the appliance appears to work normally, little or no protection will be afforded should a fault occur.

DON'TS

● Do not work on any machine that is still plugged in even if the socket switch is OFF. Always isolate fully – PLUG OUT.
● Do not in ANY circumstances repair damaged flex or cables with insulation tape.
● Do not sacrifice safety by affecting a temporary repair.

General

Consider your own safety and that of other people.
Act in a way that prevents incidents from becoming accidents.
Use your common sense and think before acting.
Tidy workplaces make safer workplaces.
Identify hazards.
Observe the rule of Safety First.
Never underestimate the dangers.

Switch off! Always withdraw plug and disconnect from mains.
Appliances vary – make sure you have a suitable replacement part.
For screws use a screwdriver, for nuts a spanner, for knurled nuts use pliers.
Examine and clean all connections before fitting new parts.
Tighten all screws and nuts firmly.
Your safety depends on these simple rules.
Fuses: Up to 250W 1A; 750W 3A; 750 to 3000W 13A.
Insulation is for your protection. Don't interfere.
Renew worn or damaged appliance flex.
Secure flex clamps and all protective covers.
Test physically and electrically on completion.

Plug wiring

Plug wiring must be connected according to the following code to ensure safety. The colours are as follows:

Live – Brown (or Red), symbol 'L'

Neutral – Blue (or Black), symbol 'N'

Earth – Green/Yellow (or Green), symbol 'E'

The colours in brackets are those used until the current international standards were introduced. They may still be found on some equipment. Plug terminals are identified either by colour (old or new) or by the letter symbols shown.

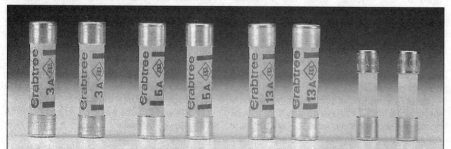

Ensure that only the correct rated fuse is used. It is dangerous to exceed the required rating. Even if the appliance appears to work normally, little or no protection will be afforded should a fault occur

Chapter 2
Basics – electrical

Special note: *Variations in supply systems used in countries other than the U.K.*

As detailed in the text in this chapter, various types of earthing systems may be encountered – one of the most popular being the PME system whereby neutral and earth are BONDED (linked) at the supply point to the property. The choice of which supply system (and ultimately which earth system your property has) is a matter for your supply authority. The requirement of a sound earth path however is common to all domestic systems.

For the sake of safety around the home or office, a basic understanding of electricity is essential. Even if you don't intend to carry out any repairs or servicing of your appliances yourself, a sound understanding of household electrical supply will prove invaluable in the long run. Ignorance is no protection against either your or a third party's errors, whether it be on repairs, servicing or the installation of appliances. It is with this in mind that this chapter has been written. It is not an in-depth study of the subject – there are many books that contain more detailed information for those who want to know more about electricity.

In this instance, the aim is to impart a safe knowledge without too much technical data. Some may argue that a little knowledge is a dangerous thing, but I believe that total ignorance is a much greater danger. To be informed is to be enlightened – to be aware of danger helps one to avoid it and to understand how and why certain safety criteria should be adopted.

The illustration below shows a simplified, but typical household supply. The substation has power supplied to it at very high voltage (400,000 volts) in three-phase form. This supply is converted at the substation, via a transformer, down to 230 volt single-phase and is then distributed to our homes. In normal circumstances, current flows from the live supply of the substation's transformer, through the electrical items being used in the house and back via the neutral conductor (cable) to the substation transformer's neutral pole (a closed loop). The neutral terminal of the transformer is in turn connected to the ground (earth – meaning in this case, the general mass of the earth), as shown in the bottom illustration. It is usual to use the armoured sheath of the electricity supply authority's cable in order to provide a low

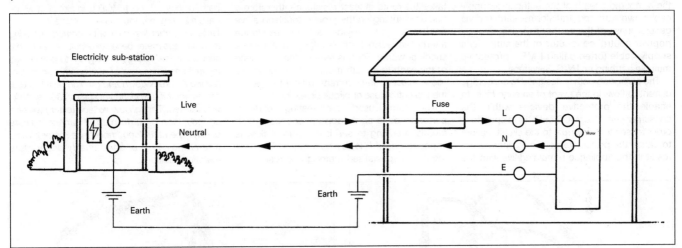

Typical household supply

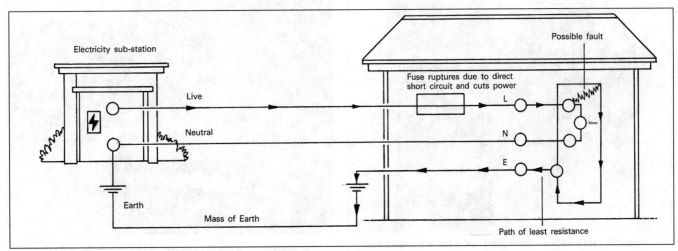

Earth path if fault occurs

Result of high resistance or break in normal earth path. Fault will find path of least resistance

impedance continuous link back to the supply transformers' start point. Various types of earthing can be encountered: connection to the armoured sheath of the authority's supply cable; own earth rod; transformer earth rod via general mass of the earth; or the increasingly popular neutral conductor of the authority's supply cable (often called PME – protective multiple earthing or TN-C-S system).

The earth loop path is designed to encourage current to flow, in the event of an earth fault, to enable the protective devices within the consumer unit (fuse, MCB or RCD) to operate in order to isolate the supply to the circuit. Failure to cause the protective device to operate will result in the appliance remaining live with the

consequence that any person touching the appliance will receive a nasty, possibly fatal, electric shock. Remember, electricity always takes the route of least resistance, therefore a person standing on the ground touching a live appliance can provide a low resistance alternative earth path resulting in a severe shock or worse. For this reason, the resistance of the earth loop path must be low enough to allow sufficient fault current to flow to operate the protective fuse or circuit breaker.

The term used for testing earthing performance is earth loop impedance, which means checking to see if the current flow is impeded and if it is, by how much. This test requires a specialised meter giving resistance

figures in ohms, the maximum reading recommended by the IEE (Institution of Electrical Engineers) being 1.1 ohms for a domestic earth path, unless a Type 1 MCB is in circuit in which case a 2 ohm maximum is acceptable.

Note: *A correct test cannot be carried out using a low voltage meter because a fault can exist that allows the low voltage of, say, 9V to pass easily (eg just one tiny strand of wire poorly connected) but would break down and go high resistance or open-circuit if a working voltage of 230V at 13As was applied. Though low voltage testing will give an indication of earth path, it cannot indicate quality. The earth loop impedance meter gives a clearer indication of earth quality under more realistic conditions.*

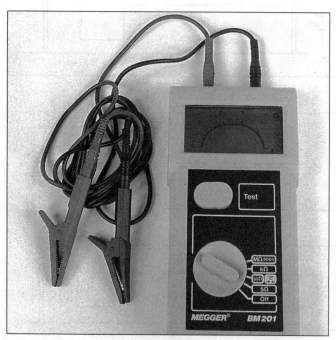

A versatile test meter incorporating 500 V DC insulation test facility

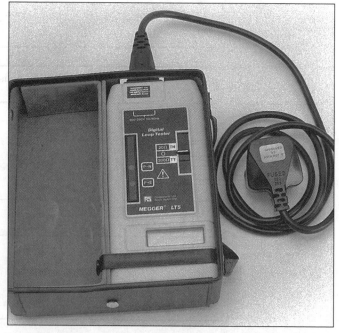

A professional earth loop test meter gives the only true indication of the earth path quality

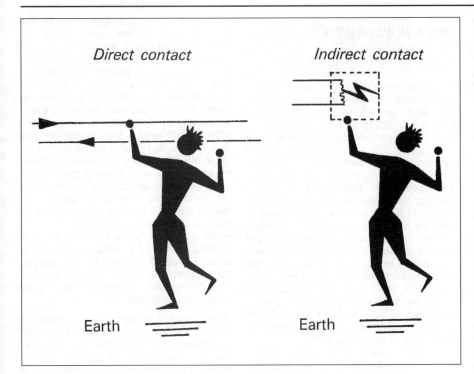

Direct contact   Indirect contact

Earth   Earth

What is an earth fault?

An earth fault is defined as the condition where electricity flows to earth when in normal circumstances, it should not do so. There are two recognised ways in which this may happen: direct and indirect.
Direct – when contact is made directly with the current-carrying conductor which is designed to carry that current.
Indirect – touching a part of an appliance, that would not normally carry current but is doing so due to a fault.

What is a consumer unit?

The consumer unit is where the supply into the house is split into separate circuits, ie those for lights, sockets, etc. It houses a main isolation switch or combined RCD which is

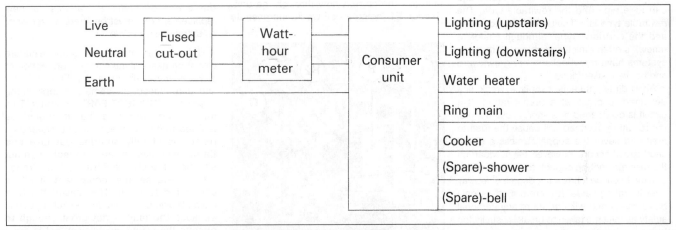

				Lighting (upstairs)
Live				Lighting (downstairs)
Neutral	Fused cut-out	Watt-hour meter	Consumer unit	Water heater
Earth				Ring main
				Cooker
				(Spare)-shower
				(Spare)-bell

A typical house insulation

Typical older-style consumer unit with isolation switch and wired fuses only

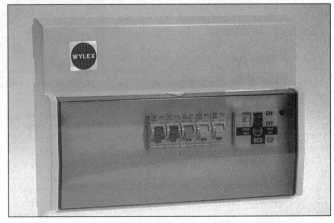

Modern consumer unit with RCD main switch and MCBs on all circuits

used to isolate (remove power from) all the circuits in the house. Also housed within the unit are various fuse-carriers for cartridge or rewirable fuses or a Miniature Circuit Breaker (MCB) in place of fuses. Each circuit leading from the consumer unit has its own rating of fuse or MCB and only that fuse rating and no other must be used.

NOTE: *Even when the consumer unit is switched off there is still a live supply to it. Do not remove the covers of the consumer unit or tackle any inspection or repair to this item without seeking further information. Faults other than fuse renewal are best left to skilled electrical engineers. Although assistance may be available from other publications, extreme care should be exercised. As mentioned earlier, it is not the aim of this book to encourage the repair or maintenance of items that are not fully isolated.*

All about fuses

Two versions of fuses are to be found: the cartridge type and the rewirable type. The rewirable type is difficult and fiddly to rewire and the cartridge type, although easier to renew, is often difficult to obtain. Both these systems have drawbacks in being awkward and not very 'user friendly'.

An ordinary fuse is simply a weak link designed to break at a preset rating. If a circuit is overloaded or a short circuit occurs, the resulting overload will cause the fuse to melt and sever the supply. Unless a direct short circuit occurs, however, the overload on the fuse may not be enough to cause the fuse to blow because it has a fair degree of leeway over its rating value. It therefore offers only basic safety and will not afford any personal safety as the time taken to break is usually too long.

To the old familiar imperial ratings for fuses and circuit breakers have now been added the international Renard ratings. A complete changeover will eventually be effected for European standardisation.

Fuse manufacturers are still using the imperial sizes whilst circuit breaker manufacturers have mostly changed to the new ratings. An equivalence chart is shown below:

Current Rating Imp	Renard	Typical Circuit
5	6	Lighting
10	10	
15	16	1mm. htr
20	20	
30	32	Ring main
45	40	Cooker/shower

Miniature Circuit Breakers

The miniature circuit breaker (MCB) is now widely used and overcomes all the problems associated with ordinary fuses. The MCB is a small sophisticated unit that affords a much higher degree of protection than an ordinary fuse. It is tamper-proof and the unit involved is easily identified when one has tripped (switch moves to 'OFF' position). Most importantly, MCBs cannot be reset if the fault still exists which eliminates the practice of putting in the wrong fuse wire or cartridge to get things working – a foolish and most dangerous practice). MCBs are available in similar ratings to ordinary fuses and operate in two ways. Referring to the accompanying photograph, current flows into the unit at H1 and along G through coil E1 and on to the moving contact D (shown here open circuit). Contact D in the ON position would be resting on fixed contact C and so current would flow to H2.

Two fault conditions may arise; firstly – short circuit. This type of fault would quickly increase the current flow through the unit. Section E1, being a coil would increase its

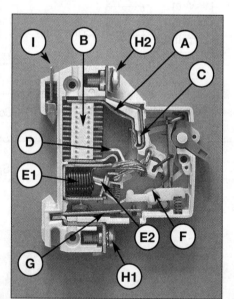

Mechanism of miniature circuit breaker

A   Arc runner
B   Arc chamber
C   Fixed contact
D   Moving contact
E1 Solenoid coil
E2 Moving core
F   Trip bar
G   Thermo-metal
H1 Wiring terminal
H2 Wiring terminal
I   Fixing

magnetic field and as a result attract E2 into the coil centre. This action trips the mechanism arm F and causes C – D to open circuit. Conductor A and arc chamber B act to suppress the arc formed on the contact point. This is done by the arc runners drawing the arc across the arc chamber where it is chopped into small arcs which are quickly extinguished. The action of the MCB is much quicker than an ordinary fuse wire. The second type of fault could simply be an overload on the circuit and, although exceeding the safe working load of the circuit, it would not cause the solenoid to trip. In this type of situation, the current flowing through G causes the conductor to heat up. The conductor is made of a tri-metal plate that bends when heated. The bending action of the conductor trips arm F, causing C and D to open circuit as before. This operation again is much better than fuse wire and calibration to higher tolerances is possible.

Note: *These units are factory-calibrated to extremely accurate tolerances and must not be tampered with nor attempts made to readjust them. The internal workings are only shown to help understand their operation. In the event of faults or failures, a new replacement unit must be fitted. No repair or adjustment is possible.*

Unfortunately, neither fuses nor miniature circuit breakers alone can give protection to anyone involved in a DIRECT EARTH situation. Indeed, the same can apply in the case of an INDIRECT EARTH contact. This may sound confusing, but it should be realised that in a 'direct contact' situation a person is literally shorting out Live and Earth, whereas in an 'indirect' contact situation, the Live to Earth path is already there because the equipment itself is connected to earth. The reason the fuse hasn't blown or the circuit breaker tripped is because the fault is not great enough to operate the safety mechanism, yet is great enough to be fatal. For instance, a 10A fuse would never blow with an 8A earth fault on the circuit, yet 8A constitutes a very dangerous level of earth fault current.

Residual Current Devices

To afford a higher degree of protection, another device has been developed, and is available in various forms.
1 Mounted within the consumer unit to protect all or selected circuits.
2 As individual socket protection.
3 An adaptor to be used as portable protection and used where required.

The name given to this device in all its forms is the Residual Current Device (RCD). It

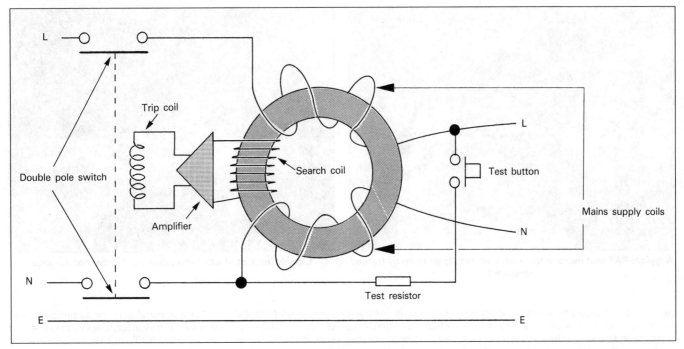

A simplified RCD circuit

may also be called a Residual Current Circuit Breaker (RCCB). In the early days of its introduction, it was known as an Earth Leakage Circuit Breaker (ELCB).

The primary protection is the integrity of the earthing, RCDs, in addition to the earthing, provide a much higher degree of protection depending upon the degree of sensitivity. For personal protection it is recommended that a sensitivity of 30 mA is used.

It is generally considered that an earth fault of 1A or more is a fire risk, 50 mA or more provides a shock risk which can have varying effects upon the human body depending upon the value of earth fault current and the body resistance of the person and, of course, their state of health. The heartbeat cycle is about 0.75 second. It is therefore necessary to cut off the fault current in less than one cardiac cycle. The Wiring Regulations stipulate that for Indirect Contact protection isolation must occur within 0.4 second.

How does an RCD work?

An RCD protects by constantly monitoring the current flowing in the live and neutral wires supplying a circuit or an individual item of equipment. In normal circumstances the current flowing in the two wires is equal but, when an earth leakage occurs due to a fault or an accident, an imbalance occurs and this is detected by the RCD which automatically cuts off the power in a split second.

To be effective, the RCD must operate very quickly and at a low earth leakage current. Those most frequently recommended are

designed to detect earth leakage faults in excess of 30 mA (30/1000ths of an amp) and to disconnect the power supply within 200 ms (the rated sensitivity); these limits are well inside the safety margin within which electrocution or fire would not be expected to occur.

It should now be apparent that RCDs are designed to sever mains current should your electrical appliance malfunction electrically, or should you cut through the mains cable of your lawnmower for instance. They are simply a fail-safe device and should be used as such. In my opinion, used correctly they are an invaluable asset to your household.

Note: *The use of an RCD must be in addition to normal overload protection, ie fuses or MCBs, and not instead of it. All residual current devices have a test button facility. It is essential that this is tested regularly to verify that the device operates. For use with adaptors or sockets, or for outside use, test before each operation. If failure occurs (does not trip, or trip appears sluggish or hard to obtain) have the unit tested immediately. This will require an RCD test meter and is best left to a qualified electrician.*

RCD's and Double Insulated Appliances

Not all appliances require earth facilities and many small appliances such as hairdryers, shavers etc., fall into this category and are classed as double insulated 'Class 2' appliances. This denotes that the design of the product incorporates special double

layered insulation construction methods that do not require an earth path connection. These products are only fitted with two-core flex at manufacture. The electrical safety of the product and the user depends on the integrity of this double layer construction. It is essential that these products be checked closely for any damage such as cracks in the plastic casings, missing covers, screws etc.

If the appliance has been dismantled for repair or inspection it is vital that all internal components be refitted correctly. Make a careful note of all the relevant parts and their correct location and orientation as you take the item apart. The electrical safety of double insulated appliances depends on the integrity of ALL its components, ensure they are ALL in good order and in their correct positions. Renew any items that show signs of damage or are missing. Although the appliance may appear to work, missing, damaged or incorrectly assembled components pose a very serious electrical hazard to the user.

You should now be aware that the use of an RCD is of great benefit when using any electrical product and this is especially so with 'double insulated' appliances.

The full electrical insulation testing of 'double insulated' appliances requires the application of very high voltages. This test is often referred to as a 'flash test' and as such must only be carried out by trained personnel using the correct test equipment in a controlled environment. If you are in any doubt as to the integrity of the 'double insulated' product you are using or have just

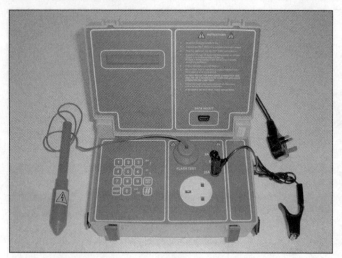

A typical PAT test meter with 'flash test' facility as used by trained personnel

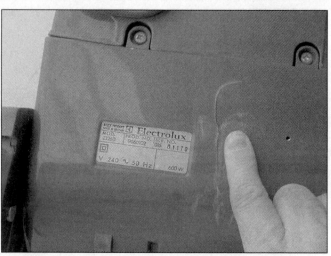

Closely inspect 'double insulated' appliances for damage

repaired, then it would be wise to have it 'flash tested'. All domestic small appliance repair businesses should conduct this type of test whenever they repair double insulated products.

The 'flash test' is often used during the routine electrical test procedures carried out under the mandatory PAT (Portable Appliance Testing) criteria laid out for commercial businesses. PAT is in essence an MOT for electrical items used in commercial environments, offices, pubs, clubs, factories etc. The testing should be carried out on a regular basis and all items logged and labelled with the results. It should not be too difficult to trace electrical or appliance repair companies in your area that can, for a small fee, perform the required tests. An interesting point to note is that it is mandatory for all businesses to have their electrical appliances safety checked and recorded (PAT) on a regular basis but no such requirement as yet exists for appliances used in the domestic environment. If you require further information on the subject of PAT testing contact the Health and Safety Executive (HSE). Large bookshops normally stock a range of HSE titles.

Chapter 3
Tools and Equipment

Most appliances found in the home do not require very specialised tools for servicing or repair, but in some instances, tamper-proof screws or fixings may have been used, eg Torx head, Allen head or unusual tops to screws which do need a special type of tool. These specialist 'bits' are now quite readily available in kit form from such manufacturers as 'Kamasa'. They can be obtained from local specialist tool shops, DIY outlets or by mail order from suppliers such as 'Maplin'. Alternatively, you can, with care, often adapt an existing tool from your kit (as described in the hairdryer and vacuum sections).

Most repairs can be completed with a selection of the following tools: a good range of cross-blade and flat-blade screwdrivers, a pair of combination pliers, ordinary pliers and a simple multimeter. Most people who are DIY-orientated will already own most, if not all, of these tools. It is not too difficult to build up a good selection of tools, which will allow you to tackle the faults that you are likely to come across on your appliances. Most of the large DIY stores will stock the tools you need, often at a good saving. When buying tools, check the quality. Cheap screwdrivers are often poorly made and finished and will soon prove to be a false economy and possibly dangerous. There are, however, many tools on the market that are of a reasonable quality and inexpensive – try to buy the best that your budget will allow. Remember that the tools that you buy are a long-term investment and should give you years of useful service. As with any investment, they should be looked after and kept in a serviceable condition. Always make sure they are clean and dry before storage.

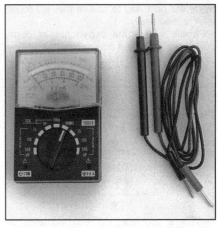

Multimeter (measures amps, volts and ohms)

Anti-tamper tool kit

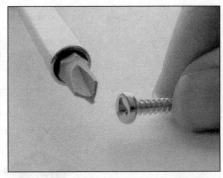

This close-up shows a tri-wing anti-tamper screw and removal bit from the kit

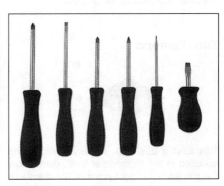

Range of cross-blade and flat-blade screwdrivers

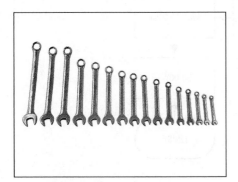

Combination open-end & ring spanners

Self-locking pliers

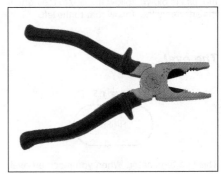

Ordinary pliers

Chapter 4
Using a flowchart

Flowcharts are used from time to time throughout this book. They are designed to help you locate the area or areas of trouble quickly and to show that a step-by-step approach to even the most difficult of faults is by far the best way to ensure they are found and rectified easily.

People with some experience of home computers may need little explanation of how to use a flowchart. The following explanation is for those who are encountering them for the first time.

How they work

At first sight, a flowchart may seem a difficult way to find faults, However, you will find it quite simple to use if you remember a few small but important points. With practice, you will discover how invaluable this method can be in all areas of D-I-Y work. Constructing your own flowchart before attempting a job will be of help when the time comes to reverse the stripdown procedure. For example, you can make notes of what was encountered at that point beside the relevant boxes on the flowchart, including such things as the number of screws and the positions of wires. These are small but essential points – so often forgotten with an unplanned approach.

Only three main types of symbols are used: a rectangle, a diamond and an oval.

The rectangle

This is a process: the box contains an instruction. Carry it out and rejoin the flowchart where you left it, travelling in the direction indicated by the arrows.

The diamond

This asks a question. If the answer to the question in the diamond is 'yes', then follow the line from the right point of the diamond. For example the diamond asks 'Is the fuse blown?'. The junction to the left is marked 'no' and the junction to the right is marked 'yes'. If the fuse is blown, follow the line to the right; if the answer is 'no' follow that to the left.

The oval

This is a terminator. When you reach an oval, you are either starting a chart or finishing one. The text in the oval indicates the action to take.

The following example flowchart illustrates the steps involved in carrying out the simple task of opening a closed door. The arrows indicate the direction to the next step to guide you through the logical sequence.

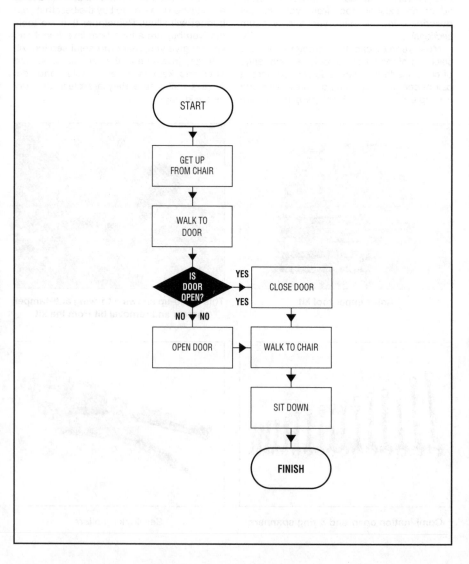

Chapter 5
Electrical circuit testing

Using a meter

Throughout this book, references are made to meters and their use in continuity testing of individual parts of the appliances and their connecting wires. All such testing and checking for 'open' (not allowing for current flow), or 'closed' circuit (allowing current to flow), must be carried out using a battery-powered multimeter or test meter. Testing should NEVER be carried out on live items, ie appliances connected to the mains supply. Remember to completely isolate the appliance from the mains supply before starting any repair work or testing.

Although some meters or testers have the facility to check mains voltages, their use is not recommended for repairs to domestic appliances. Faults can be traced easily by simple low-voltage (battery power) continuity testing, proving that the simplest of meters or even a home-made version like the one described below are quite adequate. Remember that safety is paramount and in no circumstances should it be compromised. Always double check that the appliance is unplugged – a good tip is to keep the plug in view so that no one else can inadvertently plug it in.

If you decide to buy a test meter do not be tempted to get an over complicated one as it could end up confusing and misleading you when in use. Before using your new meter, read the manufacturer's instructions thoroughly and make sure that you fully understand them. The meter used in the photographs is simple to use when continuity testing and has a scale that reads 'open' circuit or 'closed' circuit. It was purchased from a local DIY store and was very reasonably priced. The meter will also help locate faults with car electrics, but as previously stated, using on live mains circuits should not be entertained.

Some multimeters are able to show the resistance value of the item being tested as well as indicating continuity. This can be extremely useful if the correct resistance value of the item being tested is known, although this is by no means essential. Detailed use of the multimeter for this function will be found in its accompanying instruction leaflet.

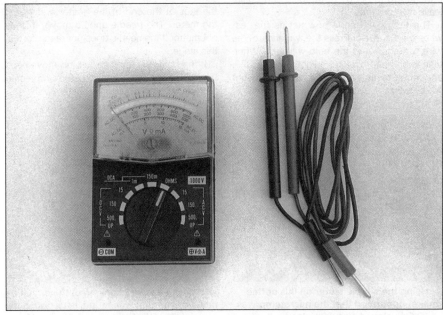

A typical analogue multimeter of the type to be bought in most DIY stores. Try to obtain a meter with a good informative booklet. The meter shown was purchased for a reasonable sum and proved to be useful for many other jobs around the house and car

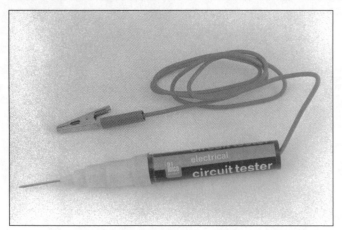

This simple continuity tester was purchased quite cheaply from a local automart. It is a manufactured version of the home made type described

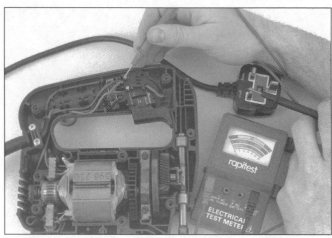

Continuity testing of this jig-saw cable identified an intermittent open circuit fault

A simple continuity tester

This simple device can be used to trace faults in most appliances and is very easy to make. It uses the lack of continuity to its full advantage. To make this tester, you will need a dry torch battery, a bulb of the same voltage and three wires – 1 x 12mm (5in) and 2 x 24mm (10in). Connect the short wire to the positive terminal of the battery and the other end of that wire to the centre terminal of the torch bulb. Attach one of the longer wires to the negative terminal of the battery and leave the other end free. The other wire should be attached to the body of the bulb and again, leave the end free.

The two loose ends now act as the test wires on the tester. Press the two ends of the wire together, and the bulb will light. When testing an open circuit the light will stay OFF, and when testing a 'closed circuit' the light will be ON.

Ensure that the machine is isolated from the main supply before attempting to use a meter. **Note:** *Low voltage bulb type testers of 1½ volts or 3 volts are not able to test the continuity of many components and should be used mainly for wiring fault finding. A test meter like the one shown is required to test components for continuity, ie motors, heaters etc.*

How to test continuity

To test for an open circuit in a component, note and remove the original wiring to the component to be tested, if this is not done, false readings may be given from other items that may be in circuit. The ends of the two probes (of the meter) should be attached to the suspect component. For example, to test a heater for continuity, place the probes on the tags at the end of the heater and watch the meter. The needle should move, it does not matter if the needle does not reach zero at this stage.

If the heater is open circuit (no movement) the heater can then be suspected and tested further. If closed circuit, the heater is OK.

Leap-frog testing – using a meter

Often the most effective way to trace a fault is to use a very simple but logical approach to the process. One such approach is called the leap-frog method and can be used to find the failed/open circuit part or parts. In this instance, let us assume that the appliance does not work at all when tested, therefore we cannot deduce where the problem lies purely from the symptoms. A quick check of the supply socket by plugging in another appliance known to be OK will verify (or not) that there is power up to that point. This confirms that the fault lies somewhere within the appliance, its flex or plug.

During normal conditions, power flows in through the live pin on the plug, through the appliance (when switched on) and returns via the neutral pin on the plug. The fact that the appliance will not work at all even when plugged in and switched on, indicates that an open circuit exists somewhere along this normal live-to-neutral circuit.

To carry out leap-frog testing, using a

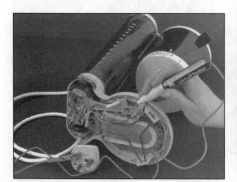

Using the simple tester on this coffee maker confirmed that the microtemp was OK, ie closed circuit, so the fault lay elsewhere

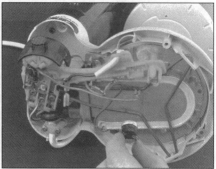

Following further checking of the circuit a faulty thermostat was found, ie permanently open circuit, when normally it would be closed circuit, opening only at 85°C

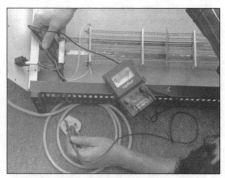

Checking that the earth path of this convector heater was satisfactory, ie closed circuit. Do not forget that the socket should also have a good earth path. See Basic and General Safety sections

continuity meter, test that the meter is working correctly, ie touch test probes together and the meter should indicate continuity. With the appliance unplugged (isolated), connect one probe to the live pin of the plug and the other on the live conductor connecting point in the plug. Continuity will be found when the pin, fuse and their connections are all OK. If this check proves to be satisfactory, move the probe from the live conductor point in the plug to the live conductor connection in the terminal block within the appliance. Again, continuity should be found, if not, a fault between plug and terminal block is indicated.

When carrying out continuity tests on flex, the wire should be moved continuously, bending it back and forth along the length, so that wire breakage internally – which often causes intermittent continuity – can be checked. If this test is OK, move the probe to the next convenient point along the live conductor, in this instance, the supply side of the ON/OFF switch. Again, continuity is required. An open circuit indicates a fault between terminal block and switch connection. The next step is to move the probe to the opposite terminal of the switch, operate the switch to verify correct action (ie ON continuity, OFF open circuit). If OK, proceed to the next point along the wire, in this instance a motor connection where continuity is again required, then move probe to the other terminal of the motor, this again should indicate continuity through the motor. At this point we will assume that an open circuit has been indicated, so go back to the

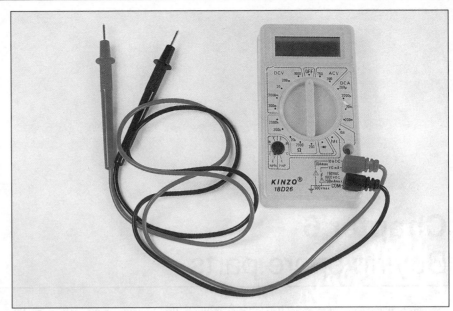

Small digital test meters such as this one are now widely available and readings are easier to interpret. They are also available in auto-ranging versions, which automatically display the correct scale

last test point and verify continuity up to that point. If found to be OK, then a fault has been traced that lies within the motor and a similar leap-frog test can now be made of the individual parts of the motor, ie field coil, brushes, etc. The fault, once located, could then be repaired.

This simple, methodical approach is all that is required to find such problems. With more complex circuits it is best to break them down into individual sections, ie motor, heater, switch etc, and test continuity of each section from Live through the individual parts and back to Neutral. This may involve moving the live probe that would normally remain on the plug live pin to a more convenient supply point within the appliance to avoid misleading continuity readings by other items within the appliance circuit. With practice, faults can be found even in complex wiring in this way.

Chapter 6
Buying spare parts

The aim of this manual is to assist you in the assessment or DIY repair of your electrical household appliances, to give you greater knowledge of how they work, and to help prevent faults from occurring.

Hopefully, armed with this information, you will feel confident enough to tackle most (if not all) of the faults that may arise with your appliances from time to time.

All the knowledge and confidence gained will, however, be wasted if you cannot locate the parts that you require to complete the repair.

In the past this would have been a problem, but over the years the availability of spares has increased. This is for several reasons.

1 The reluctance of consumers to pay high labour charges for jobs that they feel they can do themselves.
2 The general interest in household DIY coupled with the saving from call-out and labour charges, gives a feeling of satisfaction when the job is finally complete.
3 The growth in size and number of DIY stores in recent years.
4 The improvement in the availability of pre-packed spares for many products.
5 The awareness of the need to repair/recycle products and so reduce needless waste and expense.

In the past, many companies have been reluctant to supply parts for the DIY market, but the current trend is to expand the amount of pre-packed spares available to the public. The range of off-the-shelf spare parts in both retail outlets and mail order companies is most welcome, and many appliance manufacturers who do not have local dealerships will supply parts by post if requested, but unfortunately this can sometimes be a long process.

By far the best way to obtain the parts you require is to find a 'spares and repairs' dealer

through the Yellow Pages, press or the Internet. This is best done before your appliance breaks down; you will then not waste time when a fault arises. In many instances you may possess more knowledge of your machine than the assistant in the shop, so it is essential to take the MAKE, MODEL and SERIAL NUMBER of your appliance with you to help them locate or order the correct spare part for your needs.

It is always advantageous to take the faulty part with you whenever possible, to confirm visually that it is the correct replacement, ie regulators/thermostats will look the same from memory, although quite substantial differences may be seen if the faulty item is compared with the newly offered item. The casing or mounting plate, etc may be different.

Pattern parts

Certain parts that are widely available are marked 'suitable for' or 'to fit'. These are generally called pattern or patent parts. Such terms refer to items or parts that are not supplied by the manufacturer of your appliance, but are designed to fit it.

Some are copies of genuine parts and others are supplied by the original parts manufacturer to an independent distributor and are then supplied to the retailer and sold to the customer. This avoids the original manufacturer's mark-up because it is not an 'official' or 'genuine' spare part. This saving is then passed to the customer.

Many of the appliance manufacturers disliked this procedure in the past as the parts were of an inferior quality. This, however, is not now the case as the supply of parts is very big business and quality has improved

dramatically. Although great savings can be made, care must be taken not to save money by buying inferior spare parts. Check the quality of the item first wherever possible. A reputable dealer should supply only good quality pattern or genuine parts.

Many of the original appliance manufacturers are now discounting their genuine authorised spares to combat the growth in patterned spares. This is very good, as it can only benefit you, the consumer.

Genuine parts

Parts supplied by the manufacturer of your appliance, or by their authorised local agent, are classed as genuine and will in many cases carry the company trademark or colours, etc. Many of the parts in modern appliances are not in fact produced by the manufacturer of the finished items, but a subcontractor who may also supply a distributor of patterned spares with identical items.

Patterned spares producers will only take on items that have high volume sales and leave the slow moving items to the original manufacturer of the appliance. It is generally a fairly long procedure to obtain spares 'direct' from the manufacturer as many are unwilling to supply small orders direct to the public. Another system used to deter small orders is to use a 'proforma' invoicing sheet that will delay the receipt of parts until your cheque has cleared.

With the increase in DIY, manufacturers are slowly changing their view regarding spares supply. This is simply to fend off the patterned spares, by making the original parts more available and competitively priced. Again this will in turn benefit the consumer.

Chapter 7
Wiring harness faults

The term harness is used for all of the wires that connect the various components within the appliance. On large appliances they are usually bound or fastened together in bunches to keep the wiring in the appliance neat and safely anchored. Smaller appliances, however, may sacrifice neatness for safety and route the wiring to avoid contact with heat, sharp edges, etc. The correct positioning of wiring will also contribute to the double insulation of the appliance and therefore no alterations should be made to the routing or position of the wiring in double insulated appliances.

At first sight, the harness may look like a jumble of wires thrown together, but if you take the time to inspect the harness, you will find that each wire is colour-coded or numbered (either on the wire itself, or on the connector at each end). This allows the engineer to follow the wire through the appliance easily. With practice, any wiring or coding can be followed.

The connecting wires to and from a component are vital, and possibly to other components that rely on that item's correct functioning. Luckily, wiring faults are not too common, other than flex faults. When these

faults do occur, they usually seem to result in big problems, when in truth only a small fault has occurred, eg one poor connection can cause a motor not to function at all, and render the appliance unusable. Do not fall into the trap of always suspecting the worst. Many consumers, including engineers, fit parts such as a motor or a heater only to find it does not cure the problem. Stop, think and check all wires and connections that relate to your particular fault and ensure that the wire and connector has a tight fit. Loose or poor connections can overheat and cause a lot of trouble, especially on items such as heaters.

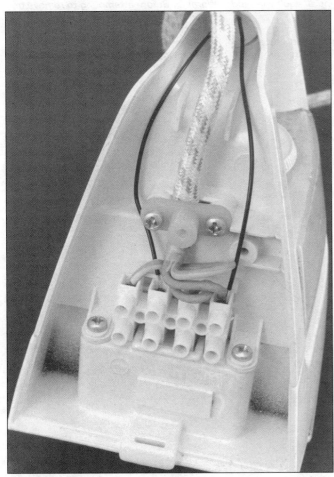

Typical internal wiring of an appliance, showing the connector block

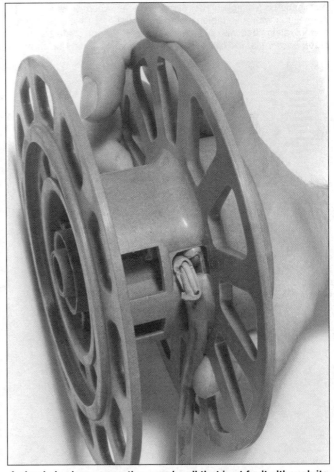

A simple broken connection may be all that is at fault although its effect can be quite major

Poor connections to items such as vacuum cleaners and hairdryers, will be aggravated by movement of the appliance when in use and may not be so apparent when a test is carried out.

One of the most easily missed faults is where the metal core (conductor) of the wire has broken and the outer insulation has not. This wire will appear perfect from the outside but will pass no electrical current. To test for this, see the section 'Using a Meter'. If a break or crack in the insulation is found renew the whole of the flex in question. DO NOT simply tape or join the damaged flex at that point. As with any repair, ensure that the appliance is completely isolated before repair or inspection is carried out.

It must be remembered that such faults may be intermittent. That is to say, that one reading may be correct and the same test later may prove incorrect. This is due to the movement of the outer insulation of the wire first making, then breaking the electrical connection.

When testing for such intermittent faults, it is wise to pull or stretch each wire tested, as an unbroken wire WILL NOT stretch, a wire that is broken WILL stretch at the break point. If an internal wire is found to be broken, rectification is a simple matter of renewing the connection with a suitable single wire of the correct rating fitted with suitable connectors.

Note: *Ensure that the harness/wiring is routed*

Always ensure that all wiring is routed as originally. Make notes before removal of components

correctly, as it was originally. Do not rush stripdowns or repairs. Double insulation relies on the correct positioning of each wire and component.

Take care that any metal fastening clips do not chafe the plastic insulation around the wires. Also make sure that wires are not in contact with sharp metal edges such as selftapping screws.

Warning: Before attempting to remove or repair the wiring harness or any other component in the appliance, isolate the appliance from the main electrical supply by removing the plug from the wall socket.

Chapter 8
Low insulation

What is low insulation?

Low insulation is best described as a slight leak of electricity to earth from the wiring of one or more of the components or wiring in an earthed appliance. If very slight, this will not harm the appliance but is an indication of faults to come and should be corrected immediately for safety reasons. The condition occurs during the progressive breakdown of the insulating properties of a normally electrically leakproof system.

How is it caused?

This can be caused by normal wear and tear over a long period, resulting in a breakdown of the insulating coating on wiring, motor windings, heater elements, etc. Such a breakdown of insulation may not result in a failure of this part at this stage and the appliance may still function as normal. This, however, is not an excuse to ignore low insulation; failure to trace and rectify low insulation is foolhardy as it compromises safety and extra expense is likely to be incurred in the long run.

Faulty covers or misplaced seals can allow dust or damp to penetrate motor windings resulting in low insulation. If not corrected, this could lead to a complete failure of the motor, or worse. A simple renewal of the cover or seal and careful cleaning and drying of the Thermal Overload Cut-out (TOC) and windings may be all that is needed to save money and improve safety for all concerned.

How can it be detected?

When an engineer tests for low insulation, he will use an instrument called a metrohm/low insulation tester. The law requires repair engineers to test for low insulation, and there is a minimum allowable level as follows:

1 Between the earth pin on the plug and all earth connection points within the appliance, the maximum resitance should be 1 ohm, ie no resistance – a perfect connection.

2 With the appliance turned on, but unplugged, test between the live pin on the plug and the earth pin on the plug. The minimum resistance should be 1 megohm (ideally no detectable reading), ie very high resistance – no connection at all.

3 Repeat this test between the neutral and the earth pins of the plug.

Testing of internal components can be carried out easily by removing connections to the part concerned and connecting one lead to one of the free terminals and one to the earth terminal. The minimum resistance should be 1 megohm. Repeat the test using the other free terminal.

These tests are carried out using a meter designed to test insulation by applying a high voltage (500V) at very low amperage (for safety). It is an unfortunate fact that many engineers do not possess such a device, and therefore do not check for low insulation. This does not mean that you should not!

A meter to test for low insulation would cost upwards of £100 and is therefore out of reach of most DIY repairers. An alternative is to utilise an in-line circuit breaker (see Flowchart). The appliance is plugged into the circuit breaker, which is then plugged into the socket. If an RCD already protects the circuit or socket then it can be used as the tester. As mentioned in 'Basics', the purpose of the device is to detect low insulation or leakage to earth and turn off the power to the appliance. Although this is not the ideal way of testing for low insulation, it will help in locating it and provide safety for the appliance and its user. If any appliance trips an RCD (or similar) system, do not use the appliance until the fault has been rectified. If tripping occurs with no appliances or load on the system, then a fault on the house wiring is indicated and the trip switch should not be reset until the fault is found and corrected.

Points to remember about low insulation

Ensure that any disconnection or removal of wires is safe and not earthing via another wire or the metal case of the appliance, etc.

Whilst disconnecting any wires during the testing for low insulation it should be remembered that the machine must be isolated from the mains at all times and the panels or covers must be replaced before the appliance is re-tested, ie **DO NOT TEST WITH EXPOSED WIRING.**

Before testing for low insulation using a circuit breaker, all earth paths of the appliance should be tested. Connecting a meter between the earth pin of the plug does this, and all other metal parts of the appliance in turn (see *Electrical Circuit Testing*).

Note: *Double insulated appliances, ie those without earth paths, cannot be tested in this way. They would normally be tested using a high voltage or flash test requiring a special test unit, see Chapter 9 for further details. As mentioned throughout the book, ensure all parts, wires, covers (both internal and external) and fixings on double insulated appliances are replaced correctly. The use of an RCD within the supply to such appliances does, however, give a high degree of safety if a fault occurs.*

A quality double pole portable (adapter type) RCD

Low insulation flowchart

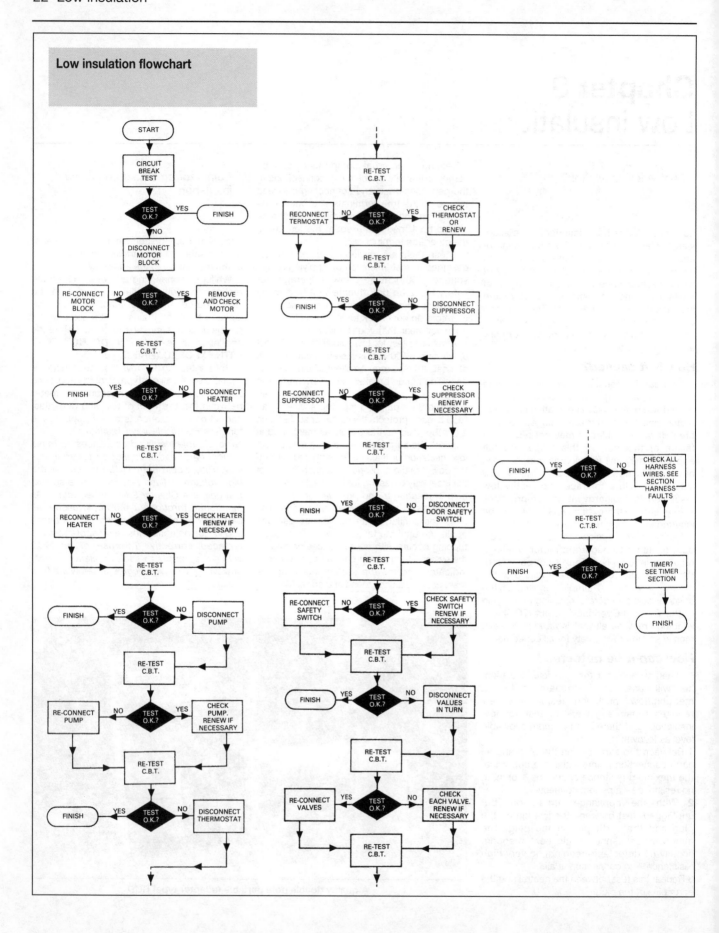

Chapter 9
Plugs and sockets

Problems with electrical appliances may not always be the result of a failure of the item itself but with the electrical supply to it via the socket. A three-pin socket must have a Live supply, a Neutral return and a sound Earth path. When a plug from an appliance is inserted in the socket, a firm contact must be made at all three points. If the live or neutral pins of the plug or connection point within the socket fail to make adequate contact or are free to move, localised heating will occur within the socket. Appliances used from spur outlets must be connected correctly and securely. The spur outlet must also have a double pole isolation switch and great care must be exercised to ensure the outlet is switched OFF prior to disconnecting or working on the appliance. It is good policy and strongly recommended to isolate the spur outlet by both its switch and by removing the relevant fuse (or switching OFF the MCB) supplying that circuit at the consumer unit. Furthermore, confirm the spur has no power by using a non-contact voltage-sensing device like the one shown. DO NOT simply rely on the fact that the appliance connected to the spur outlet does not work, power could still be present. Ensure you check before proceeding.

Problem spotting

Tell-tale signs of this type of fault often show themselves as:
1 Burn marks around one or both entry points on the socket.
2 Plug hot to the touch after use of appliance in that socket.
3 Pungent smell from socket when appliance is in use.
4 Pitting and burn marks on and around the pins of the plug.
5 Radio interference to nearby equipment caused by internal arcing within the socket creating spurious radio emissions. These may pass along the ring main to hi-fi units, etc.
6 Intermittent or slow operation of the appliance being used.
7 Failure of the fuse in the plug. In this instance, this is not caused by a fault within the appliance but by heat being transferred through the live pin and into the fuse which fails by overheating.

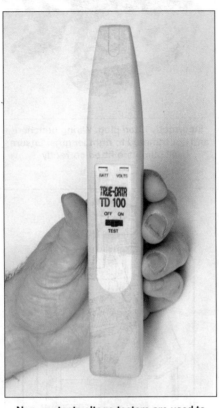

Non-contact voltage testers are used to check if a spur or outlet is isolated. This particular type of tester has a self-test facility to maximise safety and emits both audible and visual indication if voltage is detected. The use of neon test screwdrivers should be avoided at all costs

Socket highlighting overheating. Both plug and socket will require replacing

All these conditions are more likely with appliances such as washing machines, heaters and kettles, etc. which draw a high current when in use.

Why does it happen?

The reasons for such problems are various and may be caused by one or a combination of any of those listed below:
1 Repeated use of the socket, opening up the contact points within the socket. In other words general wear and tear.
2 Poor quality socket or plug.
3 Loose pins on plug.
4 The use of a double adapter.
This can cause a poor connection purely by the weight of cables and plugs pulling the adapter partially out of the wall socket. Worse still is allowing a number of high-current-draw appliances to be run through one socket thus causing overloading. Examples might be a fan heater and kettle or washing machine and tumble dryer. Whenever possible, avoid the use of adapters by provision of an adequate number of sockets and do not exceed 3 kW load on any single socket.
5 Use of a multi-point extension lead when the total load on the trailing socket can easily exceed the 3 kW load of the single socket supply.

Note: *It is unwise to use a washing machine or similar items via an extension lead. Make provision for a convenient 13A supply socket to accommodate the original length of the appliance cable.*

Rectification

First, DO NOT use the socket until the problem has been rectified. If the socket is found to be showing any of the previously described faults, it must be renewed completely. If it is a single socket it may be wise to have a double socket fitted as a replacement. Numerous DIY books describe the renewal of sockets, so I won't duplicate the instructions here. Suffice to say that caution should be exercised when tackling socket renewal. When buying a replacement socket, make sure it is a good quality one as there are many of dubious quality to be found. Price is a good indicator of quality in this field.

Internal view of severe burn out caused by poor connection to terminal. A new plug is required and the cable cut back to sound wire or renewed

Incorrectly fitted plug. Wiring bunched and not trimmed to right lengths. Ensure all plugs are fitted correctly

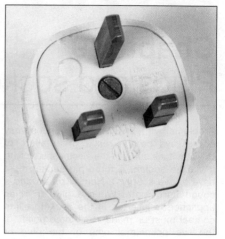

Typical resilient plug which can stand up to rugged use without cracking

High quality three-pin plug ideal for home appliances

Always look for the ASTA/BS sign when purchasing electrical fittings

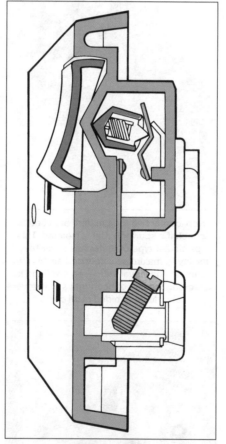

Internal view of 13A socket

It is advisable to renew all plugs that have been used in the faulty socket because damage may have been caused. It is possible, of course, that a faulty plug damaged the socket. To continue using the old plugs could result in premature failure of your new unit.

As with sockets, plugs can be found in many styles and qualities. While some of the poorer quality plugs may prove to be reliable on low current consumption items like lamps, TV and radios, they may not be so good for washing machines and heaters, etc. Although British Standards do apply to these items, quality does vary considerably. When buying plugs and sockets, go to outlets that can give advice and that carry a good selection. This will allow you to compare quality and build of the products. Look for the ASTA mark which proves that the design and manufacture has been approved by the Association of Short Circuit Testing Authorities. Replacement fuses should also carry this mark.

The earth

All of the faults mentioned previously relate to the 'live' supply and neutral return on the socket, the plug or both. There is, of course, a third pin. Although it takes no active part in the operation of the appliance, it is, however, the most important connection of all. The function of the earth system is explained in 'Basics – Electrical'. Products that have three core cable must have the yellow and green earth wire securely connected to the earth pin of the plug or pin marked E.

The earth path of an appliance can be checked easily using a simple test meter (see Electrical circuit testing). Remember, a path of low resistance is required from all items within the product that are linked into the earth path via the yellow and green cable.

Note: The earth path of an appliance from its exposed metal parts to the earth pin of the plug should be a maximum of 1 ohm (BS3456).

Checking the socket will require the use of an earth loop test meter which needs to be operated correctly. As these meters are expensive and problems could be encountered with distribution boards fitted with an RCCD, it is advisable to have these tests done by a qualified electrical contractor. A simple plug-in tester like the one shown can be found in most good electrical shops and DIY outlets. This is most useful for

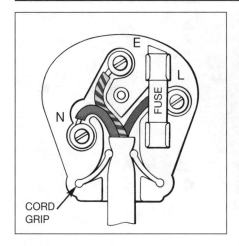

CORD
GRIP

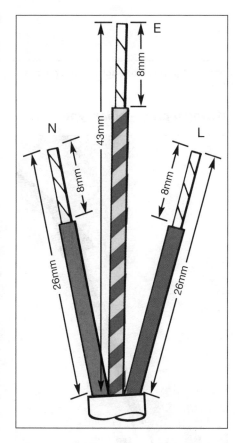

E
8mm
43mm

N
8mm
26mm

L
8mm
26mm

checking the socket for reverse polarity. In other words, it will show if a socket has been incorrectly wired. An incorrectly wired socket can still work and outwardly give no sign of any problem. This type of fault is dangerous and not uncommon. The plug-in tester also indicates if an earth path is present. However, the quality of the earth in the socket is not shown. That is to say, it may have a very high resistance but would still allow the neon of the tester to light. If the earth resistance is high, remember this may result in a failure to blow the fuse which may cause overheating at the high resistance point or allow a flow of

Typical plug in socket tester

electricity through anything or anyone else that can give a better route to earth.

Plug fitting

The fitting of a plug is often believed to be a straightforward task that needs little or no explanation. On the contrary, this is an area where many problems are to be found and dangers encountered if the fitting is not done correctly. Do not neglect this most important item.

The following text and photo sequences deal specifically with modern 13A flat-pin plugs. If your property has round-pin plugs and sockets, the indication is that the house wiring may be old and it would be wise to have it checked thoroughly by an expert.

When wiring a plug, it is good practice to leave the earth wire (yellow/green) longer than is necessary merely for connection to the earth terminal to be accomplished. The extra length is taken up in a slight loop shape within the plug. Doing this means that, should the appliance flex be pulled hard accidentally and the plug's cable grip fail to hold, the live and neutral wires will detach from the terminal first, leaving the earth loop intact to provide continued safety cover. The photo of the pillar type plug shows how the extra little bit of earth wire is contained inside the plug.

Moulded plugs

Some appliances may be supplied with one-piece moulded 13A plugs fitted to the mains cable. If for any reason this type of plug has to be removed (e.g. to allow the cable to be slotted through a hole in a work surface, or due to damage), because of its moulded construction, it is not possible to take it off in the normal way. The plug has to be cut off with suitable wire cutters and a new plug fitted correctly as shown.

Warning: Any moulded plug removed in this way must be disposed of immediately. It is wise to remove the fuse and to bend the pins of the plug as soon as it is removed to make sure that it cannot be inadvertently plugged into a socket. Do not leave it lying about or dispose of it where children can find it and plug it in.

Make sure a moulded plug removed from an appliance cannot be inadvertently plugged in. Remove the fuse and bend the pins

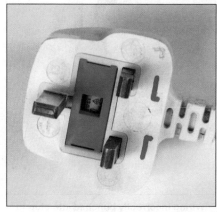

Typical moulded plug

Do's and Don'ts

● DO ensure the cable insulation is removed carefully. Use of correct wire strippers is recommended.

● DO make sure that connections are the right way around.

● DO ensure that wires are trimmed to suit plug fixing point and no bunching is present. See poorly fitted plugs illustrations.

● DO make sure that all connections are tight and no strands of wire are left protruding from terminals. To prevent this, twist the strands together as shown, prior to fitting.

● DO make sure that the cord grip is fitted correctly around the outer insulation only.

● DO ensure correct rating of fuse is used to suit appliance.

● DO ensure the plug top/cover fits tightly and securely with no cracks or damage present.

● DO NOT damage the inner core of wires when removing the outer or inner insulation. If you do, cut back and start again.

● DO NOT fit tinned ends of cables into plugs. Some manufacturers tin (dip in solder) the end of the exposed inner conductors. The tinned/soldered end, if fitted to the plug, will work loose and cause problems associated with loose connections. Although tight when fitted, constant pressure over a long period will compress the soft solder resulting in a loose joint. A second problem associated with tinned conductors is the excessive length of exposed inner wire which the manufacturer usually provides. This can protrude below the cord clamp bunch within the plug to allow the cord clamp to grip the outer insulation only. Both of these practices are dangerous and must be avoided. Always cut cable lengths to suit the plug. If this poor method of fitting is found on an appliance it must be corrected immediately.

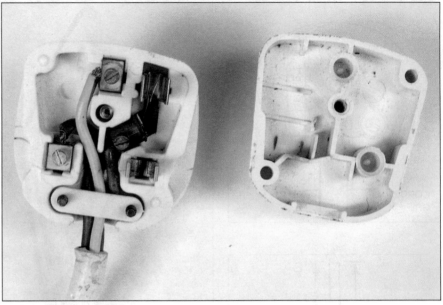

Wiring not cut to correct length. As a result the cord grip is fixed across inner wires, not outer sheath

● DO NOT allow strands of wire to protrude from any fixing points.

● DO NOT fit incorrect fuse ratings. Always match fuses to appliances and observe the manufacturer's instructions.

● DO NOT re-use overheated or damaged plugs.

● DO NOT by-pass the internal fuse.

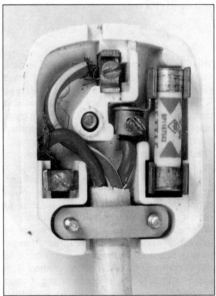

Conductor wire protruding from plug pins

Note: *All of the above photographs are used to illustrate the lack of attention to safety to this small but vital component. Always fit plugs correctly and safely. To give further assistance, a step-by-step photo guide for the two types is given.*

Wiring incorrectly bunched into plug to allow cord grip to hold outer sheath

Wiring a plug – pillar type

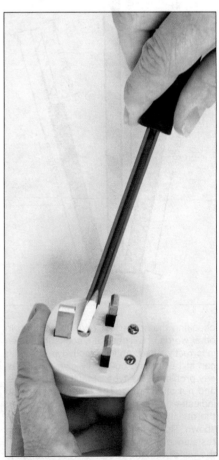

1 Remove the screw that holds the plug top-cover in position, taking care not to lose it

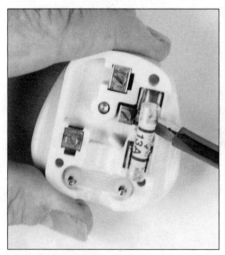

2 Ease the fuse from position (if using a screwdriver, take care not to damage the fuse)

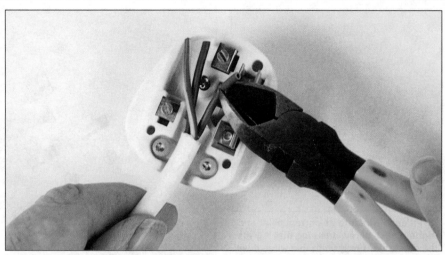

5 Offer the wiring to the plug base with the outer sheath in its correct position resting in the cord clamp area. Next, cut the inner cables as per the manufacturer's instructions, if these are not available allowing 13mm (½in) past the fixing point. Don't forget to allow a little extra on the earth cable to form a slight loop

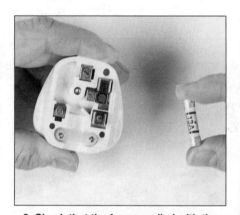

3 Check that the fuse supplied with the plug is of the correct rating for the appliance. Many plugs are supplied with 13A fuse already fitted, but do not be tempted to use it unless it is right. In this instance a 13A fuse was required

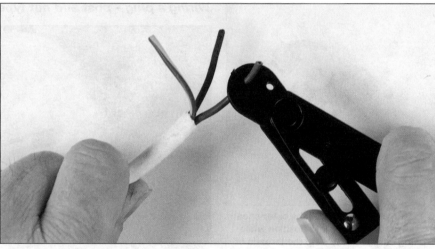

6 Carefully remove 6mm (¼in) of insulation from the end of each wire. This must be done with care to avoid damaging or cutting any strands of the conductor

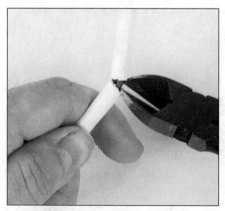

4 Carefully remove the outer cable sheath to expose the inner wires. If damage should occur to the inner wires in the process, cut back and start again

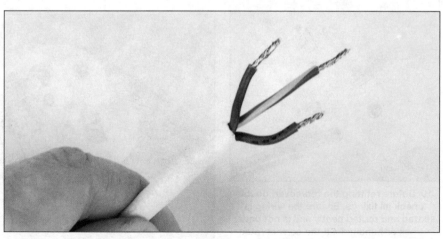

7 Twist the strands of each wire securely together. Make sure there are no loose strands

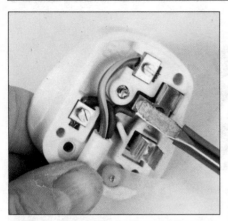

8 Fit each wire into its correct pillar and tighten each screw ensuring that it grips the conductor firmly (with thin wires it will help if they are folded over on themselves first). Make sure the wire fits up to the insulation shoulder and no wires or strands protrude from the pillar

11 With top/cover refitted tighten the securing screw

Wiring a plug – post and nut type

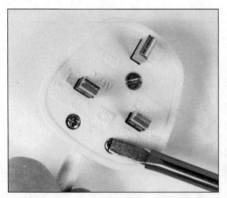

9 Fit the cord clamp over the outer sheath and screw it firmly into position while being careful not to strip the threads of the plastic grip

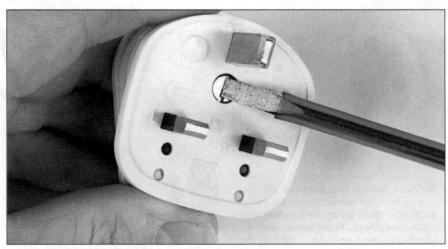

1 Remove the screw that holds plug top/cover in position

10 Before refitting the top/cover, double check all fixings. Ensure the wiring is seated and routed neatly and is not under stress or bunched. Fit the correct rated fuse, making sure that it is firmly and securely positioned

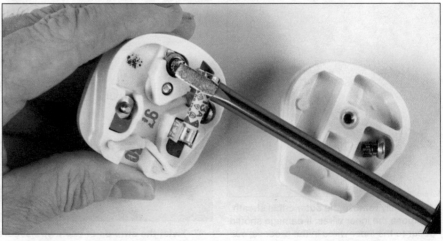

2 Remove the knurled/slotted nuts and place them safely in the top

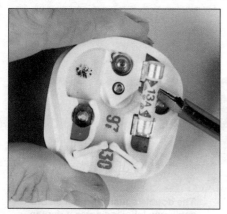

3 With the plug top/cover removed, the fuse can be eased from its position. If using a screwdriver, take care not to damage the fuse

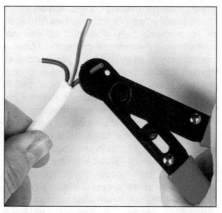

6 Now remove 15mm (⁹⁄₁₆in) of insulation from the end of each wire. This must be done with care to avoid damaging or cutting any strands of the conductor

9 Fit each conductor (wire) to its correct terminal. Make sure each is fitted in a clockwise direction, otherwise it will be pushed out as the nut is tightened. Ensure only the conductor is gripped and not the outer insulation

10 Securely tighten all three nuts. Ensure that the wire fits up to the insulation shoulder and no wires or strands protrude from the terminal. Before refitting the top/cover, double-check all fixings. Ensure the wiring is seated and routed neatly and is not under stress or bunched. Fit the correct rated fuse, making sure that it is firmly and securely positioned

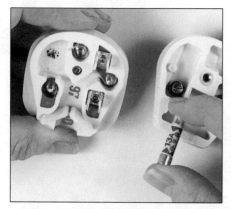

4 Check that the fuse supplied with the plug is of the correct rating for the appliance. Many plugs are supplied with 13A fuse already fitted but do not be tempted to use it unless it is right. In this instance a 13A fuse was required

7 Twist the strands of each wire securely together. Make sure there are no loose strands

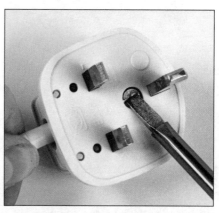

11 With top/cover refitted tighten the securing screw. This type has a captive screw with a shockproof washer to prevent it working loose during use

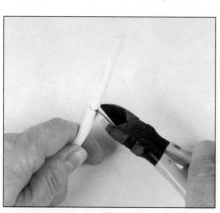

5 Carefully remove 43mm (1¾in) of the cable sheath to expose the inner wires. If damage should occur to the inner wires in the process, cut back and start again. Next, cut the inner cables as per the manufacturer's instructions, in this instance trim the live and neutral wires to 34mm (1⅜in)

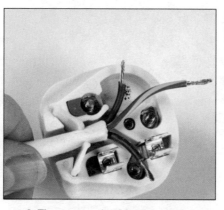

8 The prepared cable can now be inserted into the cord grip ensuring only the outer sheath of the cable is gripped

Double insulated appliances

Not all appliances require earth facilities and many small appliances such as hairdryers, shavers, vacuum cleaners, DIY and garden tools etc., fall into this category. Such appliances are classed as 'double insulated' and as such carry a 'double square' logo on the rating plate of the appliances (see photo). This denotes that the design of the product incorporates special double layered insulation construction methods.

Such products are only fitted with two-core flex at manufacture. The electrical safety of the product and the user depends on the integrity of this double layer construction. It is essential that these products be checked closely for any damage such as cracks in the plastic casings, missing covers, screws etc. If the appliance has been dismantled for repair or inspection, it is vital that all internal components be refitted correctly. Make a careful note of all the relevant parts and their correct location and orientation as you take the item apart. The electrical safety of double insulated appliances depends on the integrity of all its components, ensure they are all in good order and in their correct positions. Renew any items that show signs of damage or are missing. Although the appliance may appear to work satisfactorily, missing, damaged or incorrectly assembled components pose a very serious electrical hazard to the user. Information relating to the electrical testing of double insulated appliances can be found in Chapter 2.

The double square symbol on the appliance label indicates a double insulated product

Plugs and sockets flowchart

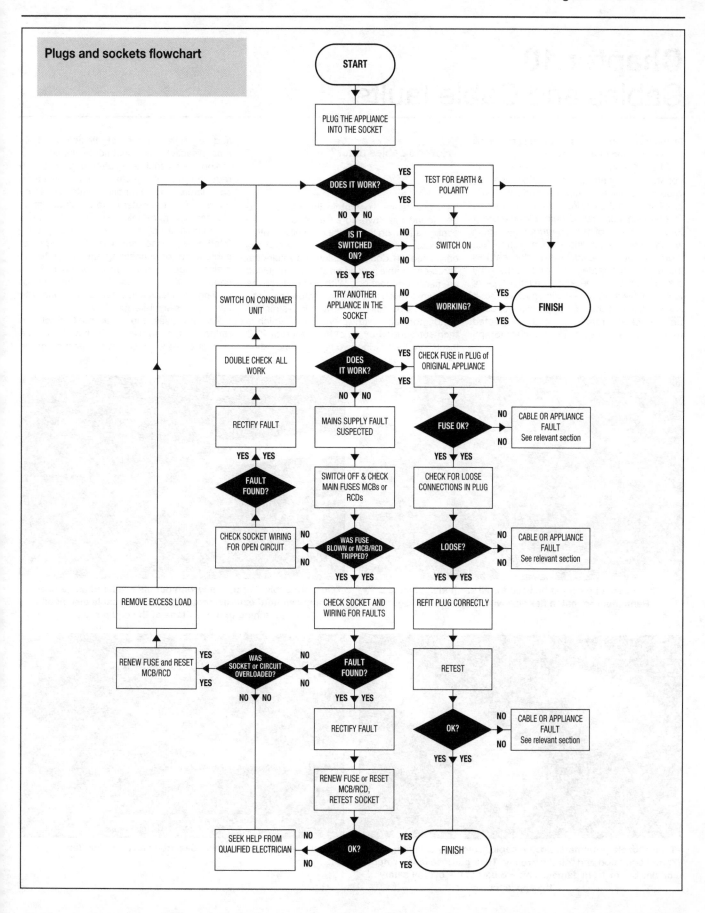

Chapter 10
Cables and Cable faults

All the mains appliances featured in this book have some kind of mains cable.

When the appliance is portable and is constantly moved around during use, eg vacuum cleaners, hedge cutters, etc., problems with the cables are not uncommon. The problems can range from a simple break in one or more of the conductors – which would render the appliance open circuit – to a more serious breakdown of the cable's insulating properties caused either by damage, fatigue or neglect. The latter type of fault could lead to an electric shock or fire. It is essential for cables and extension leads to be checked regularly and inspected thoroughly as shown in the photograph sequences.

How do cables differ?

Several different types of flexible cable are to be found in two-core and three-core configurations on the appliances shown within this book. Remember that two-core cable is only used on double insulated appliances. Three-core cable is used on all items requiring an earth connection. With items such as vacuums, mixers, drills, lawnmowers, etc., flexibility is obtained by using multi-stranded conductor cable with a PVC cover which is then surrounded by an outer sheath of PVC insulation, thus giving two layers of insulation

and a high degree of flexibility. It is recognisable by its smooth outer surface.

Appliances such as heaters and irons also require three-core multi-stranded insulation conductors within a rubber sheath covered by a braided cotton outer cover. This design is classed as non-kink flex; it is therefore essential that only the correct cable type be fitted as a replacement. The various types of cable used for connecting appliances to the mains supply via a socket or spur outlet should not be confused with the type of cabling used for the internal house wiring. The latter type is semi-flexible only.

As with fuses, the cable must match the rating of the appliance. Failure to fit the correct cable will result in overheating of the

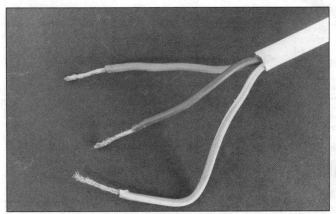

Three-core cable must be used for all earthed appliances. Remember to match flex size with appliance wattage

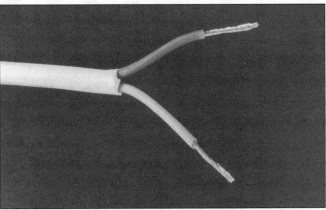

Two-core cable. For use only with double insulated appliances or lamps without external metal fittings. This cable also needs matching to the wattage of the equipment

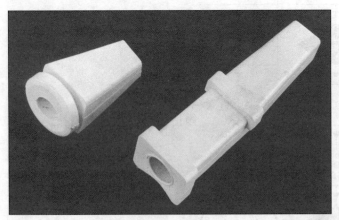

Typical cable grommets. Ensure cable grommets/sleeving are in good condition and fitted correctly. Their purpose is to protect cables or flex from damage and are part of the overall safety of the appliance

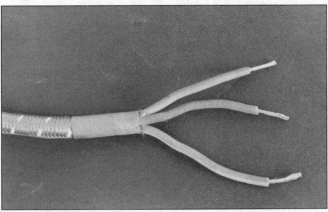

Braided cable, also described as non-kink flex

cable and possibly in failure of the appliance, fire or shock.

Flex size	max wattage*
0.5 mm	700
0.75 mm	1400
1.00 mm	2400
1.50 mm	3000

* see rating on appliance

When obtaining an extension or replacement cable for portable outdoor equipment such as lawnmowers, strimmers, etc., the bright orange or yellow coloured cable is recommended because it is easier to see in grass and therefore easier to avoid. Do not extend the lead of the appliance itself, as it is advisable to have the plug connection point within easy reach when using this type of appliance. See also the descriptions on RCDs in 'Electrical Basics'.

Internal wiring to cookers and heaters will require heat resistant cable. This is illustrated in the relevant sections.

Avoid having appliance leads too long or too short. Too long, and the excess cable may rest across a cooker hob or similar dangerous areas, or if on the floor it could also cause someone to trip. Too short a cable may result in stress at either end caused by pulling which can result in damage to the cable, internal connection points of the appliance, plug or supply point.

When using an extension lead, make sure that its total load does not exceed its stated maximum. Some extension leads may use 0.75mm cable and must only have a total load of 1400W. To power, say, a 3000W (3kW) fan heater with such an extension lead would overheat the cable and be extremely dangerous. Be aware of such basic limitations. Some trailing sockets on extension leads have up to four outlet sockets. Even if the supply cable is 1.5mm the total load must not exceed 3000W (3kW). This would only be sufficient for the one 3kW fan heater and nothing else. Although three sockets would be free do not be tempted to use them and cause an overload.

Many extension leads are now conveniently stored on a drum or reel system. It is important that when in use, these extension leads are fully extended even for jobs not requiring the full length of cable. If an extension cable is used whilst still wound on the storage drum, heat is generated in the cable which will damage the insulation, possibly causing a short circuit or fire. Many modern extension cable drums like that shown, have internal overheat/overload protection (TOC) as a safety measure. Do not rely on all extensions having this protection. Understand the limits of sockets, cables and extension leads and avoid overloading and incorrect use.

If you wish to extend the lead of an appliance, **never** make a joint by twisting the

Regularly inspect cables for faults, damage, and wear and tear; do not use equipment with such faults

conductor wires together and binding them with insulation tape. To extend a lead, a correct flex connector **must** be used together with the correct rated cable. Ensure that the socket side of the connector is on the supply side and the plug half of the connector is on the appliance cable. As with all cable fixing, it is important to connect it correctly. All electrical connections should be tight and the cord grips in the correct position and tight. Replacing the whole flex with the length

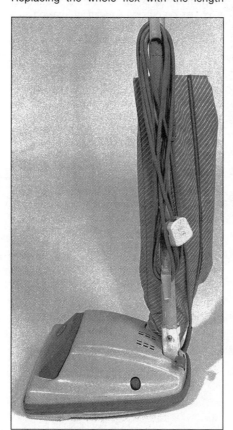
Store cables neatly to prevent problems and accidents

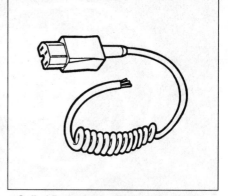
Coiled flexes for appliances like kettles avoid loops. Ensure the flex used is suitable for this type of high wattage appliance

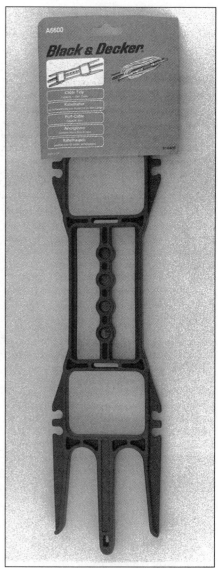
A cable holder is useful for outdoor equipment

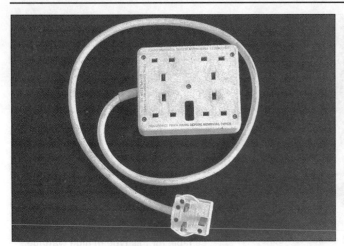

Simple extension lead

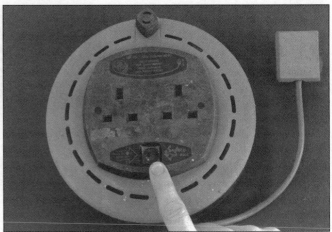

Some extension leads have overheat/overload protection similar to this one which requires manual resetting when tripped, ie push raised area to reset

required would be a much better and safer solution.

Damage to cables

Damage to the outer insulation sheath of any kind is impossible to repair satisfactorily. **Never** use insulation tape around cuts, splits or cracks in cables. Inspect the whole length of cable and if there is no other defect and the damage is near either end, it may simply be a case of cutting the cable on the good side of the damaged area and reconnecting the socket or plug to that point. This makes a much safer repair, but obviously with some loss of cable length. If the loss of cable is too great, a fixed waterproof cable connector could be used, but remember, if such a connector is used on a drum-stored cable, retraction of the cable would be restricted.

It is worth remembering that bulky joints (like those mentioned in the previous paragraph) on outdoor cables used on lawnmowers, hedge trimmers, etc., can cause obstruction to free movement of the cable through grass and debris. This may pose a 'physical' hazard in the use of the appliance so extra care should be taken if such joints are used. Damp and rough outside conditions could cause damage to extension leads and connectors, so it is therefore wise to check the cable thoroughly before and after each use. Remember to isolate the cable before inspection: 'Switch off, plug out'.

Do's and Don'ts

DO check extension leads and appliance cables and fittings regularly – at least once a year on household appliances. Extension leads need to be checked before and after each use on outside equipment, making sure that all conductor paths are correct.

DO make sure the appropriate fuse is used. For outdoor use of equipment use an RCD socket or adaptor if your main consumer unit does not have one.

DO make sure the correct size and type of cable is used. It must match the load and the stress it will have to endure.

DO store cables neatly and safely. If the appliance has a cable storage position then use it. Otherwise, make sure the cable is stored without kinks and that it is not in a position that would damage the outer insulation of the cable, eg by wrapping the cable around an iron that is still warm, or leaving cables or extension leads with other tools such as chisels and saws on a bench.

DO think of others when using extension cables or appliances with long flexes. Accidents can easily happen to others or yourself if precautions are not taken to prevent them.

DO make sure that any damaged cable is renewed before using the appliance.

DO NOT run cables under carpeting or similar floor coverings. Appliance and extension lead cable is not designed to be walked over and damage will inevitably occur and if unseen can become a fire hazard or cause a shock.

DO NOT extend cables to power tools. This type of equipment should have its plug within easy reach at all times. If required, use a suitable extension lead with a suitable socket.

DO NOT use extension leads to enable usage of mains powered appliances in a bathroom or shower room. Electrical appliances should **NEVER** be used in these areas.

NOTE: This does not only apply to extension leads. No provision for mains voltage portable appliances should be made in bathrooms/ shower rooms. **DO NOT** fit a 13amp socket outlet in these rooms in any circumstances. The only socket found in bathrooms should be the special one for an electric shaver supply (such outlets contain a transformer supply) and on no account should they be used for any other electrical appliance.

DO NOT handle electrical appliances, sockets, plugs or cables with wet hands. When cleaning or wiping down equipment after use, make sure the item is isolated and not just switched off. **REMEMBER** – 'Switch off, Plug out'.

DO NOT compromise safety for any reason.

DO NOT allow ignorance to jeopardise safety.

IF IN DOUBT- FIND OUT

Chapter 11
Electric motors

Most of our labour-saving household appliances will contain an electric motor of some description. The motor can be classed as the workhorse of the appliance and most are well capable of coping with the workloads inflicted upon them. Some motors, however, through poor design or cost limitations, are inadequate for the job they are required to do. Adequate or not, at some point it is almost inevitable that they will fail or simply wear out. To prevent this happening, give a little care and attention whilst using the appliance, be aware of its limitations, and carry out regular inspection and servicing. This will prevent small problems escalating into major problems due to misuse or neglect.

Not only does the size of motor vary greatly between products; the way in which it works can also be different. To diagnose faults successfully and to service or repair appliances, a working knowledge of motors is essential. What follows is a basic introduction to various types of motors that may be encountered, a description of how they work, the machine that each may be found in and its advantages and drawbacks. Specific problems can be found in the relevant sections on appliances.

Three types of motors are used in the larger mains-powered appliances: brush motors, induction motors (capacitor start), and induction motors (shaded-pole). Any one of these three types of motor may be found in a hairdryer, but it is more likely that a fourth type, the DC (direct current) powered permanent magnet motor will be used as they are smaller than the three other types. For the operation of this type of motor please refer to the section on hairdryers after having first read the section on general motor principles. Electric shavers are also covered in a separate section.

Brush motors

This is by far the most common type of motor used in mains-powered household appliances. Variations of size, power and speed are many, as are the applications. Brush motors are to be found in vacuum cleaners, (upright and cylinder styles), food mixers, electric drills, hedge trimmers, strimmers and spin dryers.

The brush motor consists of two sets of electromagnets: an outer fixed set called the 'field coil', and an inner free set called the 'armature'. The armature is made up of many separate windings. It is configured in such a way that power is only supplied to one set of windings at a time. The corresponding movement induced in the armature, continuously brings a new set of windings into circuit, whilst the previous winding circuit is broken. The windings are continuously out of synchronisation, therefore inducing continuous rotation of the armature whenever power is supplied. Reversal of the motor is achieved simply by reversing the power flow through the field coil winding. This type of motor can be used with alternating current (AC) from the mains or with direct current (DC) via a transformer or battery.

Typical brush motor from an upright vacuum cleaner

Just one of the many variations of brush motor used in cylinder vacuum cleaners

Typical cylinder vacuum cleaner motor

A. Fan housing
B. Moving fans
C. Motor end frame (front)
D. Static fan
E. Front bearing
F. Rear bearing
G. Bearing securing plate
H. Armature
I. Field coil
J. Motor brush and slide
K. Suppressor
L. Motor end frame (rear)
M. Spacers and nut

A brush motor can be readily identified by its shape, because its length is greater than its width. Due to the switching device, a brush motor can be used either with AC from the mains or DC from a battery. The switching device is called the 'commutator', and is made up of many copper segments. Each segment is connected to a winding in the armature and is supplied with electricity through two stationary pieces of graphite, called 'brushes'. These are pushed onto the commutator by springs.

When power is applied to the motor, current flows to the field coil and through the brushes to the commutator. This magnetises the armature coils, inducing rotation. As the armature rotates, the next two segments of the commutator come into contact with the brushes. This operation is repeated many times a second.

Speed control of this type of motor is usually achieved by interruption of the AC power being supplied to it. The alternating current supply waveform is interrupted at precise points on each cycle. Where and for how long it is interrupted is proportional to how much voltage actually gets to the motor, the lower the voltage supplied the slower the motor runs. The interruption of the AC waveform in this way is not as straightforward

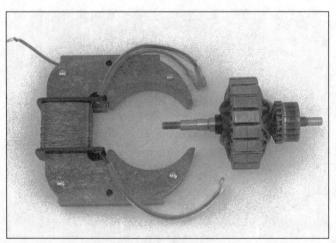

Large field coil and armature from a Hoover senior cleaner

Typical small induction motor

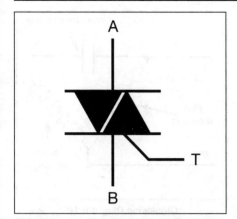

This is the symbol used to indicate a Triac. Applying a low voltage to point 'T' will allow a higher voltage to flow between points A and B. Voltage can only flow between A and B when 'T' has a trigger voltage applied to it

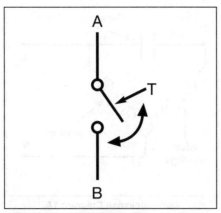

The Triac shown in the previous diagram can be likened to a simple on/off switch like the one above. Applying pressure at point 'T' would close the switch and the circuit between A and B. In the Traic mechanical pressure is replaced by voltage pressure

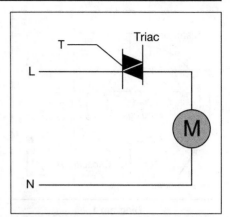

The rate at which the triac trigger 'T' is pulsed is governed by the speed control circuit. Pulses are varied according to the speed selected by the user of the appliance

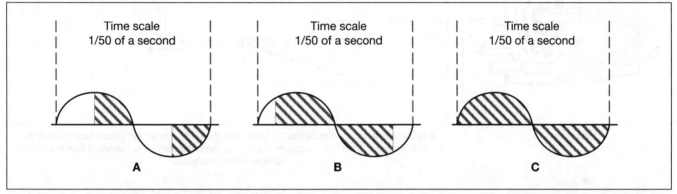

In diagram 'A' the triac trigger 'T' is pulsed at the mid-point on both halves of the AC waveform. This results in the motor receiving half the normal supply voltage. On a 230V supply only 115V would reach the motor and as a result the motor would run slowly

In diagram 'B' the triac is pulsed at the end of the first quarter of each half of the waveform. This results in the motor receiving three quarters of the supply voltage, in this instance around 172V

In diagram 'C' the triac trigger 'T' is supplied with a continuous voltage. The waveform and supply are not interrupted and full mains voltage reaches the motor allowing it to run up to full speed

as it may seem as the interruption must occur 50 times* a second and at exactly the correct point on each cycle to create the required output. This is achieved by a speed control circuit (often referred to as a module), the main component of which is a large 'triac'. The triac is a solid state switching device controlled by the other components on the circuit board. Control of the triac is by means of a low voltage 'trigger' to allow mains power to flow through it. In essence the triac is rapidly 'pulsed' on and off at the required points in the AC cycle. See diagram. However, this is not as straightforward as it may seem, because the pulse has to be smooth to eliminate jerky action at low speeds. This is achieved by other electronic components on the speed control circuit board. Many appliances have variable speed control and more detail will be found in individual appliance sections.

*Note: *This figure relates to cycles per second of the AC mains supply which in the United Kingdom is 50Hertz (50 cycles per second). It must be remembered that some countries have a 60Hertz supply. However, the speed control principle described above remains the same.*

The induction motor

The asynchronous induction motor is quite simple and uses the absolute basic principles of electricity. Its apparent complexity stems from the need to use extra windings to control its speed. Although modern electronics have allowed for variable control, this is the basics of asynchronous induction motors used without module control.

Induction motors (capacitor start)

Unlike brush motors, induction motors can only operate on alternating current (AC), and are technically called asynchronous induction motors. Single-phase household induction motors consist of two main items – an outer wound coil called a 'stator' and a rotatable core made of high-grade cast aluminium with internal metal lamination (which are slightly skewed to aid torque for starting purposes) called the 'rotor' (see diagram). The rotor is isolated from the windings and receives no power at all.

The most simple stator would consist of two sets of windings set 180° to one another (see diagram) Two windings are needed to induce the rotor to turn when power is applied. One coil would not induce movement, though if the rotor were started by

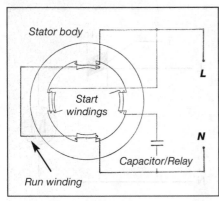

Diagram 1

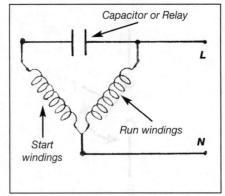

Anti-clockwise Diagram 1A

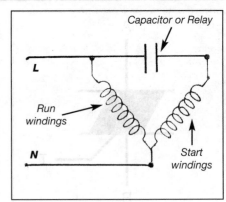

Clockwise Diagram 1B

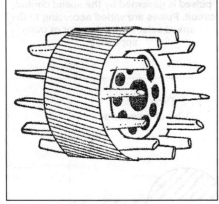

Diagram 2

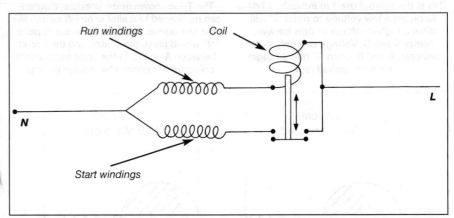

A relay may be placed in circuit to cause the phase displacement necessary to start the induction motor. This is a mechanical delay as described and it is essential that the relay is upright when energized

mechanical means, it would continue to turn as long as power was being supplied to the stator coil. In reality, motion is induced by placing one set of the windings 90° out of phase with the other. This is done by introducing a delay in the current flow to one

winding using a relay or, more usually, using a capacitor, the rating of which is matched to the windings. (The rating is given in microfarads (μF) on its casing.) Being out of phase due to the delay caused by the capacitor/relay, a rotating magnetic field is

created, causing the rotor to accelerate up to working speed. At this point the start windings, as they are known, can be switched out if required. Reversal of the motor is achieved simply by reversal of current flow through the starting winding or the run winding, but not both (see diagrams).

When a motor is supplied with 240V at 50Hz (ie mains voltage) its speed is a function of the phase cycle (50 cycles per second) and the number of poles in the unit. A two-pole motor mimics the phase cycle and rotates at 50 revolutions per second, 3000rpm, a four-pole motor 1500rpm, an eight-pole motor 750rpm, and a 16-pole 375rpm. Variable speed motors require complex stator windings and are inevitably expensive. Ensure that faults with motors are checked and rectified promptly. A loose motor block connection may allow power to one winding only and cause overheating and failure of the whole motor. A faulty capacitor or a malfunction of a selector switch or internal TOC can also have the same result. *Warning: When checking for faults, the appliance must always be isolated from the mains. Turn off at the wall socket and remove the plug. The capacitor(s) will still contain a charge although the mains have*

Two larger shaded-pole induction motors similar to those found in some fan assisted ovens

been isolated. This must be discharged by using an electrically insulated screwdriver. Using this, 'short' the terminals of the capacitor with the shaft of the screwdriver ensuring that you are only in contact with the insulated handle. It is not safe to proceed further until this has been done.

If the stat or windings of an induction motor are faulty, it may continue to run, although appearing sluggish and getting extremely hot even when used for a short time. Therefore, if you have been running the machine to determine the fault, proceed with care, as the motor will remain hot for some time. If the windings are faulty the unit will have to be replaced.

The capacitor

Capacitors used for motor starting can have either metal or plastic outer casings with an insulated top with two terminals (see photo).

How does the capacitor work?

What follows is a simplified version of what happens within a capacitor in an AC circuit.

The two terminals of the capacitor are in fact completely insulated from one another. Internally they are connected to two sheets of metal foil and between this foil is an insulator. This package of large surface area is rolled into a cylinder which fits into the shell of the capacitor. If the two terminals and their connected sheets of foil are insulated from one another, how, you might ask, do they pass a current when in use? The answer is that as the voltage supplied to one terminal is in fact alternating (at 50 times per second), so does the polarity of its connected foil. An opposite movement of electrons is induced in the other foil even though they are insulated electrically. This effect causes a delay in the electrical path at this point, and this, in the

Typical capacitor for use with induction motors. Do not confuse capacitors and suppression units. They may look similar but their functions differ

case of an asynchronous induction motor, gives the out-of-phase feed to the start winding.

The storage capacity of a capacitor is measured in microfarads (μF) and is displayed on the shell. Any replacement must be of the same rating.

Note: *It is possible for a motor start capacitor to retain voltage even when the appliance is isolated. It is therefore essential to discharge the capacitor prior to any service or inspection work being carried out. This is preferably done with the appliance isolated and the use of a capacitor discharge lead which is connected across both terminals of the capacitor. However, if a capacitor discharge lead is not available an alternative method is to use an insulated screwdriver or insulated pliers to short out the terminals of the capacitor. This will also discharge the capacitor. ALWAYS ensure that you are only holding the insulation and that it is sound and in good order.*

The relay

What is a relay? A relay is an electro-mechanical device used in this particular instance for induction motor starting in place of a capacitor.

What does it look like?

The most common relay consists of a plastic moulding with three terminal tags, two at the top and one at its base. On the centre section is a wire wound coil (see photo). However, on products such as fridges and freezers the relay may have smaller electrical connections (see photo).

How does it work?

The main aim of the relay in the context of asynchronous induction motors is to cause a

A relay may be placed in circuit to cause the phase displacement necessary to start the induction motor (often used on refrigeration equipment). This is a mechanical delay as described. It is essential that the relay is upright when energised

Close up of later type fridge/freezer motor relay

Fridge motor unit with relay arrowed

delay in the start winding supply, similar to the capacitor. The main difference is that the relay achieves this operation mechanically. The wound coil section is connected in series with the run winding. When power is supplied to the motor, the current to the run winding passes through the coil and on to the motor run winding. This current induces a magnetic force in the coil, which in turn attracts the metal core of the relay. The metal core is linked to an internal contact switch and when 'made' allows current to pass to the start winding (see diagram). This operation gives the required delay to induce starting of the induction motor.

When power is switched off, gravity resets the relay core. It is, therefore, essential that the relay be in its correct position and the machine upright for this item to function correctly.

The relay may also be matched to the run winding of the motor, ie, as initial power draw of the stationary motor is high the magnetic attraction of the relay coil is great enough to attract the core. When the motor is running, the initial high power draw drops and weakens the magnetic pull of the coil, the core drops and open circuits the start winding allowing the motor to continue running more efficiently. Always make sure that the correct replacement is obtained by quoting model numbers and manufacturer when ordering.

Faults to watch for are: open circuit of the coil, metal core sticking (in either position), overheating and contact points failing. Renew any suspect relay immediately as the failure of this item, like the capacitor, can lead to motor failure (if it has not already done so).

If you have to renew a damaged stator coil or motor and it is relay started, it is wise to change the relay at the same time as it may (a) have caused the original motor fault or (b) have been subsequently damaged by the motor failure.

Solid State Relays (PTC)

A solid state relay is a motor starting relay with no moving parts. Solid state relays are popular with manufacturers of motors for fridges and freezers.

What does it look like?

The size and outward appearance of solid state relays can be very similar to the mechanical relay described earlier. However, closer inspection will reveal that there is no coil, moving rod or relay switch, although some units will house an overload (TOC) switch.

How does it work?

A solid state relay is essentially a large resistor. However, the particular type of resistor used within the unit has an unusual property, its resistance changes with temperature. Resistors that have this particular property are called 'thermistors' and there are two versions: Negative Temperature CO-efficient (NTC) - with this type the resistance drops as the temperature of the resistor rises.

Positive Temperature CO-efficient (PTC) - with this type the resistance increases as the temperature of the resistor rises. It is this later

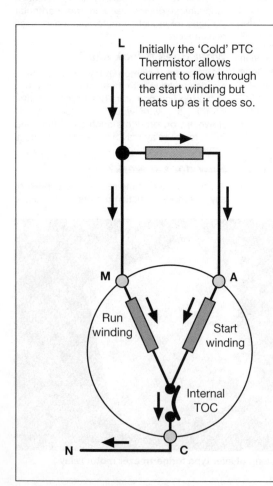

Initially the 'Cold' PTC Thermistor allows current to flow through the start winding but heats up as it does so.

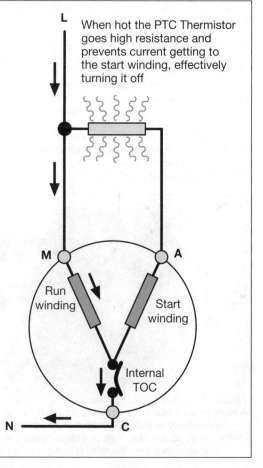

When hot the PTC Thermistor goes high resistance and prevents current getting to the start winding, effectively turning it off

Relay/overload unit highlighting the simple 3 pin push on 'plug and socket type' fitting

Typical solid state PTC motor starting device

characteristic that is utilised in the solid state relay, which operates in the following manner. When the motor it is connected to is initially switched on the thermistor will be cold and therefore have low resistance to the electrical flow. This allows a high current to pass through the 'start' winding and if all is well the motor will start. The flow of current passing through the thermistor causes it to heat up and the version used is PTC (see above) therefore as its temperature rises so does the resistance. The increase in resistance of the thermistor reduces the flow of current through it (Ohms Law). The properties the particular thermistors used within these relays allow them to reach very high resistances which in effect reduces the current flow through the start winding to virtually zero allowing the motor to run efficiently on only the run winding.

Common problems with this unit are that they can overheat due to loose/poor internal connection and a loose fit to the compressor connecting pins. In common with all motor starting devices it is essential to renew a solid state relay with an exact replacement.

Induction motors (shaded-pole)

The shaded-pole motor is the simplest of all induction motors and is similar in basic format of rotor and stator to the capacitor start induction motor. However, only one stator coil is used to create the magnetic field. Obviously this alone would not induce rotation of the rotor, only a constant magnetic field.

To start rotation, an imbalance in the magnetic field is required which is created quite simply by copper band inserts at the pole ends of the stator laminations. The copper band within the mild steel stator laminations distorts the magnetic field in a given direction, therefore inducing rotation in the stator. Reversing the supply to such motors does not affect any change in motor direction as this is governed by the direction of the fixed shaded poles. These motors do not have a high starting torque and because of the magnetic

imbalance being fixed, heating of the stator occurs which, in normal conditions, creates no problems. Nevertheless most stator coils are protected by TOCs for safety.

Benefits of shaded-pole motors are their cheapness and quietness; the drawbacks are heat and low starting torque.

Note: Because these motors are fitted with TOCs, if the safe working temperature is exceeded, this device will sever the power supply to the motor. Most TOCs are now self-resetting, resulting in constant heating up and cooling down of the motor. If the fault is not spotted quickly, the TOC itself will fail, therefore causing motor failure.

Note: *If a shaded-pole stator is inadvertently fitted back to front, it will cause the main motor to run in the opposite direction. Always note orientation prior to stripdown.*

Details of types of motors used, motor faults, fault finding and fault correction relating to particular appliances will appear in individual sections throughout the book. This section should therefore be used in conjunction with the information given for individual appliances.

This room heater uses a shaded-pole motor to drive the air circulation fans

Shaded-pole motor stator as used in fan-assisted ovens. The copper banding can be clearly seen

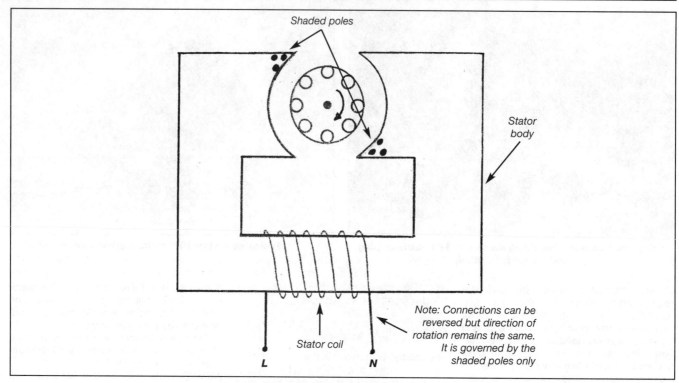

Shaded pole diagram

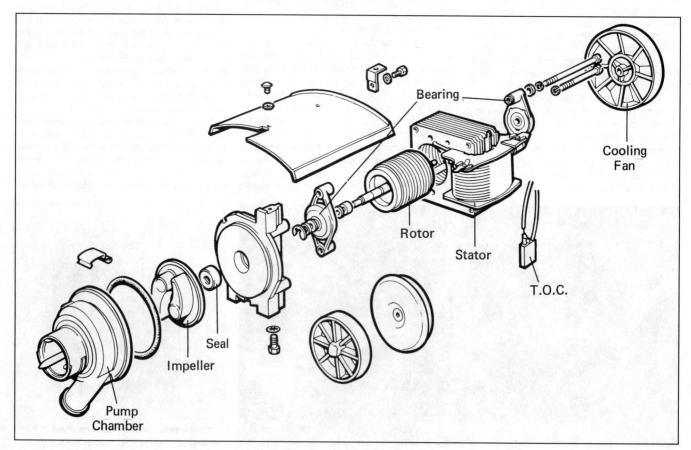

Typical shaded-pole induction motor

Chapter 12
Suppression

What is a suppressor?

When an appliance is in use, small sparks are generated at mechanical contacts such as those found in switches and the junction between motor brushes and commutator. The sparks result in the emission of spurious radio waves that can be heard as crackles on radio or TV receivers or, passed down the mains circuit, to audio equipment.

A suppressor is a device designed to eliminate the formation and transmission of these spurious radio waves.

By law all domestic appliances must be suppressed to conform with the regulations on radio interference, and it is an offence to use an appliance that is not suppressed to these standards.

Suppressors vary in style, shape, position, size and colour. Sometimes individual parts are suppressed, but more often the mains supply is suppressed at, or just after, the entry point into the appliance. This is called in-line suppression because both the live and neutral supply goes through the suppressor and on to supply the whole of the appliance with power. Do not confuse suppressors with capacitors that may be used in the appliance for induction motor starting. They might look very similar but they carry out distinctly different functions. Suppressors may also be called mains filters because of their ability to remove spurious radio transmissions.

Faults with suppressors

The main fault is one of short circuit to earth (if in an earthed appliance) usually resulting in the unit blowing both the main fuse and itself (on both double insulated and earthed appliances). This is often accompanied by a pungent burnt smell. Remedy is a straightforward one of replacement. Open circuit problems can occur and the unit will fail to allow current to pass through as normal. The suppressor can easily be checked for continuity using a meter. When checking, inspect the insulation closely and if cracked or at all suspect, renew the complete unit. As many in-line suppressors use the earth path as part of their filtering circuit (although very little power passes through it), it is essential for all such appliances to have a good earth path. If an appliance with an in-line suppressor has a break in its earth path (due to cable, plug or socket fault), small electrical shocks may be experienced when the user touches metal parts of the appliance, especially if they are in contact with a good earth themselves, eg holding a metal sink or worktop. It is essential that such faults are traced and corrected immediately.

An alternative means of suppression may be found where a choke type suppressor is used, fitted in series between live and neutral positions or individually in-line on both live and neutral supplies to individual components. Such units consist of a ferrite core or ring around which the conductor is wound. Some appliances may also use one or more small capacitors linked across live and neutral to obtain suppression in small double insulated appliances. On some appliances, a combination of different types of suppressor may be found.

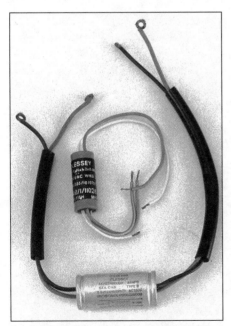

A selection of vacuum cleaner suppression units

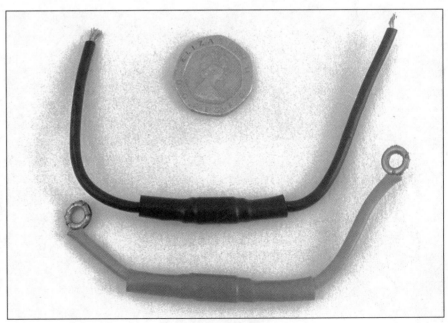

Typical 'choke' suppressors

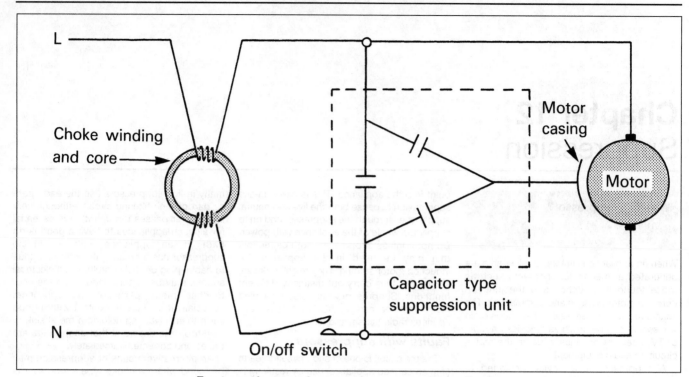

Two types of suppression as used on vacuum cleaner circuits

Chapter 13
Heating elements

There are a very wide variety of household products that contain heating elements. The two basic types are: the exposed single-wire element, most often used in hairdryers, fan heaters, toasters, etc., and the metal sheathed element used in ovens, grills, iron sole plates, immersion heaters, etc. Additional information relating to heating elements can be found in Chapter 18 Ovens and Hobs.

Exposed element

This type of element is simply an exposed length of conductor that heats up when a current is passed along it due to the resistance properties of wire. Being an exposed conductor means that it must be housed and supported in such a way as to avoid accidental contact, which could cause electric shock or burns. It must also be housed in such a way that it can dissipate the heat generated and do the job intended. For instance, a toaster needs an aperture large enough for the bread to go in and also to allow it to rest near the exposed element for it to function correctly. This causes no problem during normal use, but if jamming occurs or the appliance is tampered with whilst still plugged in, contact with the exposed conductors carrying mains voltage is possible. Metal objects or fingers must **never** be used to unblock or probe the loading area of such an appliance whilst it is still plugged in. Even the simple action of wiping it down with a damp cloth after use must be done with the appliance isolated completely: SWITCH OFF, PLUG OUT. This applies to all appliances but is stressed more with items like toasters, hairdryers, irons, etc., as this is an area where carelessness due to

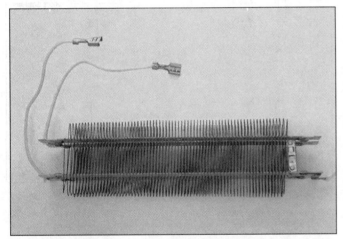
The fan heater element is wound on to two mica supports and has an integral TOC on the right of the picture

Modern kettle with concealed heating element sealed into flat metal base

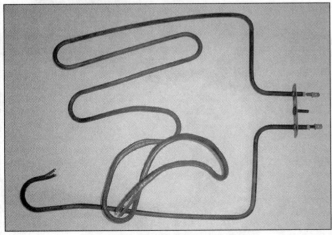
This grill element failed dramatically

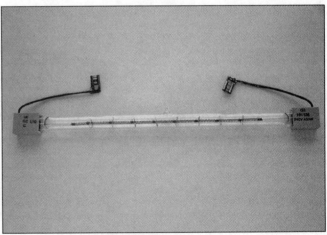
Halogen heating tube

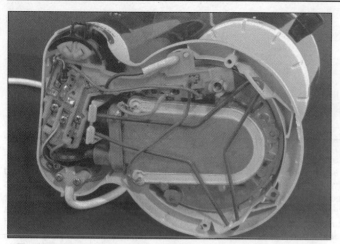

The base plate of this coffee maker has the element set into it. The complete unit is therefore required for a simple open circuit element

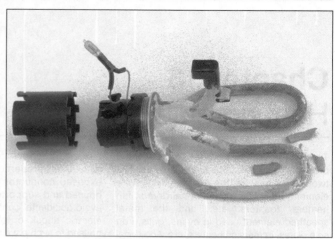

This badly scaled element failed due to infrequent descaling. For advice on descaling, see main section

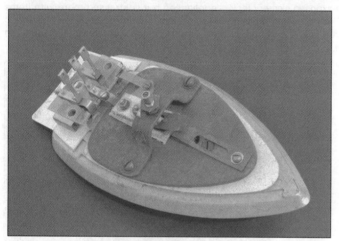

Most modern irons have the heating element set in the soleplate. Older irons like the one above have elements clamped to the soleplate; these, therefore, can be renewed separately

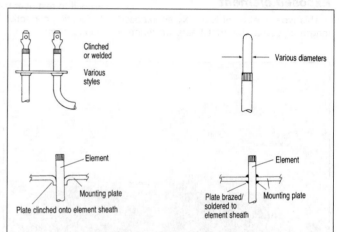

Types of element terminal connection

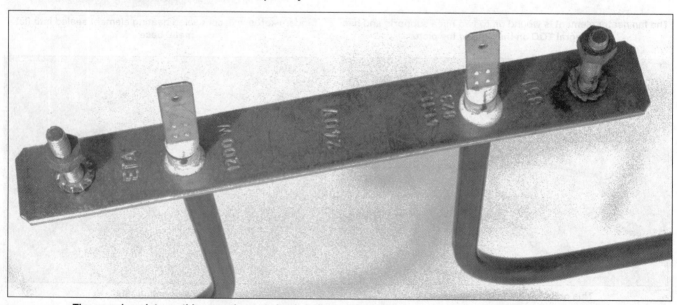

The securing plate on this oven element clearly indicates the voltage requirement and wattage (240V, 1200W)

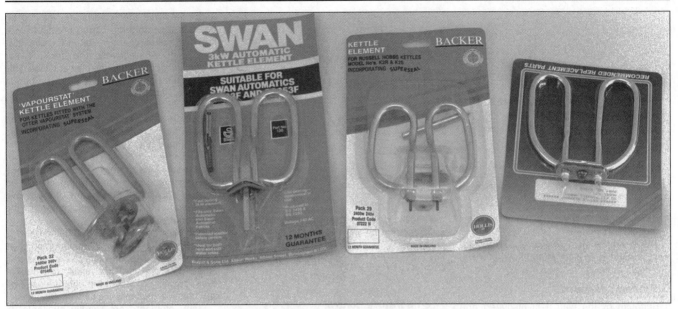

These prepacked kettle elements give a clear view of the shape and fixing along with voltage and wattage details to assist when obtaining a replacement

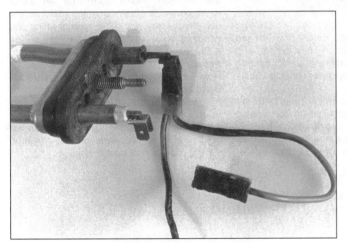

Overheated terminal due to loose connection on live supply

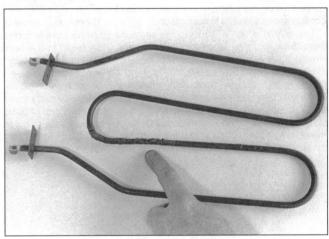

Blown oven element due to short circuit of conductor to outer sheath

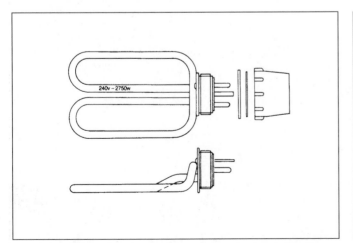

Kettle immersion element (copper sheath, nickel plated)

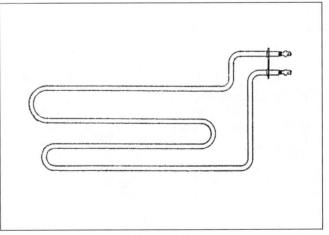

Oven element (mild steel sheath)

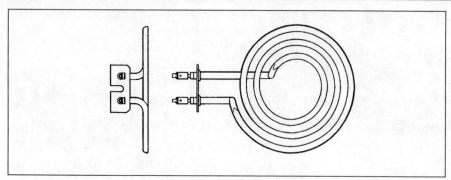

Cooker hotplate (incoloy sheath)

thoughtlessness leads to so many incidents that could be avoided.

The design of elements varies enormously from product to product, but the way in which they work remains the same.

Covered element

Because of the way it is insulated and supported by its solid outer sheath, the metal-covered (shrouded) element can be bent and shaped during manufacture into a multitude of configurations to suit any application.

The way in which it works is the same as described for the exposed-type element. However, the conductor in this type of element is housed within a tube and surrounded by an insulating material (magnesium oxide). Heat is transferred to the outer sheath but the current cannot pass. Outer sheaths are made from various types of metal to suit the particular requirements and conditions. Some are designed for use with the heating portion of the element submersed in water (kettle, immersion, shower, etc.). Others used in cookers, sandwich makers, etc. are designed to radiate heat.

Temperature control

There are several ways in which the temperature is controlled, details of which can be found in the section on *Thermostats*, and also in the relevant appliance sections along with details on care, repair and specific faults on each item.

One of the most common faults with the heater is that of open circuit, ie no current flow through the heater, therefore no heat is produced. This can be due to a broken or loose connection to one of the heater terminals. This then overheats, leaving an obvious discoloration of the connection or terminal, resulting in a break in the circuit at that point. Alternatively, the break in the circuit can occur within the element itself. This can be tested for continuity as described in *Electrical Circuit Testing*.

Another fault that can occur is that of low insulation. In this case, please refer to the section *Low Insulation*. Accompanying this fault is that of the short-circuiting of the heater caused by a complete breakdown of insulation. This results in the appliance blowing fuses or earth tripping (if it is an earthed appliance). Should any of the above faults occur, a complete replacement of the component is required.

Two basic terminal types are found on solid elements and are shown in diagrams on page 46, along with support plate fixing variations. Those on the left are used for cooker elements, etc., those on the right are used on submersible elements like kettles, etc.

Many elements are readily available as spare parts and blister-packed for ease of identification. Make sure that an exact replacement is obtained which matches the original in every way. Size, type of fitting and wattage must match. For kettles, coffee makers, etc., new seals will be required to replace those disturbed during repair.

Note: *Ensure the appliance is isolated – Switch off, Plug out – before commencing any checks or repairs. Clean all connections thoroughly and renew any suspect or overheated connections. Failure to do so will quickly lead to problems due to the high current draw of heating elements.*

Chapter 14
Temperature control and Thermostats

Many of the appliances that feature in these pages have some means of governing the temperature at which they operate. For example, the regulation of high temperature ovens, heaters, etc., by switching elements on or off, and at the other end of the scale, the control of low temperatures in refrigerators, freezers, etc., by turning the compressor motor on or off.

Thermostats range in type from the simple single-action switch which turns off or on at one precept temperature and may be entirely non-adjustable, to the fully adjustable type which can be regulated anywhere within a given range.

The first type might be found in use in a kettle, and the second in an iron or fridge. The TOC (thermal overload cut-out) may be thought of as a thermostat although its purpose is safety only, ie to ensure the power supply to an item is cut off if the safe working temperature is exceeded. All these devices rely on direct or indirect contact with a heat source and are known as thermostats, or simply 'stats'.

The following is an explanation of several types of fixed thermostats, variable thermostats and TOC thermostats. References are made in the various sections which relate to specific appliances and one or more combinations of these devices, so a knowledge of their operation, application and reason for use will be of great assistance when fault finding and repairing.

Fixed thermostats

A thermostat is an automatic device for regulating temperature. A fixed thermostat will either 'make' or 'break' a circuit at a predetermined non-adjustable temperature.

Temperature ratings are usually marked around the metal perimeter on the back of the stat, and also marked NO or NC to indicate normally open contact – that is, closing and making a circuit at a given temperature, or normally closed – opening at a given temperature. Some thermostats combine both variants.

Thermostats are held in position by metal clips or clamps. Make sure of a good contact point and check that the clips or clamps do not trap or touch wires or connectors. Often a white paste is used on the face of the stat; this is a special heat sink compound, so must be renewed if disturbed.

The operation of a fixed thermostat involves the use of a bi-metal strip or disc that consists of two dissimilar metals bonded together. The metals have different expansion rates when subjected to heat. This causes a corresponding distortion or bending of the strip/disc, the movement of which is transferred into a switching operation.

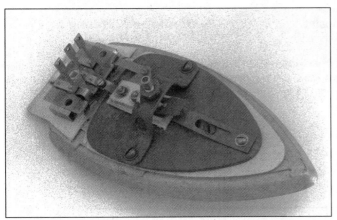

Iron stat in situ

Fixed stat (used in coffee makers, etc.)

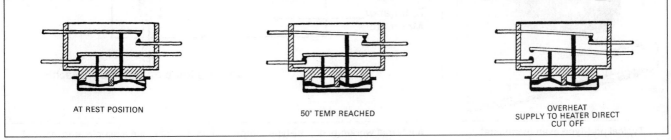

AT REST POSITION

50° TEMP REACHED

OVERHEAT
SUPPLY TO HEATER DIRECT
CUT OFF

A typical fixed thermostat

Variable bi-metal plate-type stat (often used in convector heaters)

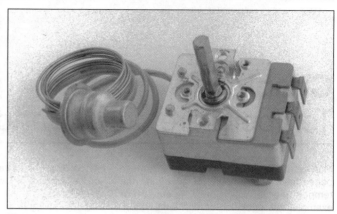

Variable thermostat showing the switches, capillary tube and pod

The temperature at which bending occurs is governed by the make-up of the bi-metal strip/disc and cannot be adjusted in fixed thermostats. Although the external appearance of stats may be similar, it is essential that the correctly rated stat be fitted. Details of a double thermostat are shown although temperatures are for demonstration and do not represent a given appliance.

The accompanying series of three diagrams show a typical thermostat, in this instance with a 50°C (NO) normally open contact and an 85°C (NC) normally closed contact. The latter is a safety thermostat, which operates if overheating should occur within the appliance. The first diagram illustrates the position of a thermostat at rest. Bi-metal discs are mounted directly behind the metal front cover of the stat and are pre-set to distort at given temperatures (in this instance 50°C and 85°C). They are linked to contact switches by pushrods. Distortions of the discs either make or break the corresponding contacts as shown. When removed from the appliance, the thermostat's operation can be tested by placing the metal cover in contact with a known heat source, such as a radiator, hot water, etc. which matches or slightly exceeds the required temperature. Allow a little time for the heat to

warm the stat and bi-metal discs. Establishing the closing or opening of the thermostat can now be carried out by testing for continuity as described in *Electrical Circuit Testing*.

Check temperature with a household thermometer and allow a few degrees either way of the marked temperature on the outer rim of the stat, and remember to check if the stat is normally NO or NC. When cool, check that the stat returns to its normal position as indicated on the rim, ie NO or NC.

Warning: Before attempting to remove or repair any component from the machine, isolate the machine from the main electrical supply by removing the plug from the wall socket.

The variable thermostat

Figure A (below) shows a schematic diagram of the internal workings of a pod-type

thermostat. This is found on appliances that have a variable temperature control. The stat consists of an oil/gel filled pod that is connected to the switch by a capillary tube. When the oil/gel in the pod is heated or cooled, it expands or contracts in the tube and operates a diaphragm. This diaphragm acts on the switchgear thus breaking the circuit and in this instance, 'making' the other. When the oil cools it contracts, pulling the switch in the opposite direction. The switch is then in its original position and the process repeats if necessary. A device that works on a similar principle as the variable thermostat is the pan sensor, for details of this component see *Chapter 16 Ovens and hobs*.

Removing and refitting a pod-type thermostat

The pod that is found at the base of the capillary tube must be eased from its position gently, taking care not to kink or pull unduly on the capillary tube itself.

Typical pod-type oven thermostat

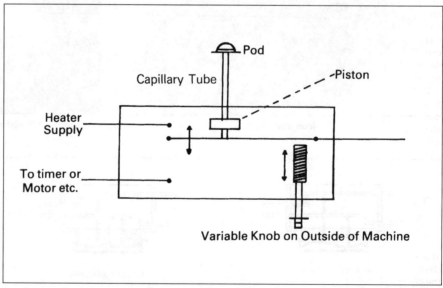

A Internal workings of pod-type thermostat. In this instance a simple auto-defrost thermostat

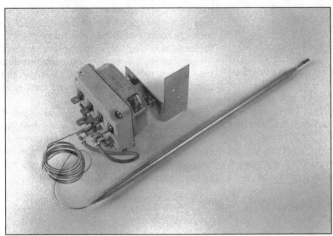

Pod type thermostat

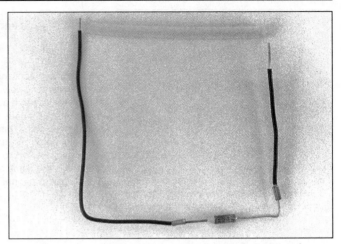

Micro-temp (now used in a wide variety of equipment)

Note: *When fitting or refitting this form of thermostat, the capillary tube must not come into contact with any electrical contacts such as the heater terminals, or with any moving parts or sharp edges. When fitted, the tube should be checked along its entire length for contact with these items. Any coiled sections should be duplicated in the replacement unit.*

The iron stat shown is a variable thermostat that uses the bi-metal strip principle. A large bi-metal strip that has one contact point on it can be seen. The opposing contact point is mounted on a movable threaded shaft, which is linked to the temperature control knob. Heat causes the bi-metal blade to distort which causes the contact to make or break depending on the degree of distortion required relevant to the position of the movable contact point. This is a simple yet effective means of temperature control. Unfortunately, the constant operation and flexing of the bi-metal during normal use can quickly tire the bi-metal resulting in ineffective control or temperature regulation. In some cases, a degree of adjustment to the stat is possible and recalibration will often be necessary. A pyrometer is required if an iron needs to be recalibrated.

With many appliances, it may be advisable to obtain a new thermostat that is factory calibrated. Take care when handling such stats as the bi-metal blades can be very sharp and can also be easily knocked out of calibration.

Thermal Overload Cut-out

The thermal overload cut-out (TOC) is a safety device that is generally connected in-line with the item it is protecting, ie power supplied to a heating element will first pass through the TOC and on to the heater. If the safe working temperature of the heater is exceeded, the TOC will operate and go open circuit and cut power to the element. There are two ways in which the TOC can reset when normal working temperature has been reached. The simplest is a self-setting version similar in operation to the fixed stat described previously, which works on the bi-metal strip principle. This type can give rise to cycling of the fault, that is to say constant heating and cooling of the element via the TOC, tripping on overheat and resetting when cool. If not spotted and the cause for the overheat rectified, failure of the TOC will occur. This may simply be a failure to reset, or worse, the contacts of the TOC may short or weld together and effectively render the device useless. The result of the latter could cause serious problems.

The second type of TOC is a version that requires manual resetting once tripped. It cannot reset itself thus eliminating the possibility of cycling. Resetting is usually by pressing a reset button. Remember to unplug the appliance before doing this and check for the cause of the tripping and rectify as required.

Shapes, sizes and styles of bi-metal TOC vary. Some look identical to fixed thermostats and are housed in an insulated container. In other types the bi-metal disc or blade is not covered. Such exposed types can also trip if overload current occurs; eg if a motor fails to run due to seizing up, current loading would be higher than normal causing the TOC in circuit with the motor to heat up and trip out. Obviously TOCs must match the equipment they protect. Although they all perform a similar operation, each has its own temperature setting. When renewing the TOC, ensure that an identical replacement is used. **Never** by-pass a TOC.

Note: *Take care with the blade/disc TOCs because they can be very sharp.*

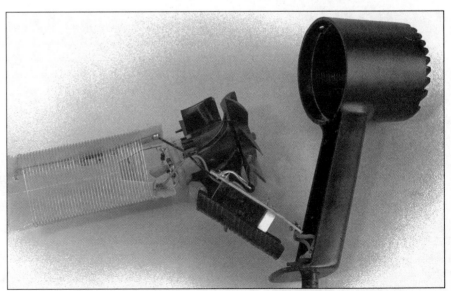

The overheat thermostat (TOC) can be seen set inside this hairdryer element

Bi-metallic discs are used to mechanically operate two safety switches on the jug kettle

Thermal Fuses and Micro Temps

Many modern appliances requiring protection from overheating now use a different overheat fail-safe device that avoids the use of moving parts and contact points that may in themselves fail. This device also has the benefit of being very small. It has many names – thermal fuse, micro-temp, safety diode. Its function is the same as any TOC, but once it has tripped it cannot reset itself or be reset manually and renewal is the only answer. This type of system gives a high degree of safety to many items that in the past could give rise to dangerous situations through overheating. Though small, it is easily recognisable but it may be housed in a protective sheath in the appliance. The outer shell gives details of operational temperature.

Testing is as before: if OK, closed circuit, if tripped, open circuit. Make sure that an identical replacement is fitted and crimp-fit securely, ensuring that the new fuse is in the same direction and fitted in the same position as the original. **DO NOT** bypass this item.

Chapter 15
Waste Disposal Units

Although not found in every kitchen at present, waste disposal units are becoming more popular. Essentially a waste disposal unit is a vertically mounted induction motor (see *Chapter 11*), shaft seal, shredding disc and chamber. The shaft of the induction motor is used to directly drive the shredding mechanism which breaks/cuts the waste into pieces small enough to pass through the normal kitchen waste system.

There are two ways in which the shredding action is produced:

Early systems have the cutting blades mounted directly onto the motor shaft. When switched 'ON' the blades simply rotate and shred almost anything that comes into contact with them.

Later and more current models now use a disc with pivoted metal weights attached to the upper surface. The disc is again attached directly to the induction motor shaft. A set of fixed (stationary) cutting blades surround the disc. When the motor runs the metal weights not only help break up the waste, they propel pieces of waste material onto the ring of cutters around the disc.

Many of the problems that occur with waste disposal units can be attributed to misuse of one type or another. The following text therefore contains both repair and preventative guidance.

Safety warning

It is essential that the unit is isolated from the mains electrical supply before any inspection or work is undertaken. **Do not** rely on the isolation switch, ensure the supply plug is removed or if fitted to a spur outlet that the circuit supplying that outlet is turned off at the consumer unit (fuse removed or MCB switched off). See *Basic Electrics* Chapter.

Basic use and care

A common failure of the unit is caused by cooking utensils or bones blocking/jamming the rotating disc. Care must be exercised, when using the unit, to ensure that such items are not allowed to enter. Jamming the unit in this way not only damages the disc but also puts strain on the motor, resulting in overheating. The unit will have a TOC (thermal overload cut-out, see *Temperature Control and Thermostats* Chapter). This will normally be a manual reset type with the reset button located on the body of the unit. If the TOC has operated do not simply press the reset button. Isolate the unit and investigate the reason why it tripped in the first place. If during use an unsuitable item enters the unit and jams it, do not reach in or grab an exposed item. Always fully isolate the unit first as described earlier. A loud buzzing noise from the stalled motor often precedes the tripping of the TOC which will have tripped due to overheating of the jammed motor and quite a period of time will be required for the motor to cool sufficiently to allow the device to be reset.

To help the unit work correctly always ensure that a continuous flow of water is used before, during and for a period after shredding is completed. The noise of the motor will change (it runs much quieter) when the unit has completed the shredding action. Running water through the unit in this way has several benefits. It helps the shredding action, flushes the residue from the disc chamber and helps the waste to flow completely out of the pipe work.

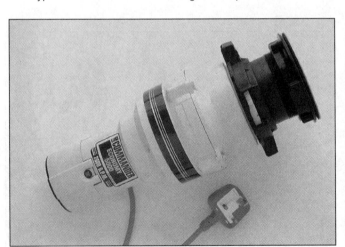

1 Firstly isolate the unit as described earlier. Note: To aid the photographic sequence this waste disposal unit is not shown *in situ* and is shown complete with sink fixing collar

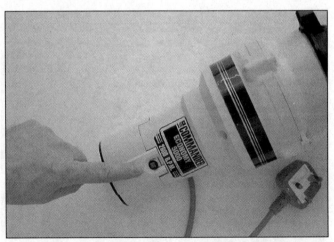

2 Check the reset button. If it has tripped, only reset it when the reason for it tripping has been identified and corrected

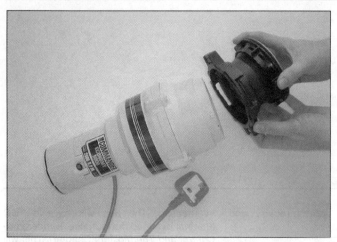

3 Separate the waste disposal from the sink support collar. In this instance a locking collar is used which is turned anti-clockwise

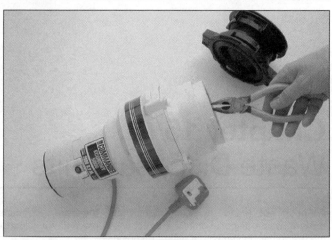

4 With the cover removed check to see if there are any objects jammed in the unit. If so remove them with pliers or grips. DO NOT place your hands inside even though the unit is isolated as there are very sharp edges inside

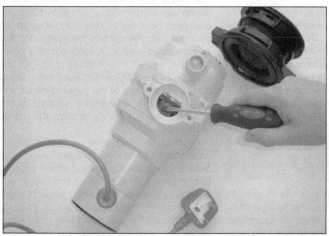

5 If the item is below the disc it may be possible to gain access to it via the drain hole

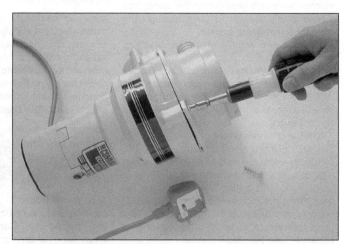

6 To check the disc for damage or to get at difficult items remove the grinding/shredding chamber fixing screws

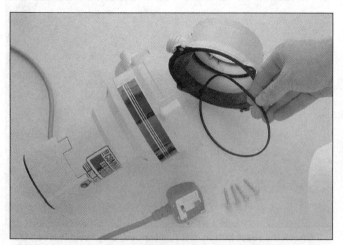

7 When removing the grinding/shredding cover take care not to damage the chamber seal. Renew if required

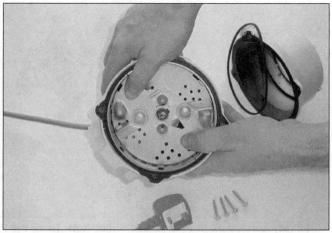

8 Check that the disc is secure on the drive shaft and cannot be rocked from side to side

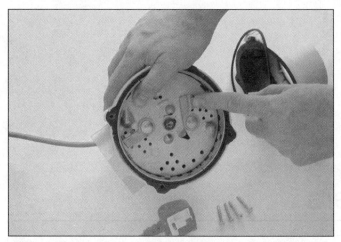

9 Check that the disc arms (often referred to as hammers) move freely

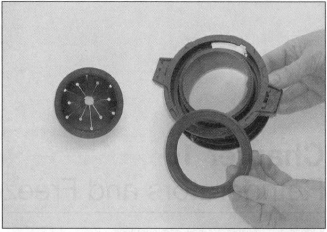

10 Periodically check the sink coupling gasket and splash guard cover as they inevitably deteriorate over a period of time especially if they come into contact with dishwasher discharge and/or kitchen bleach

Another helpful tip is to avoid the use of bleach or caustic cleaning agents as these can shorten the life of the motor shaft seal and gaskets within the unit. If the shaft seal between the shredding chamber and the motor shaft fails (even slightly) water can penetrate the top bearing and the motor. This can cause the motor to run noisily, vibrate, seize up and possibly short circuit. It is best to renew shaft seals as soon as they are found to be faulty.

If the unit develops an unpleasant odour and you wish to avoid the use of chemicals, you can run a combination of ice cubes and lemon or orange peel through it to clean the interior of the unit.

Even when used correctly it is still possible for the disc mechanism to jam. Occasionally some makes supply a special tool that can be inserted into the loading aperture and allows you to manually turn the disc. Another method is

the use of an Allen key, which is used on the base of the unit to manually turn the motor shaft. It should go without saying that these and any other methods of freeing a jammed disc must only be done with the unit fully isolated. If your unit was supplied with a special freeing tool then follow the instructions that came with the unit. If, however, your unit was not supplied with a freeing tool or you have mislaid it then the following should be of help.

Fault finding - Waste disposal units

Won't work at all

Possible causes

a. Faulty supply, plug, socket or outlet

b. Reset button tripped

Action

Check, isolate and check for blockages, seal damage, seized bearing(s), faulty motor (see *Motors*)

See *Plugs and sockets*

Makes a noise but does not work

a. Jammed disc

b. Seized bearing

c. Cutters worn/damaged

d. Motor/capacitor problem

Check for blockages see this Chapter

Check shaft seal, bearing and disc fixing, see this Chapter

Check condition of cutters and disc. Renew if worn or damaged

See *Motors* chapter

External leak

a. Sink gasket weeping

b. Motor shaft seal worn/damaged.

Check condition of gasket. Renew if required

Check condition of motor/chamber shaft seal and the motor for water/detergent ingress

Works but does not drain waste or water away

a. Blockage in chamber/outlet

b. Blockage in sink drain

Check for blockages in shredding chamber or its outlet

Check sink drain pipework for blockages. Strip the pipework down or use rodding to clear blockage. Avoid the use of chemicals for this process

Chapter 16
Refrigerators and Freezers

Fridges and freezers are now commonplace items in the home. Faults can be inconvenient and expensive when the contents thaw out. Most, if not all, contain CFC gases for the cooling system and within the insulation materials. Although efforts are now being made to eliminate the use of these gases in new machines, it will be a considerable time before non-CFC use becomes the norm. Whilst CFCs are still in widespread use there are a number of things you can do to minimise their associated problems.

Firstly, regular servicing of your appliance will reduce failure and the need to renew it prematurely – at the moment, probably with another CFC-using appliance. At present, CFC free fridges and freezers are expensive, but time and demand should see a reduction in costs.

If faults occur that render your appliance uneconomical or unsafe to repair, its disposal **must** be carried out correctly. The refrigerant gas should be extracted and collected in cylinders for safe disposal or recycling. This cannot be done without specialist equipment and knowledge, but local councils and firms will advise on the availability of this service. Remember, even the foam insulation may contain CFCs so it must also be disposed of properly. All this may seem pointless for one scrap machine that is no longer of any use, but depletion of the ozone layer can *only* be halted by taking these seemingly insignificant steps.

It is not possible for you to repair some faults that may occur because expensive specialist equipment is needed for the sealed system. Do not attempt repairs to the sealed pressurised pipework. However, you can, by elimination, trace and repair many of the common faults found in fridges and freezers. If, after carrying out all normal checks, a fault is suspected in the sealed system, it is advisable to call in a qualified refrigeration engineer. A competent engineer should collect any gas that he needs to bleed off during the repair and also use inert gas as opposed to refrigerant to test for leaks. It would be advisable to check this with your engineer before he starts any repairs.

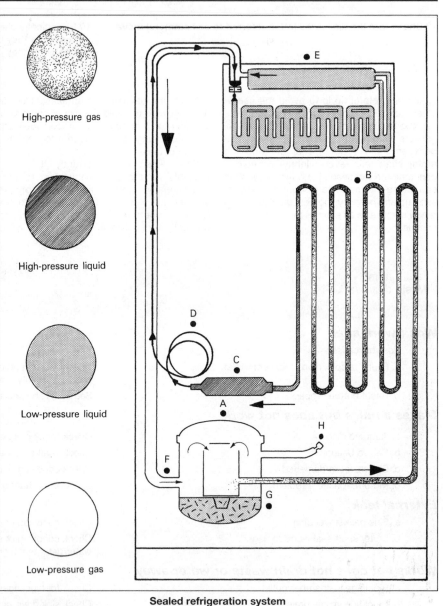

High-pressure gas

High-pressure liquid

Low-pressure liquid

Low-pressure gas

Sealed refrigeration system

A   Induction motor
B   Condenser matrix
C   Dryer/filter
D   Capillary tube
E   Evaporator
F   Tube
G   Reservoir
H   Evacuation tube

This rear view of a fridge unit clearly shows the motor/compressor unit to the base and the condenser matrix above

Internal view of fridge compartment showing the evaporation unit and drainage channel below for auto-defrost

How do fridges and freezers work?

Although there are many different types of appliance on the market, most of them work on the same principle of compression and expansion within a sealed system like that shown.

At the heart of the sealed network of pipes and tubing lies an induction motor (usually relay start) (A) connected directly to a piston operated compressor with which it forms one complete unit. The motor/compressor unit also acts as a reservoir (G). When the motor is supplied with power, operation of the compressor begins. Low pressure gas is drawn into the compressor chamber via tube (F) and compressed by a rapidly moving piston which forces the now compressed gas into the condenser tube system (B).

Reed valves are situated on both the inlet and outlet of the compressor unit and operate in opposition to each other by the pressures produced. Heat generated in the compression sequence and any that has been absorbed from the sealed motor is dissipated in the condenser matrix (B). This cooling allows the refrigerant gas to liquefy. The liquefied gas then passes through a dryer/filter (C) designed to remove any traces of water vapour or crystals prior to passing through a capillary tube (small bore) and on to the evaporator.

A small-bore capillary tube is used to control the flow of liquid to the evaporator. When the high pressure liquid gas from the capillary tube enters the large network of the evaporator (E) the sudden expansion of the liquefied gas results in dramatic cooling of the unit as the liquid reverts to a lower pressure gas once more. Being a sealed system, this is a continuous operation as long as the motor and compressor unit run, the system remains sealed and there is enough gas within the system. The tube (H) is used to evacuate the system during manufacture and to introduce

The internal view of this freezer section shows the evaporator unit forms two of the shelves in this model (in common with several other makes), and in this instance requires defrosting

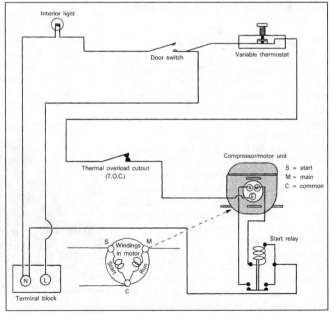

A simple refrigerator circuit with relay motor start

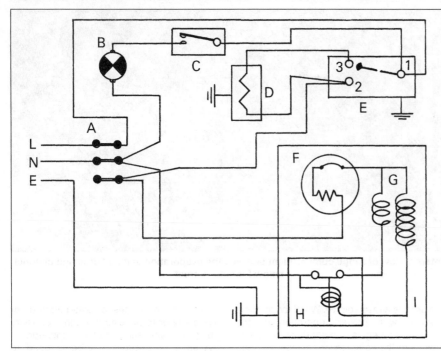

Typical auto-defrost circuit

A	Terminal block	D	Defrost heater	G	Motor windings
B	Interior light	E	Thermostat	H	Relay
C	Door micro-switch	F	Motor overload protection	I	Motor/compressor unit

Typical solid state PTC motor starting device. Refer to: Motors chapter for function details

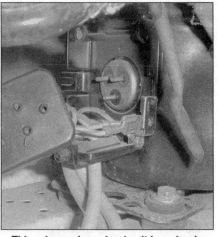

This relay and overload unit is a simple push fit on to the compressor's motor pins

the coolant gas then or during servicing by qualified personnel.

Note: *Most systems allow for a length of the capillary tube from the filter to be fixed on the outside (or inside on some machines) of the return from the evaporator. This is done to improve the efficiency of the sealed system and keeps the return tube from forming condensation due to its being colder than the surrounding air.*

Refrigerator auto defrost

The automatic defrost operation is done simply by warming the evaporator area via a small heater unit. This melts the build-up of ice particles that run off the base of the unit into a catchment channel. The channel is designed to funnel the liquid through a small hole at the rear of the appliance on to a dished area at the top of the compressor unit. The heat generated by the normal operation of the compressor/motor unit evaporates the small but regular amount of water to the atmosphere. The switching of the heater unit is linked to the thermostat operation, working in opposition to the cooling sequence.

Note: *The small hole from the collection channel to the exterior dish mounted on the compressor/motor unit can easily block. This would cause water to accumulate in the base of the refrigerator, which may mislead you into thinking the appliance had a serious fault. Periodically check that the vent hole and channels are free from debris. Clearing of this*

hole can be done with a pipe cleaner or something of similar flexibility.

Temperature control

Temperature variations in fridges and freezers are governed by a simple thermostat arrangement. Nearly all manufacturers use variable capillary thermostats and replacement units are generally available. When obtaining a new thermostat, make sure it is identical to the one you will be replacing. It is advisable to fit the new unit on a one-to-one basis. As with all repairs, ensure the appliance is isolated (switch off, plug out) before checks or repairs are carried out.

A guide is given to the most common faults that occur and ways in which they can be

diagnosed and ultimately rectified. Many faults can be avoided and the life span of the product extended if a few simple checks and maintenance routines are carried out.

1 Check that all the seals around the door are in good condition. Renew split or poor seals immediately, otherwise warm moist air will

Checking of the internal induction motor circuit. In this instance the lower pin is the 'common' neutral connection and marked (C). When testing between this and each of the other two pins in turn you should have one resistance higher than the other. The start winding which is often called the auxiliary winding (A) should have a higher resistance than the run winding - often called the main winding (M). Measuring between pins A and M should result in a resistance reading higher than both of the previous readings ie the sum total of both windings in series

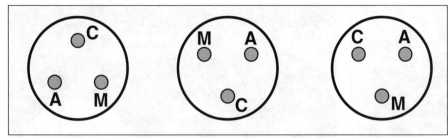

Compressor pin connections vary in position between manufacturers. Shown are three popular variations. The connections are often marked C - common, A - auxiliary (start winding), M - main (run winding). If not you can use the testing sequence shown in the accompanying photograph to work out which winding is which to ensure the correct fitting of the relay/starting device

enter, producing a quick build-up of ice on the evaporator and surrounding areas, incorrect temperature, and damage to the lining of the cabinet. All this contributes greatly to making the unit inefficient and uneconomical to run.

2 Do not leave the door open for long periods at a time. Kitchens, especially when cooking is in progress, can have a high degree of moisture in the air. This moisture-laden air is attracted to the coldest parts of the room; if left open moisture in the atmosphere will inevitably condense on the cold interior.

3 Some appliances are designed to defrost automatically, but many have to be regularly defrosted manually. Make sure you are aware which type of fridge or freezer you have and read the instructions regarding defrosting.

4 On auto defrost models, check regularly that the vent hole and channel are clear (as described earlier).

5 Ensure that the correct setting is used for the type of foodstuffs stored and for the length of time you expect to store them. The correct storage of foodstuffs is most important. If the temperature is not cold enough, a build-up of bacteria in a product could result, whereas if the temperature is too cold, ice crystals will form in the food. This can also produce higher running costs. The correct storage of food in freezers is most important and the temperatures must be considered carefully. A star rating system operates and is shown below. Pre-packed frozen foods will show their star rating on the packet and should be strictly followed. Your appliance manual should be consulted so that you are aware of its capabilities. Star rating, temperature and storage times are as follows:

* – 6°C or below. Short storage (1 week)
** –12°C or below.
    Medium storage (1 month)
*** –18°C or below. 3 months
**** –18°C 3 months with fresh food freeze
    down capability

Freezer compressor with relay/overload plastic cover removed

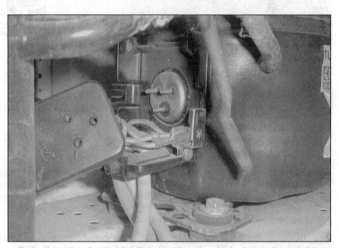

Relay/overload unit highlighting the simple 3 pin push on 'plug and socket type' fitting

An alternative combined PTC relay and bi-metallic overload unit

Internal view of this combined PTC relay and bi-metallic overload unit shows a severe overheat and burnout of the internal connections and components. This is a common cause of failure

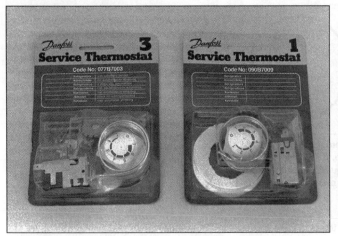

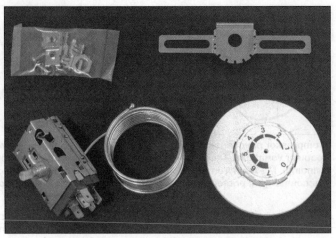

Various types of thermostats are available - make sure that a direct replacement is obtained which matches the original

Typical thermostat kit now widely available

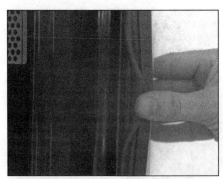

Check door seals regularly for signs of wear, cracks or splitting, etc, and renew if suspect. Adjust door if out of position

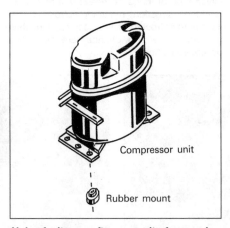

Compressor unit

Rubber mount

Noise faults are often a result of excessive movement of the compressor/motor unit during operation. Check that it is mounted correctly on its rubber supports

6 Regularly clean the interior of the appliance. When cleaning a freezer ask a friend or neighbour to store your food. If this is not possible, wrap the contents in blankets and store them in a cardboard box to insulate them. As with any maintenance or repair, completely isolate the appliance and defrost. The interior can then be thoroughly cleaned using a recognised fridge/freezer interior cleaner. Alternatively, a weak solution of bicarbonate of soda can be used and rinsed off with lukewarm water. The interior plastic parts must not be washed in water hotter than lukewarm. Dry with a clean cloth only – heaters of any kind should not be used. Strong chemicals, perfumed cleaning products or abrasive cleaners are not advised and should be avoided. In no circumstances should salt be used to speed up defrosting. This would cause damage to various metal parts within the compartments.

7 It is essential for fridges and freezers to stand on a firm base capable of carrying the weight of the appliance *when full*. Make sure that the appliance is as level as possible (most have adjustable feet) and that it does not rock. If it is a freestanding unit, care must be taken that it does not rest on, or touch other fitments,

otherwise you will have to suffer vibrating noises when the compressor unit operates!

8 Freestanding appliances should have adequate space between the rear of the cabinet and the wall. The pipe work matrix on the rear of the unit requires good air circulation for it to operate efficiently.

Frost free systems

As the name implies, this system does not produce an ice build-up during the refrigeration or freezing process.

Cooling is by compression and expansion with the addition of a motorised fan that circulates the air evenly throughout the compartments to give a more even distribution of cold air. Included in the system is a means of dehumidifying the air which is being circulated (it condenses on the coldest part of the system and then is drained away to evaporate outside the load compartment). This is a simple operation that works extremely well. The main benefits are that

there is no ice build-up within the compartments thus eliminating manual defrosting. Due to the reduced humidity level, fresh food lasts longer and keeps its flavour and texture longer. Constant air circulation helps keep a more even temperature throughout, and reduces food odours.

Mechanical and electrical problems encountered will be much the same as conventional appliances with the addition of possible faults with the circulation fan and motor. Although faults associated with excess frost build up are eliminated with this system, the running cost and the initial purchase price are higher.

Fault finding – fridges and freezers

The following is a compilation of the faults most likely to occur in both refrigerators and freezers. Seven general symptoms are listed with the possible causes in the most likely failure order printed beneath. Alongside the likely causes are notes on action to be taken. Regular checks and maintenance of equipment will make you more aware of the operation and workings of your particular machine. This in turn will help greatly in diagnosing and isolating any faults that occur. **Remember**: *Safety is paramount and in no circumstances should it be compromised. Always double check that the appliance is unplugged. A good tip is to keep the plug in view so that no-one else can plug it in without your knowing.*

DO NOT jump to conclusions and commence work in a haphazard way. Calmly sit down and start to work out what the problem may be and form the plan of attack in a logical and concise manner. It is assumed that you will already have read the main section *Refrigerators and Freezers*.

Freezer noise when running flowchart

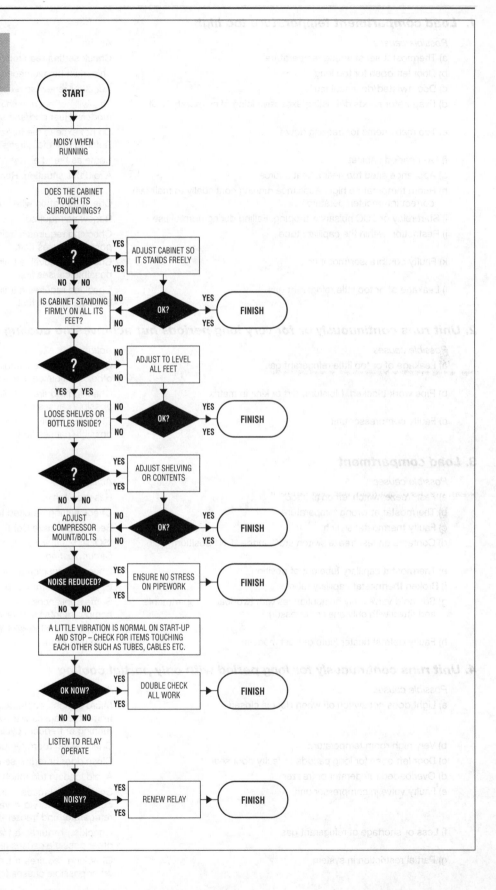

START

NOISY WHEN RUNNING

DOES THE CABINET TOUCH ITS SURROUNDINGS?

? — YES/YES → ADJUST CABINET SO IT STANDS FREELY

NO / NO

IS CABINET STANDING FIRMLY ON ALL ITS FEET?

OK? — NO/NO ←   YES/YES → FINISH

? — NO/NO → ADJUST TO LEVEL ALL FEET

YES / YES

LOOSE SHELVES OR BOTTLES INSIDE?

OK? — NO/NO ←   YES/YES → FINISH

? — YES/YES → ADJUST SHELVING OR CONTENTS

NO / NO

ADJUST COMPRESSOR MOUNT/BOLTS

OK? — NO/NO ←   YES/YES → FINISH

NOISE REDUCED? — YES/YES → ENSURE NO STRESS ON PIPEWORK → FINISH

NO / NO

A LITTLE VIBRATION IS NORMAL ON START-UP AND STOP – CHECK FOR ITEMS TOUCHING EACH OTHER SUCH AS TUBES, CABLES ETC.

OK NOW? — YES/YES → DOUBLE CHECK ALL WORK → FINISH

NO / NO

LISTEN TO RELAY OPERATE

NOISY? — YES/YES → RENEW RELAY → FINISH

1. Load compartment temperature too high

Possible causes	Action
a) Thermostat set at wrong temperature	Check setting required for contents
b) Door left open for too long	This must be avoided for reasons stated in text
c) Door twisted/door seal faulty	Adjust or renew as required
d) Evaporator needs defrosting/excessive icing of evaporator unit	This will not occur with regular defrosting or on auto defrost models. Heat pod/stat suspect. Check and renew if required
e) Too many items for freezing down	Do not exceed the freeze-down capability of your appliance. Refer to manufacturer's instruction book for details
f) Overloaded cabinet	Same as b and e.
g) Appliance sited too near a heat source	Avoid this situation. Reposition appliance
h) Room temperature high. Appliance running continually to maintain correct internal temperature	Check operation when room temperature returns to normal
i) Start relay or TOC nuisance-tripping. Failing during normal use	Renew as required
j) Restriction within the capillary tube	Checking requires a trained engineer. Check and eliminate possible causes first.
k) Faulty compressor/motor unit	Checking requires a trained engineer. Check and eliminate other possible causes first
l) Leakage of or too little refrigerant gas	Checking requires a trained engineer. Check and eliminate other possible causes first

2. Unit runs continuously or for very long periods but achieves no cooling at all

Possible causes	Action
a) Leakage of or too little refrigerant gas	Checking requires a trained engineer. Check and eliminate all other possible causes first
b) Pipe work blocked. Moisture, dirt or kink in matrix	Checking requires a trained engineer. Check and eliminate other possible causes first
c) Faulty compressor unit	Checking requires a trained engineer. Check and eliminate other possible causes first

3. Load compartment

Possible causes	Action
a) Fast freeze switch left on (if fitted)	Reset switch
b) Thermostat at wrong temperature	Check setting required for contents
c) Faulty thermostat switch	See Temperature Control and Thermostats
d) Contacts on fast freeze switch stuck in the "ON" position	ISOLATE. Check switch and renew if required. See Electrical Circuit Testing
e) Thermostat capillary tube out of position	Check. Reposition as required
f) Broken thermostat capillary tube	See Temperature Control and Thermostats
g) Solenoid valve (only on appliances with two-load compartments and fitted with only one compressor)	Some appliances use one compressor for two load compartments via a valve, which alternates cooling between refrigerator and freezer via the thermostats
h) Faulty defrost heater (auto defrost models)	Heat pod or thermostat suspect. Check and renew if required

4. Unit runs continuously for long period with only partial cooling

Possible causes	Action
a) Light does not switch off when door is closed	Micro switch or actuating arm sticking. ISOLATE and test. Heat from bulb causes warming of the interior, hence the continual running or frequent cycling
b) Very high room temperature	Check when room temperature returns to normal
c) Door left open for long periods or faulty door seal	Close door or renew seals as necessary
d) Overloaded refrigerator or freezer	Avoid loading too much at any one time
e) Faulty valve in compressor unit	Some appliances use one compressor for two load compartments via a valve, which alternates cooling between refrigerator and freezer via the thermostats
f) Loss or shortage of refrigerant gas	Checking requires a trained engineer. Check and eliminate all other possible causes first
g) Partial restriction in system	Checking requires a trained engineer. Check and eliminate all other possible causes first

5. Compressor/motor unit fails to start/run

Possible causes	Action
a) No power from wall socket	Check house fuse. See *Safety Guide* and *Plugs and Sockets*
b) Faulty thermostat	See *Temperature Control and Thermostats*
c) Faulty start relay or overload protector	See *Electric Motors*. Renew as required
d) Open circuit or shorted wiring harness	See *Wiring Harness Faults*.
e) Faulty or burnt out compressor windings	See *Electric Motors*
f) Seized compressor – mechanical	Checking and rectification requires a trained engineer
g) Insufficient ventilation for condenser causing the compressor/motor unit to overheat and trip the TOC	Adjust position to allow airflow
h) Extremely low room temperature (below freezing)	No need for appliance to operate

6. Intermittent TOC operation when motor starts (nuisance tripping)

Possible causes	Action
a) Faulty thermostat	See *Temperature Control and Thermostats*. Renew if required. See photo sequences
b) Faulty start relay or overload protector	See *Electric Motors*. Renew if required
c) Faulty motor compressor	This requires a trained engineer. Check and eliminate all other possible causes first
d) Restriction within the capillary tube	Inspect capillary tube for kinks. Internal faults require trained engineer
e) Overloaded cabinet	Avoid loading too much at any one time

7. Symptom: Load compartment odours

Possible causes	Action
a) Appliance stored/left switched off for long time with door closed	Always store appliances with door left slightly ajar to allow air to circulate around the interior
b) Unclean load compartment	Clean interior regularly
c) Uncovered foodstuffs	Cover strong-smelling foodstuffs when storing

Fridge thermostat renewal

1 Ensure the appliance is isolated before commencing any repair or servicing - Switch OFF, plug OUT

2 The fault with this fridge was that it continually ran and would not regulate temperature. The fault was traced to a broken capillary tube on the thermostat behind the evaporator plate

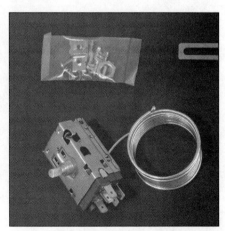

3 A thermostat was obtained and checked for compatibility prior to fitting

4 To remove the old thermostat, the selector knob was eased off the shaft (push fit only in this instance). With the bulb cover and bulb removed, access was gained to the securing screw on the rear

5 With the fixing screw removed the cover was eased carefully from its position to expose the thermostat. A note of the wiring was made prior to removal

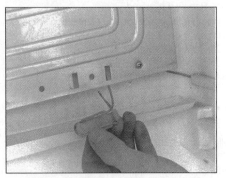

6 The end of the capillary tube was secured to the evaporator by means of a plastic clip and was easily removed. Note the way in which the tube is fitted

Refitting was a reversal of the removal procedure. Great care was taken to ensure that all the capillary tubes and wiring were refitted as original and all covers repositioned correctly. Earth continuity tests were done prior to functional testing via an RCD protected supply

Chapter 17
Dehumidifiers

Dehumidifiers are closely related to both fridges/freezers and air conditioning units. To prevent repetition it is essential that you have read and understood the previous chapter on Refrigerators and Freezers with specific emphasis on how the sealed system operates.

In recent years the purchase price of domestic dehumidifiers has reduced and this has in turn led to an increase in their numbers. They can be found in many combinations, shapes, sizes and prices but all work on the same principle. The principle being that moisture in the atmosphere will readily condense on cold surfaces. No doubt you will have witnessed this principle in action many times and thought nothing of it. When you pour a very cold drink into a glass, beads of water form on the outside of the glass. What is happening is that as the air in the immediate vicinity of the glass is cooled the moisture within it condenses on the even cooler surface of the glass. If you kept the glass cool by adding ice cubes quite a pool of water would eventually surround the glass. The volume of water that condenses is dependent on the amount held within the air (the humidity). Hence the term 'de-humidify' ie remove the water from the atmosphere.

A similar effect can be seen when you open the door of a freezer in a humid kitchen, small clouds of moisture form in the very cold air escaping from the interior. Moisture from the atmosphere also enters the cabinet and freezes on the very coldest parts and creates ice inside the freezer.

Why do we need dehumidifiers?

The simple answer is that under normal situations we don't. However, there are times when there can be an excess of water in the

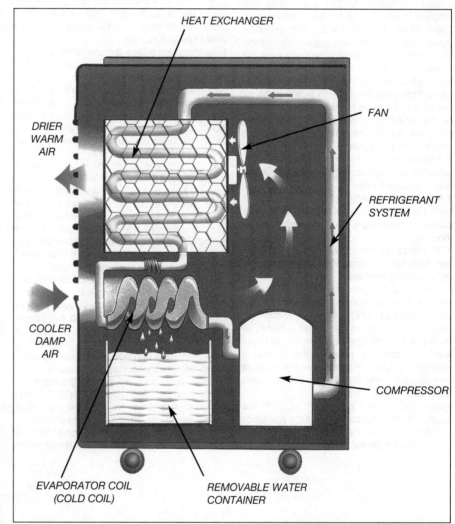

Air from the room is drawn in through the front grille by the fan. It passes over the cooling coils/surface and the water droplets in the air condense on the cool surfaces. The water drips from the coils and collects in the container below. The cooler but drier air then passes over the warm compressor matrix and is warmed before it re-enters the room. A humidistat situated in the incoming airflow detects the level of humidity and will turn the appliance off when the required setting is reached. A simple but effective system

atmosphere and the surroundings in general. This can lead to damp walls, floors, furniture etc., which in turn can lead to the growth of mould. High levels of humidity can have a knock on effect and cause health problems for those living in such damp conditions. The solution to this problem is to remove excess moisture from the atmosphere and surroundings by using a dehumidifier.

How do they remove moisture?

Dehumidifiers use the cold glass and condensation principal mentioned earlier. In simple terms a dehumidifier is a fridge without a cabinet. Please refer to the sealed system diagram in Chapter 16 for the following text. The cooling coils, where the high-pressure liquid expands back into a gas, creates the cold surface (E) to attract moisture from the air passing over it. The cooled but now dry air leaving the cooling coils is passed over the warm compressor matrix (B) to warm the air before it is returned to the room. Depending on the model, a number of other components complete the product. The three below are standard on all models.

1 A fan is used to ensure that as much air as possible from the surrounding area passes over the cooled surface.

2 A means of controlling the required level of humidity. The device used for this purpose is called a humidistat (not standard on all models).

3 A container to collect the water (the condensate) removed during the dehumidifying process.

Additional components and features may also be found on some models, which are a combination of dehumidifier and room (fan) heater. Other features include air purifiers, air fresheners, drainage kits and condensate level switches to prevent the container overflowing. Many models have auto-defrost thermostats should the cooling coils accumulate ice and freeze up.

Note: *This is not usually a fault of the appliance. Freezing can occur if the appliance is used in situations below 18°C (65°F) Refer to correct use for details.*

Repair and servicing

In reality dehumidifiers require little in the way of maintenance and DIY work must be restricted to external compressor motor problems such as relays and PTC's (see *Motors* chapter), humidistats, thermostats, fan motor and level switch renewal. As with fridges and freezers **do not** attempt to work on the sealed pressurised system, leave this work to a refrigeration specialist. When the appliance reaches the end of it's working life it is essential that it be disposed of correctly by the relevant authority. Contact your local waste disposal department for details of how this is done in your particular area.

As with most appliances, a little care and attention at the right time can help prolong the useful life of the product and help maintain peak performance. The following is a list of useful tips and advice.

1 By their very nature dehumidifiers are used in damp conditions, it is therefore essential that both the appliance, and the supply it is connected to, be in good condition. Both must have a sound earth path (see: *Basic Electrical Chapter 2*). Ensure the supply lead, plug and casing are complete and in good order and avoid the use of an extension lead to power the appliance.

2 Dehumidifiers work best at a room temperature of 21°C (70°F). Below 18°C (65°F) ice may form on the cooling coils/surface. If your model has an auto defrost system it should automatically go into defrost mode if icing is detected. However, if the ambient temperature remains below 18°C (65°F) the process will repeat itself (cycle). If your model does not have the auto defrost facility then you will have to turn the appliance OFF and allow it to defrost fully before turning it back ON again. As before, if the temperature is still below 18°C (65°F) then frosting will simply happen again. Continuing to use a dehumidifier that keeps freezing up in this way may ultimately damage the sealed system. When dehumidifying very damp areas/rooms ensure that the room temperature is maintained at around 21°C (70°F) thus allowing the unit to operate at peak performance. Another point to remember is that it may take quite some time to reduce humidity levels as when the moisture in the

atmosphere is removed, it is replaced by moisture from the damp wall, floor and furnishings. Given time your dehumidifier will reduce the overall level humidity in the whole of the room and its contents.

3 Where you place your dehumidifier relates directly to how efficient it will be. It needs to be positioned at least 15mm (6in) from the nearest wall as this will allow a free flow of air to circulate through the system. If possible do not place the unit in a corner, centre of the room or close to soft furnishings.

4 When dealing with very damp situations ensure the windows are closed or you will be trying to dehumidify an ever-changing atmosphere. Close all doors and windows and try to restrict access to the room to the periodic emptying of the water container (See: following note e.) This simple action greatly improves the process as each time you open the door a large volume of new moisture laden air may be entering.

5 Always ensure that the appliance is isolated ie unplugged prior to removing the water container.

Routine Maintenance

As with all electrical appliances, before any repair or routine maintenance ensure that the item is fully isolated from the mains supply, switch OFF, and plug OUT.

To prevent the growth of mildew and mould within the appliance, wash the water container in a mild detergent solution on a regular basis.

At least once a year (more if the appliance is used frequently) carefully clean the inlet and outlet grilles and if required the cooling coils/surface. It is best to use a small soft brush and vacuum cleaner. However, take great care not to knock or scrape the pipe work of the sealed cooling system.

Check the circulation fan and motor for free rotation and gently remove any fluff build-up. Most manufacturers use sealed fan motor bearings that do not require lubrication. In fact lubricating the bearings may cause more fluff to accumulate around the shaft and cause problems. If you do decide to lubricate the motor bearings use only a very small amount and remove any excess. If the bearings appear tight it is best to renew the motor and clean/renew any filters.

Chapter 18
Ovens and Hobs

Ovens and hobs are amongst the most used items in the home. On the whole, reliability is very good, but when a problem does occur, it is usually at the most inconvenient time. Over the years, ovens and hobs have become more and more complex with the addition of digital timers, touch controls, etc. However, many still function with parts that have changed little from their early predecessors and it is these appliances that are covered in this text and following photo sequences.

It is most important to remember that these appliances are connected directly to their mains supply and as with any repair, cleaning or service must be completely isolated. In this instance, the main double pole isolation switch for the appliance must be switched off and also the fuse for the cooker/hob circuit removed from the main distribution board. If an MCB is fitted in place of a fuse, ensure it is in the off position. **Do not** proceed with any repair or service if both these requirements are not met. Advise others, who may use the switch, of your intentions.

The cable used within cookers and hobs is a special heat resistant type and generally sleeved/shrouded for additional protection. Make sure all cable runs are routed correctly and not trapped or allowed to foul sharp or hot surfaces. All metal parts must be part of the earth path and the appliance must be earthed in accordance with the manufacturer's instructions. See *A General Safety Guide*.

The Hob

Cooking on the hob of the appliance is by means of heating elements (usually four). There are several different types, the most popular being, radiant ring, solid hot plate, ceramic plates and halogen. Each variation has its own benefits and drawbacks. However, some means of varying the heat output is common to all. The way in which this is done depends upon the type of element and the following sections give details of the various types, followed by the different methods used to vary heat output.

Radiant Hob elements

These can be of various patterns and either double or single operation. The fixing plate on the element will generally give details of wattage and a simple inspection of the

Check hob element closely for signs of failure such as this defect

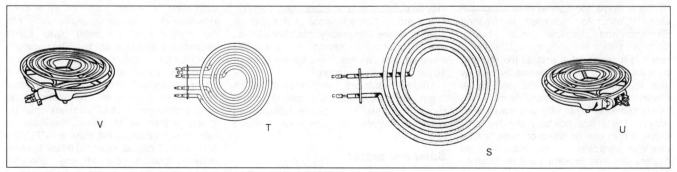

Types of hob element

Swivel-type element (V)   *Double element (T)*   *Single four-turn (S)*   *Lift-up type (U)*

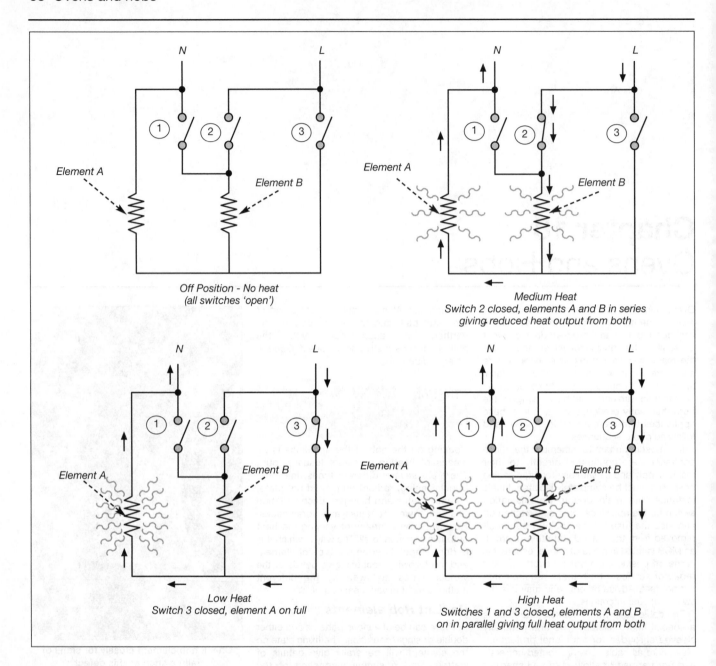

Off Position - No heat
(all switches 'open')

Medium Heat
Switch 2 closed, elements A and B in series
giving reduced heat output from both

Low Heat
Switch 3 closed, element A on full

High Heat
Switches 1 and 3 closed, elements A and B
on in parallel giving full heat output from both

element will determine size and style, ie double or single and number of turn/rings the element has. As explained in *Heating Elements* and *Electrical Circuit Testing*, continuity testing is simple. If a replacement is required it is essential that all the relevant criteria of the old element be met by the new one, ie, wattage, size, turns, etc. Some elements come as separate items whilst others come complete with their own dished recess. These are normally the types of element that can be tilted or swivelled for cleaning purposes. In common with all heaters, it is most important that the push on or screw on connections to the element are fitted securely and all cables and covers are sound.

When renewal of an element is required, it may be possible to fit an economiser element. These are available in most of the popular sizes and are completely interchangeable. The fitting of such elements in place of the standard type can result in a saving of up to 10 per cent in consumption.

Energy regulators (also referred to as 'simmerstats') are generally used to control radiant hob elements. Some radiant ring elements may also incorporate pan-sensing units.

Solid hot plates

Solid hot plates are easily recognised as having a large flat area of cast iron for the heating surface. Being cast iron they can be either rectangular or circular, the latter is the most common design. Normally two or three individual elements are set permanently into the underside of the solid plate. Basic temperature output is obtained by turning a rotary switch to select various combinations of the internal elements. See diagrams. With a rotary selector with three switches connected to two internal elements, four heat settings can be obtained. With all switches open (1, 2 and 3) there is no circuit, therefore no heating can occur, ie the plate is OFF. With only switch 2 closed, power can flow through elements A and B in series (in line – one after the other) and the combined resistance of both elements in this way results in a 'Low' heat output. To obtain a 'Medium' heat

Solid hot plate

Solid hot plate with pan sensor hole

setting only switch 3 is closed. This allows power to flow only through element A, the resistance of which equates to a medium heat output. 'High' heat is achieved by closing switches 1 and 3, allowing power to flow through both elements A and B in parallel (together – both at the same time). This parallel configuration results in the highest heat output as the heat output is combined.

The above is a simplified circuit layout used to illustrate how the elements within a solid hot plate are switched, both in parallel and series configuration. The circuit does not relate to any particular make or model.

To help in understanding the principle, the theoretical circuit shown has only a single pole switch in the live supply. Within most appliances double pole switching (a switch in both live and neutral) is used. With a double pole configuration it is possible to obtain a sequence of four heating circuits, therefore the selector switch in this instance would have five positions including the off position. If a third heating element is moulded into the plate, it will have four terminals and a 7-position selector switch resulting in six heat circuit configurations, plus an off position.

Due to the variations that may be encountered, it is essential that a careful note of all wiring connections be made prior to removal/replacement. Obtaining the correct

replacement part is also very important. This is not too difficult when it comes to the plates themselves, as the differences in diameters and either three of four terminal configurations are relatively obvious. However, there are many more variations of rotary control switches and they all look very similar in appearance but have very different switching sequences. Ensure you obtain the exact replacement.

When renewal of a solid plate is required, it is essential that the correct replacement be obtained. The circular plates are available in two basic diameters and either two or three internal element combinations. The latter gives an even more variable heat selection range. Solid hot plates with pan sensors have a centre hole where the spring-loaded pan-sensing head attaches from below and protrudes above the face of the plate.

A common problem associated with solid hot plates is that due to constant heating, cooling and the odd spill, they quickly lose their original lustre and become unsightly, even rusty. This can be prevented and their appearance enhanced by the use of special protective products such as *Electrol* by Collo. Alternatively a *very small* amount of cooking oil can be applied to the top surface of a *cold* element and spread over the surface with newspaper or kitchen towel. The idea is to

leave only a slight smear of oil on the surface. Ensure that any excess is removed before use. If done correctly, this will leave a protective film over the surface of the element, preventing rust and greatly enhancing the looks of the hob. Unfortunately, if you wish to keep the hob looking good, this will need to be done each time the hob is used as the protective layer is removed when the element fully heats up.

Rotary selector switches are normally used to control basic element selection sequence. However, additional control such as pan-sensors and thermostats may be used to give greater control.

Halogen

Halogen heating elements are found in most, but not all, ceramic /glass topped hobs. Some hobs are a combination of elements, two halogen and two ceramic, see following section. The halogen elements operate very quickly and glow very brightly when switched ON. Each halogen heating area is made up of several long halogen bulbs, similar in looks to those used in the popular outdoor floodlights. It is a combination of the separate elements (bulbs) that result in the variable heat output. They are controlled in series and parallel circuits, which are, in essence, the same as that described in the previous section on solid hot plates. Some manufacturers use a ceramic element and halogen bulb combination to obtain a balanced heat output. Refer to the following section on *Ceramic Elements* for details.

All variations have rotary selection switches to control basic heat output. In addition to the selector switch, each series of elements will have a long glass covered temperature limiter resting across the top. As its name implies, the temperature limiter is used to prevent overheating and works by simply turning off all the elements until the limiter resets. The limiter works by the expansion and contraction of a glass encased metal rod actuating (opening then closing) switch with

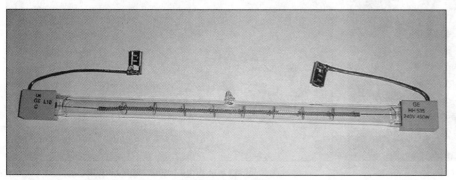

Single halogen tube

Single ceramic element

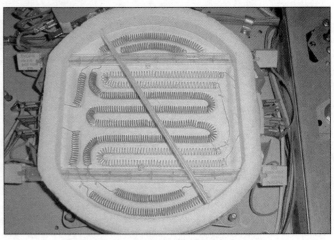

Combined ceramic and halogen elements

contacts connected in series with the heating elements.

Repair of a halogen element unit depends very much upon the manufacturer of the appliance. Some supply individual elements (bulbs) whilst others only supply complete sets and it is not always possible to obtain the temperature limiter as a separate component. If you can obtain a separate halogen element, ensure you make a note of the wiring before you change it, as all the wires to each element are the same colour. **Do not** directly handle/touch the glass envelope of halogen elements or temperature limiters as this will drastically shorten their working life.

Rotary selector switches are normally used to control basic element selection sequence.

Ceramic elements

Ceramic elements consist of a coiled (spring like) element inserted into a maze-like channel, formed in a soft ceramic or mica-like support medium. The channels are designed to create the largest heating surface area possible from the element. Passing a current through the element coil creates the heating effect. The exposed ceramic element can be likened to the solid elements (see *Chapter 13*) but without the outer metal cover in place. In the case of the ceramic unit, a break in the element can normally be easily seen. However, if a break is detected **do not** be tempted to simply twist the broken ends together, a faulty element should always be renewed. As with radiant elements ceramic elements can be single or double configurations.

Energy regulators (also referred to as 'simmerstats') are generally used to control ceramic elements. Temperature limiters are also used.

Energy regulator control

This is probably the most common type of control and can be found in many appliances. An energy regulator may also be referred to as a simmerstat for reasons that will become apparent later in this section. Typical control applications are radiant rings, ceramic elements, grills and water boilers. Because each manufacturer may use different wattages, sizes and styles (double or single) of element, it is essential that only the correct replacement be obtained. They are widely available, but make sure you obtain one of high quality. Make a note of all wiring positions and routes prior to removal. Some replacement controls will come with sticky labels for the purpose of marking the wiring prior to removal. This is especially helpful for older appliances, where the new unit may have a different wiring configuration due to improvements in switch design and operation, and will therefore require modification to the new version. If this is the case, ensure the new switch is supplied with the relevant modification details.

The function of the regulator is quite simply to turn the supply voltage to the element on and off periodically. The temperature variation is, therefore, in direct proportion to the rate of

Double ceramic element unit

Glass sheathed temperature limiter

Internal view of regulator showing switch contacts, cam and internal heater on bi-metal strip

Typical energy regulator

the on/off sequence. Variation of the on/off sequence is by our old friend the bi-metal strip. Within the unit is a large bi-metal plate with a small heating element secured to it. On early regulators a small wound element was used and open-circuit faults were common. The new control (shown) now uses a thick-film resistor to heat the bi-metal plate and prevents problems associated with the early wound-element type. The control includes a switching action at the 'off' position. When turned on, the live contact is allowed to rest on a cam linked to the shaft of the unit. The cam varies the distance required for the bi-metal to move before operation of this switch takes place, ie the more deflection required, the longer the power is supplied to the element. When the bi-metal plate has moved enough to cause the switch to go open circuit, thus removing power from the element, the same switching action removes the supply to the small element/resistor, therefore allowing

the bi-metal plate to cool and reset the switch. This process repeats for as long as the switch is in the 'on' position. The varying lift of the cam is proportional to the visual heat setting indication on the hob switch control panel, ie low, medium, high.

Remember that the outward appearance of controls may be similar but internal operation of switching may be different, eg single-ring or double-ring controls. Make sure the correct replacement only is obtained and fitted. Match up all numbers – model number of appliance, number on switch, etc. Do not remove any wiring without first marking connection points and positions. Ensure as always that the appliance is **isolated**. Do not attempt adjustment or repair to regulators. A faulty unit **must** be renewed.

Checking an energy regulator (simmerstat)

The information given in this section will

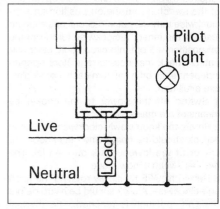

Typical wiring circuit for regulator (grill or hotplate)

also apply to the grills on many cookers. What follows is a simple way to ascertain if the control is faulty or not. Short circuit failures on

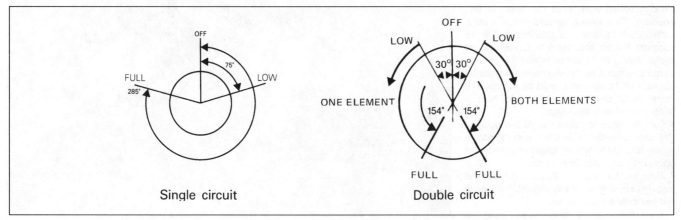

Single and double circuit regulators

Typical rotary selector switch clearly showing cams and switches

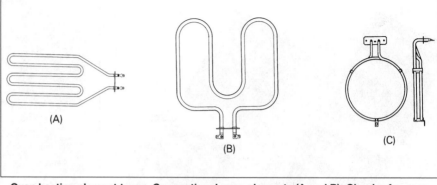

Oven heating element types. Conventional oven elements (A and B). Circular fan oven element (C)

elements may damage regulators, in which case, if you are in any doubt after thoroughly checking the regulator, renew it.

A simple test sequence is given below to help in checking a regulator. The following test is for a single circuit application, ie a single element. For double regulators, ie double element, the same procedure will be required on both single and double operations of the switch. From the off position an anti-clockwise turn will put into circuit one element (usually the inner), a clockwise turn from the off position will put into circuit both inner and outer. Check that double regulators operate independently on a half turn each. For singles, use a full turn.

1 Switch off the power to the cooker by means of the mains switch.
2 Rotate the knob slowly clockwise from OFF. A click should be heard when the knob is at ON or at the lowest mark on the dial. The thermal switch is now made.
3 Return to OFF by slowly rotating the knob anti-clockwise. A click should be heard before the OFF position is reached. The thermal switch is now broken.
4 Ensure that the knob is left in the OFF position.
5 Switch on the power to the cooker by means of the mains switch.
6 Turn the knob slowly clockwise until the click is heard and leave the knob in this position. The switch should break with a further audible click in approximately 5 to 10 seconds. If there have been no further audible clicks after 5 to 10 seconds and the heating element remains full on, the regulator must be considered faulty and should be replaced. If there is a pilot light, it should remain illuminated during this check.
7 Turn the knob to position 3. At this position ON and OFF times will be approximately equal, and clicks will be heard at intervals of approximately 10 to 25 seconds.
8 Turn the knob to the FULL position. The element controlled by this regulator will glow red-hot after a few minutes.

Take care to avoid the elements during this test sequence. If the above checks prove negative, that is to say, the control appears to be functioning correctly, the element should be checked. See *Heating Elements*. If a fault is found in either the control or the element, do not attempt adjustment as only renewal of the unit concerned is possible.

Rotary switch control

Rotary switch controls consist of a series of switches, each of which rest upon a profiled cam barrel. Each switch rests upon its own cam and turning the selector knob to the required setting also turns the barrel. The cam barrel can be turned to a series of fixed positions, each of which lift the switches into a combination of different positions. This combination of closed switches relates directly to the range of parallel and series circuits needed to provide the required heat output. For a simplified explanation of this action refer to the solid hot plates section and accompanying diagrams.

Faults with rotary switches include loose connections, worn cams (causing poor or intermittent switch contact) or pitted switch contacts. These faults often lead to overheating of the switch or its contact. Always inspect the switch closely and renew any switch that appears to show signs of wear or overheating.

Pan sensors

Pan sensor control can be found on both radiant ring and solid hotplate elements. They consist of a spring-loaded sensor head connected by a thin capillary tube to a bellows within the element selector switch. The sensor head unit clips into a hole at the centre of the element with only the spring-loaded top of the sensor protruding above the

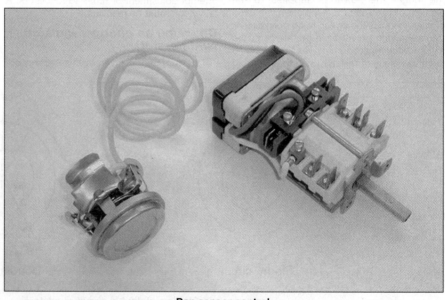

Pan sensor control

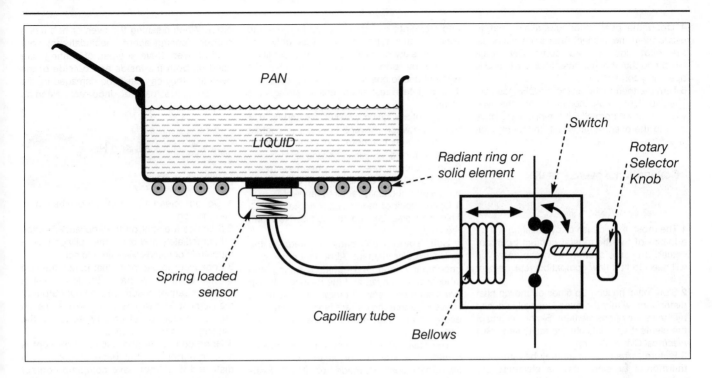

surface. When a flat-bottomed cooking pan is placed on the element, the spring-loaded sensor is pressed down, and in doing so, makes a positive contact with the base of the pan. In this position, the sensor head can now detect the temperature of the pan and its contents. The sensor, capillary tube and bellows, within the control switch, operate in a similar manner as the variable thermostat described in *Chapter 14 Thermostats and Temperature Control*. The sensor, capillary tube and bellows form an oil/gel filled sealed

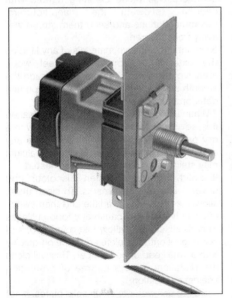

Variable oven thermostat with auxiliary switch (directly behind mounting plate) used for additional switching such as double oven or fan-assisted variations

system. As the temperature of the sensor rises the oil/gel within the sealed system expands and extends the bellows within the control switch. Expansion and contraction of the bellows switches the element OFF when the predetermined temperature is reached, and back ON again when the sensor temperature falls below a predetermined point. This action effectively reduces the heat output of the element by turning it ON and OFF. 'Cycling' the element (turning it ON and OFF) in this way, results in the ON time getting shorter as the temperature of the pan rises. The design and calibration of the unit prevents liquids such as milk from boiling over.

As with energy regulators, there are many variations of pan sensor. Ensure you obtain a direct replacement and double check this by making sure the serial number from the old unit matches that of the replacement.

Ovens

Regulating the temperature in an oven is done by a pod-type thermostat, which allows the high degree of temperature variation required for the oven to function correctly. The operation of a variable thermostat is described in *Temperature Control and Thermostats*. Heating is by radiant elements, the size, shape and wattage of which vary enormously between makes and individual models. It is therefore essential that any replacement matches the original in every way.

Two of the most common ovens used today are firstly, the conventional oven, which has two or more elements situated either at the sides or top and bottom of the oven (usually behind the oven's inner lining). Secondly, the fan oven, which usually consists of one circular element that surrounds, or is positioned in front of, a fan driven by a shaded-pole motor (see *Electric Motors*). This particular system provides a uniform heat distribution within the oven by means of air circulation. Element failure is not uncommon in both types of oven, due to the high degree of usage. Generally, repairs to the oven are not too difficult although access to ovens that have been built-in can prove difficult. Many ovens now have plug-in elements, but others will require removal of panels to gain access to fixing screws, nuts and push-on connections. Care must be exercised when removing the panels and insulation materials. Ensure that the appliance is ISOLATED. With appliances such as ovens and hobs, the double pole isolation switch should be switched to the OFF position and its fuse/MCB at the consumer unit should be removed or switched off as required.

Five simple tests to help diagnose oven thermostat faults:

1 Switch on the power to the cooker by means of the main switch.

2 Turn the oven thermostat knob from OFF to a low dial setting.

3 Within about 10 minutes the oven should have warmed up sufficiently to cause the thermostat to switch off. Often a pilot light is provided on the appliance, in which case the light should go out indicating that the thermostat has switched off.

4 Open the oven door and allow heat to escape into the kitchen. After a few seconds, the pilot light should come ON again indicating that the thermostat has cut in and is operating correctly.

5 Turn the thermostat dial to the OFF position. The pilot light should then be out and the oven will cool down normally. If the pilot light stays on and the oven remains hot, the thermostat is defective and should be replaced.

Conventional ovens - faults

1 The most likely cause of overheating will be a failure of the thermostat contact points or sealed pressure system, in which case you will need to fit a new compatible replacement unit.

2 Slow initial heating-up times or uneven heat distribution within the oven is usually caused by the failure of one element. Simple testing of the element will highlight the faulty item. See *Electrical Circuit Testing*.

3 Failure to heat up at all may be either the thermostat or elements. As elements are easier to check for continuity, a simple process of elimination will indicate where the fault lies.

4 Poor cooking results or under-cooking of food can also be caused by a faulty thermostat, by turning off elements at too low a temperature. As stated in 3 above, the elements are relatively easy to check, so eliminate them first.

Isolate the appliance before removing covers or panels for any reason. All tests for continuity, etc., are carried out using a battery operated test meter only.

Fan oven – faults

Faults on fan ovens will be similar to those found on conventional ovens. The thermostat

Check door seal position and condition

and elements can be checked in the same way. As this type of oven has only one element, slow or undercooking is most likely caused by poor air circulation over the element due to one of the following reasons:

1 An air intake restriction. Ensure airways are clear.

2 Fan motor running slowly. This can be due to bearing wear, allowing the rotor to contact the stator (new fan motor required), debris on fan or distorted fan (clean or renew).

3 Complete seizure of main bearings, ie no airflow at all over element – may be possible to free off but usually requires renewal.

4 Open circuit of motor stator or stator TOC. This may also be due to fault 3. New unit required.

Both 3 and 4 can cause damage to the coiled circular element. Abnormal noise may accompany fault 3. Regular cleaning and lubrication of the fan and the bearing will help avoid such problems. If renewal is required, it is essential that the correct fan unit is fitted as each make and model have their own variation.

The main non-electrical fault with ovens, whether free standing or built-in, is the door seal. These seals are made from flexible heat-resistant rubber or woven fibre tubing. Many variations of cross sectional shapes and methods of fixing are used by the various cooker manufacturers. It is most important that the door be sealed correctly, not only for the efficient operation of the cooker but also for safety reasons, especially in ovens which are built-in, where the door sides may be close to fitted units. Door seal kits are available for all of the leading makes and the removal of old seals and the fitting of new ones should not cause any problems. Make sure that the correct replacement seal is obtained and make a note of how the old one is fixed before removing it. If your door seal is held by spring clips it would be advisable to get the kit which includes the new springs, rather than just the door seal. Make sure the new seal is trimmed to the correct length and all the fixing points are used and secure. Renew seals that become hard, cracked or brittle to keep the oven at peak performance. Regular cleaning of both oven and seals will also help keep the appliance in good working

Older type braided oven door seal kit

order. When cleaning the oven or hob use a proper cleaning agent specifically for your type of oven. Several types of coatings are used on both the inside and outside of the oven and they can easily be damaged by the indiscriminate use of incorrect cleaning products.

Care of Cookers and Hobs

1 Do not clean the appliance when it is switched on.

2 If liquids are spilt on the appliance, switch off immediately and clean the spillage before foodstuffs or liquids have time to set.

3 Endeavour to use pans that match the size of the element. A pan with too small a diameter cannot absorb all the heat output of the element. This results in heat loss and such inefficient use of electricity adds to the running costs of your home.

4 Good contact of pan base and element is also important. If the base of the pan is distorted it will not have complete contact with the element therefore resulting in poor transfer of heat into the pan. This then allows hot spots to develop within the element due to heat retention, which will reduce its lifespan. Solid hob plates are more susceptible to this problem and must not be left on without a pan being placed on them, otherwise they will burn out or distort.

5 Avoid using harsh abrasive cleaning products for general cleaning. Products formulated for hobs and oven exteriors and specialised interior oven cleaners should be used. Use these cleaning agents with caution, following the manufacturers' recommendations and keep them stored well away from children.

6 Do not use abrasive materials of any kind on the exterior of appliances. Steel wool, abrasive pads, etc., will quickly damage the smooth surface and lead to discoloration and deterioration of the surface finish.

7 When using a recommended cream cleaner, it is advisable to finish by wiping over with a dry paper towel. This will help remove any calcium used in the cleaner. If left, the calcium may stain the surface yellow when heated.

8 Solid hob plates often discolour and develop unsightly rust marks. To clean them, allow them to heat up a little and then switch off. The heating will cause any food spillages to carbonise. Next, allow just a few drops of cooking oil onto the plate and wipe off quickly with a small pad of newspaper. This will clean the plate and give a degree of protection against oxidisation.

Do not use water to clean solid plates. If not cared for, these plates can become unsightly. When new, their appearance is a uniform dark greyish colour which can be maintained if cleaned correctly and regularly. There is a branded product on the market specifically for solid hobs, designed to clean them and keep the dark uniform colour.

Self-cleaning ovens

The interiors of many ovens are classed as self-cleaning. The inner panels, which can be easily removed, are coated in a special porous enamel compound. The compound has a catalytic action on the normal build-up of grease and dirt from cooking which eliminates the need for chemical cleaning associated with normal oven linings.

The catalytic coating causes grease and dirt to oxidise on the panel's surface while the oven is in use. Some models have a 'clean only' setting which requires a very high temperature, whereas other ovens are designed to work at lower temperatures during normal operation. Consult your instruction book.

As oxidisation takes place, a combination of carbon dioxide and water is produced which escapes through the normal oven vents.

Stubborn stains caused by milk and sugar may take longer to break down by this process, reducing gradually with each subsequent use.

Do not be tempted to use normal oven cleaning products or abrasives because they will cause considerable damage to the surface and reduce the catalytic properties of this type of panel. If the need for cleaning is absolutely necessary, then rinse the panels with lukewarm water only.

Self-cleaning oven panel with catalytic coating

OVEN ELEMENT RENEWAL

1 Switch off at isolation switch

2 Double check that power is OFF

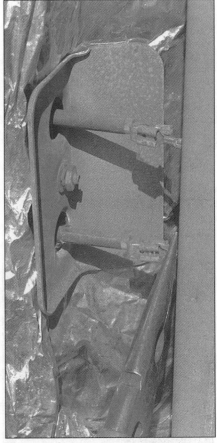

5 Carefully remove terminal connectors with pliers, do not pull on the wires

3 Remove fuse or switch off MCB

4 Lifting the hob gave access to the side panel screws. Remove panel to gain access to elements

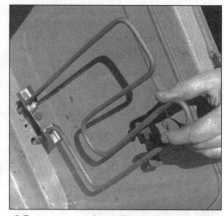

8 Remove oven inner liner to gain access to element. Ease from support clip/slides carefully

NOTE: Check for earth continuity prior to functional testing

Refitting is a careful reversal of the stripdown procedure. Make sure all connections are tight and in their original positions to prevent contact with sharp or hot surfaces or covering panel when refitted. Double check all work carried out prior to functional testing. The new element may give off a little smoke when first used as it has a protective coating applied to inhibit tarnishing during storage. Smoking will cease within a few seconds

6 Note wiring and positions. With wires removed, test element for continuity. This one is OC (open current) and therefore requires renewal

7 Remove centre fixing nut

FITTING A NEW REGULATOR

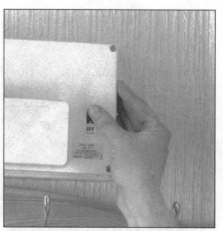

1 Switch off at isolation switch

2 Double check that power is OFF

3 Remove fuse or switch off MCB

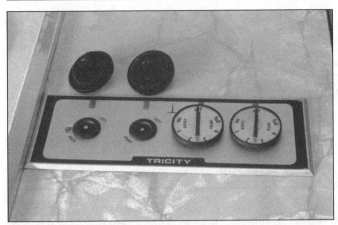

4 This unit has a separate switch bank for the hob. Access is gained by removal of push-fit knobs and two securing screws. Lay out knobs in sequence and make a note of their correct positions prior to removal

5 The third switch from the left required changing because it failed to control the top RH ring on the hob. This was found by using the test sequence for regulators. Take care with the exposed switch bank fixings and connections. As always, make a note of all connections and cable positions prior to removal

6 The make and model number of the appliance, along with knowledge that it controlled a single element, made sure that the correct replacement was obtained. The replacement regulator came with useful information confirming that it suited all requirements. Read all such information thoroughly along with information in the relevant sections

7 The regulator is secured by a single nut to the mounting plate or bar

9 A thorough inspection of all the connections and condition of the wiring was carried out. All exposed metal parts were tested to make sure they were part of the earth path, ie metal plate to earth pin of a socket. Finally, refit covers ensuring all seals are in position and that screws do not come into contact with cables or connections. Refit knobs in correct order. Hob is now ready for functional test as described previously

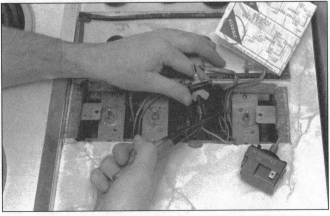

8 This regulator was a direct replacement. Even so, all wires were marked prior to removal and positions of wires noted

Chapter 19
Cooker hoods

Cooker hoods are becoming a standard fitting in many new and refurbished kitchens for alleviating cooking smells and reducing steam from boiling pans.

The extraction function of the hood is achieved by means of a motor, usually a shaded-pole or capacitor start induction type, which drives a normal or tangential (barrel like) fan. Variable speeds are often included for coping with different conditions during use. A light to illuminate the hob is another addition to the hood. It is switched independently of the extractor.

When the hood is switched on, air is sucked by the fan through a filter system to remove grease particles and odours. Most hoods come with the option of being vented externally or having the air recirculated into the kitchen. Although the recirculating version is useful, better results are obtained through external venting. Kits like the one shown are widely available and are simple to install. All hoods, whether recirculating or vented, require regular filter renewal. Failure to do this will greatly impair the operation of the hood and possibly lead to failure of the motor in the long term. The type of filtration system used depends on whether you vent the air outside or recirculate it back into the kitchen after filtration and deodorising it.

Note: *If your hood has a cartridge filter and you are connecting it to vent the air outside, then you normally do not want the cartridge in place as they are usually only used for recirculation (non-vented) installations. If you are unsure check your instruction manual for details.*

Some hoods use pre-formed filter replacement cartridges that combine a grease and activated carbon filter in a disposable unit (see note above). Replacement cartridges can be found in many shapes and sizes and it may not always be easy to find the exact replacement.

In instances where a direct replacement cannot be obtained it is worth considering renewing the internal charcoal granules that make up the filter. Replacement tubs of activated charcoal granules like the one shown are now available. Remove the filter cartridge from the cooker hood and look closely at how the unit is fixed together. Taking a filter apart and refilling it can be a messy job so cover the work area with old newspaper or a blanket. To prevent the possibility of carbon dust going everywhere it may be wise to carry out the stripdown of the filter cartridge outside although, with care, this should not be necessary.

Most cartridges are made from two pieces of plastic clipped together and with care the two halves can be separated. Once opened, the old granules and any additional polyester filter material can be removed. With the filter medium removed the cartridge housing can be washed carefully in warm soapy water and allowed to dry completely before moving on to the next stage. When the casing is completely dry it is then ready for refilling. If the unit also has cloth/foam filters these will also need to be renewed with a kit as described in the following paragraph, using the old filters as templates. When the replacement cloth/foam filters (if fitted) are in place the casing can be filled with the granules and carefully refitted.

The alternative to filter cartridges is the use of polyester tangle fleece material which has open weave to the exhaust side which may be used in conjunction with a carbon impregnated filter cloth/foam. The open polyester weave of the primary filter removes grease particles from the steam laden air by trapping them within the material. If recirculation is used in place of venting, the air may then be passed through a secondary carbon filter or carbon impregnated foam matrix to remove odours.

Note: *Vented hoods with the cartridge filter removed will still require the primary filtering medium of cloth/foam like that described.*

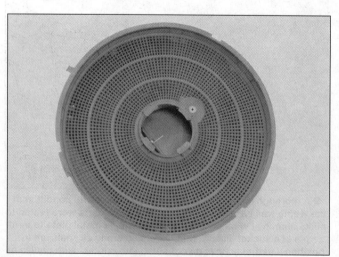

Cooker hood replacement filter cartridge

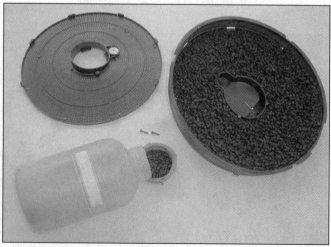

Carefully opening the filter cartridge allows the old filter medium to be removed

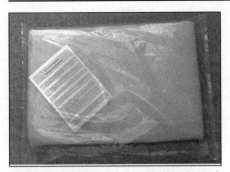

This cooker hood filter kit can be adapted to fit many makes by cutting the filter medium to the correct size. Such kits are available with or without carbon. The one shown above is without carbon

The life expectancy of a cloth/foam grease filter is only 2 – 3 months depending on the usage; after this period the absorption capacity quickly diminishes and the filter will become brownish in colour and fail to suppress odours. Consult your instruction book for the recommended interval between replacing the filter. If the specific filters for your particular hood are difficult to obtain, there are several types of filter kits available that only need cutting to the size required. Follow the instructions in the pack and make sure the filter is the correct way round.

Mechanical and electrical problems with cooker hoods are few, the most frequent one being the failure of the hood light. This is usually a straightforward job, but remember to isolate the hood prior to changing the bulb and be sure to refit all parts correctly. Other problems that may arise are motor failure, bearing wear on motor or fan and switch failure. Simple checking for continuity is all that is required to ascertain the fault (see *Electric Motors* and *Electric Circuit Testing*); this also applies to switch faults. The first sign of bearing failure is usually an increase in the normal operating noise. This may be gradual and go unnoticed for quite a while. The bearings of both fan and motor are usually more than capable of coping with the light demands upon them, but faults can occur if filter replacement is ignored or irregular. This could allow grease deposits to build up on the fan and cause it to turn out of balance.

Mounting the cooker hood too close to the hob is a common problem. This could result in a faulty switch, a motor fault due to overheating, trim damage, or a sticking switch. It is also dangerous to mount equipment below the minimum height recommended by the manufacturer. Consult your instruction manual and check the correct height of the installation for the hood. Remember, the hob may have four elements in use at the same time, the wattage of each being between 1200W and 1800W, giving a possible total heat output of between 4800W and 7200W.

Note: *Minimum height recommendations also apply to gas hobs. Ensure the hood has its own fuse and isolation switch or socket.*

Cooker hood – tips

1 Renew filters at 2 to 3 month intervals, unless otherwise stated in manufacturer's instructions.
2 If the cooker hood has been fitted for recirculating only, but has the facility to be vented externally, consider fitting a vent system.
3 Ventable models are identifiable by having a blanked off circular hole in the back or top of the hood. By removing the blanking piece the ducting system can be inserted.
3 Start the hood fan a few minutes before using the hob. This allows an air flow over the hob to be established prior to odours or steam being produced. This simple operation will allow the hood to work much better whether recirculated or vented.
4 Leave the fan running for a few minutes after use of the hob. This will also allow the hood to function much better and remove residual odours and moisture from the atmosphere.
5 When installing or using extractors and vented cooker hoods, or any ducting system in a kitchen, a back flow of air, ie ventilation, must be provided to replace the air extracted from the room. In locations where appliances such as Aga cookers, gas central heating boilers or other gas-powered appliances are present, it is essential that adequate back flow is provided to prevent exhaust gases being drawn into the room.

THE ORACSTAR COOKER HOOD VENT

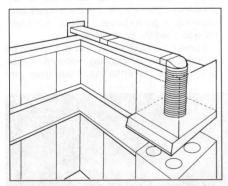

This new flat vent kit system fits neatly into position and is adaptable to most hoods (top or rear vent). It is available in kit form or as individual parts for longer or more complex installations (A)

Being square, the ducting is easy to fit through the wall. The removal of a brick is all that is required (B)

An anti-draught cover is included. Make sure it remains clear by checking it regularly (C)

Chapter 20
Irons

In the past, the electric iron was a simple appliance consisting of an electrical heating element pressed on to the sole plate of the iron and controlled by a simple variable bimetal thermostat. Due to its rugged construction this type of iron proved to be long lasting. It had little in the way of styling or gadgetry, but it was popular and gave good service for several generations of housewives. The basic iron may still be found, but the modern iron has changed greatly in recent years with attention to styling and reduction in weight, making it much more attractive and easier to use. In addition many irons have the added sophistication of a variable steam facility, a steam release valve to deal with heavily creased materials, and a plain water spray to dampen items that are too dry to iron easily.

Common to all irons is the need to heat the metal sole plate (the part that comes into contact with the clothes), and to accurately control the temperature to a given setting.

Earlier irons used replaceable heating elements, but most modern irons now use sole plates with the heating element bonded within them. This means that the simple fault of an open circuit element requires the fitting of a new sole plate unit. The cost of this is usually very high in relation to the cost of a new iron. Thermostats have changed little and are still predominantly bi-metal. One main difference is that most replacement thermostats now come pre-calibrated, unlike early irons where setting of temperatures was a fiddly job and required a pyrometer to ascertain correct functioning of the new thermostat. In common with early irons, there is usually an indicator light that goes out when the iron sole plate reaches the selected temperature. This action is carried out by the thermostat in conjunction with the element control.

For the steam spray facility, the iron needs to be able to store water. It is essential that the seals and the water container be checked

regularly for leaks, especially after repair or inspection has been carried out. Irons require earth connections, and a three-pin plug and socket must be used for these appliances. See *A General Safety Guide*; *Plugs and Sockets*; and *Cables and Cable Faults*.

When water is heated to produce steam, mineral scale will inevitably build up; the degree of which depends on the hardness of water being used (if from domestic supply). Some irons allow for tap water to be used whilst others do not, so it is wise to know which type of water you should be using in your particular iron. Using the incorrect water will promote blocking due to scaling and is likely to cause a complete failure of the appliance. Some irons are classed as self-cleaning. A powerful jet of steam is usually used to clean the scale away.

Some irons have steam valves that can be removed easily for cleaning, allowing the use of tap water. Nevertheless, if you have very

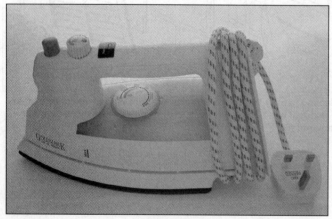

Simple iron

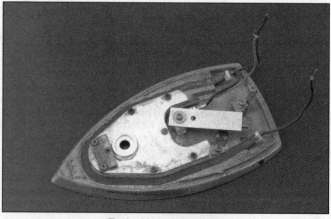

Typical iron thermostat

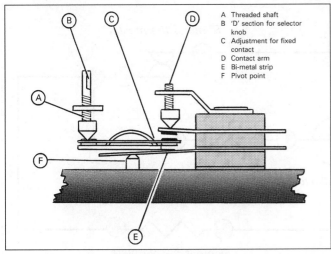

A Threaded shaft
B 'D' section for selector knob
C Adjustment for fixed contact
D Contact arm
E Bi-metal strip
F Pivot point

Bi-metal thermostat

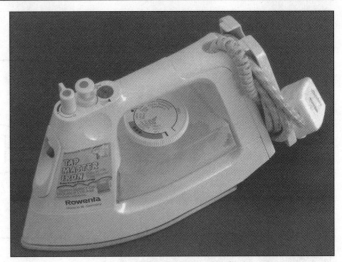

Steam iron with spray facility

hard water in your area, it may be unwise to use tap water. With irons that cannot use tap water, it is important to use only distilled or de-ionised water. Do not use melted water from defrosted fridges or freezers and avoid using battery top-up water supplied from garages. Although some manufacturers may recommend its use, others do not – so check the instruction book.

Many modern steam irons have silicone-coated valves and jets or demineralising crystals within them that prevent scaling, thus allowing them to be filled straight from the tap. Demineralisers are available separately and convert tap water into fully de-mineralised water suitable for all steam irons. Irons that are not self-cleaning require regular descaling. Keeping a steam iron free from scale will allow it to perform much better and longer. The regularity of descaling varies according to whether tap water is used and the degree of hardness of the water.

Descaling

Use a proprietary brand of descaler, which is specially formulated for irons (like the example shown), and follow the instructions carefully. This particular product is one of the most popular and readily available. It is non-toxic, non-caustic, non-corrosive and fully biodegradable. More than one treatment may be necessary if the iron has been used regularly without being descaled. The descaler works by breaking down the bond between the scale and the host surface. The residue is then rinsed away. Before using a descaling product, check the iron's instruction book; some self-cleaning irons should not be descaled in this way even though when used in very hard water areas, they still tend to scale up.

Irons – tips

1 Check the condition of the mains flex regularly and renew at the first sign of any deterioration at any point along its length. Closely inspect the grommet at the iron end of the flex.
2 Help alleviate flex wear by using a flex holder.
3 Descale regularly if using tap water.
4 If you accidentally melt nylon or any other synthetic material on the sole plate (usually by having the temperature set too high) DO NOT let the iron cool down or the residue will set and damage will be caused to the sole plate when you try to scrape it loose. The correct course of action is to turn the thermostat up to HOT (if it wasn't already) which will keep the residue of the fabric on the sole plate soft. You will then be able to remove most of it with a paper towel. Next, allow the iron to cool to WARM and use a sole plate cleaner to remove

Descaling products

Check the condition of the flex and grommet regularly for damage. (This problem should have been rectified a long time ago!). If a fault is found, do not use the appliance until it is rectified

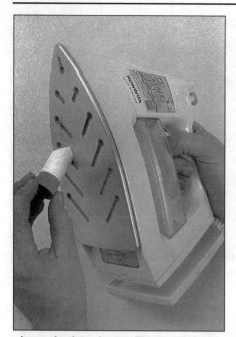

Iron sole plate cleaner. This type is used on a warm iron so care is required. Isolate as usual when carrying out this or any repair, inspection or maintenance

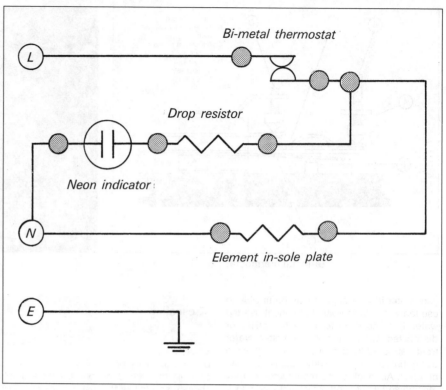

Typical wiring circuit of iron

the remainder (this comes in stick form and is a must). The liquid that forms should be wiped off immediately – **DO NOT** let it run into the steam vents on the sole plate.

5 The sole plate cleaner will also remove starch stains and fabric conditioner marks.

6 Damage to the sole plate can be caused by running over sharp objects such as zips, metal buttons, rivets on jeans, etc. Take care as most sole plates are made of aluminium and are easily scratched.

7 Iron low temperature items first and work up to higher temperatures. If working down, you must allow time for the iron to cool. Wait for the light to come on and then off again before continuing. If you don't, make sure you have read TIP 4!

8 Never leave an iron switched on and unattended for any reason.

9 Always unplug a steam iron when filling or emptying its water tank.

Electrical problems

The most common fault is the deterioration of the flex caused by its constant movement when the iron is being used. This can result in the inner conductor being broken giving rise to a plain open circuit fault, or more commonly, an overheating fault due to the movement of the flex causing a make-break action. Heat is generated at this point and will eventually lead to a short circuit within the cable or exposure of the inner wires. This problem occurs more often at the entry point of the cable sleeve on the iron.

It is essential that the flex be checked regularly for signs of wear or damage, often caused by careless use (eg. allowing the flex to come into contact with the hot sole plate). At the first sign of damage renew the whole flex with non-kink iron flex. See *Cables and Cable Faults* and the cable replacement photo sequence. The flex problem has been alleviated a little by better designs such as the inclusion on some models of a storage facility for the mains lead and easier adaptability for use with either hand. The introduction of the cordless iron solves the flex problem to a point, although the base unit still requires a mains-powered lead. When the iron is placed on the base unit, it receives power that heats up the sole plate to the correct temperature (via the iron's own thermostat). Sole plates on these irons are thicker and normally use a higher wattage element to retain the heat between charge periods. Most models have the same facilities as the corded irons, but it is most important to return the iron to the base unit regularly, especially if the steam setting is in use.

FITTING A NEW IRON FLEX

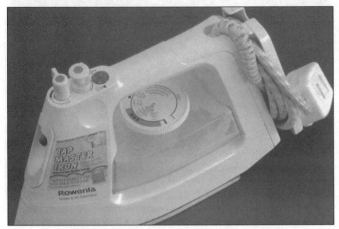

1 On testing, iron indicated Symptom 1. The appliance was isolated before further checking was carried out

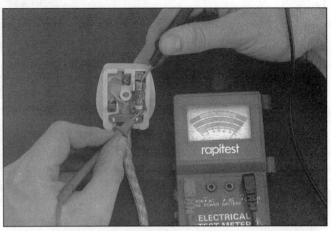

2 A check of the socket proved to be OK so the plug and fuse were then checked

3 All connections within the plug were sound and the fuse was found to be OK in step 2. The rear cover of the iron was removed so that continuity testing of the cable could be carried out

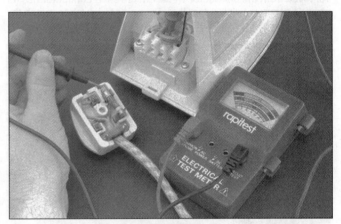

4 Continuity of all three conducting wires was made and the live conductor was found to be open circuit. This occurred intermittently when the cable near the grommet was moved. The fault found clearly indicated fatigue of the flex and the fitting of a new length of flex would be required

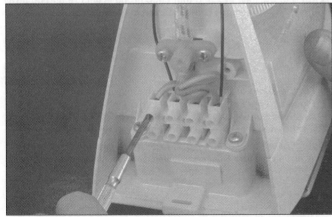

5 A note of the position of the wiring and covers etc, was made prior to removing the damaged flex. A matching length of flex was obtained. Two choices were available – a straightforward length cut from a roll or a pre-dressed cable ready to fit. A cut length of flex will require dressing (preparing) at both ends to match the original flex

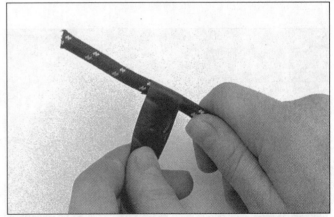

6 Before removing the outer braiding, wrap a length of insulation tape around the outer of the flex just below the trim point. This prevents fraying of the outer cotton braid. Alternatively, if the original flex had a rubber collar, this may be rolled down in place of the tape

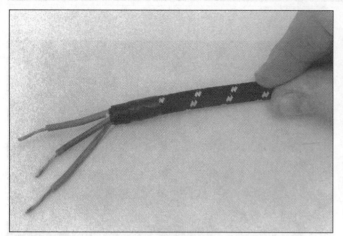

7 Carefully remove the outer braid and inner sheath to expose the 3 inner wires. Take care not to damage the insulation of the inner wires in the process, if you do, cut back and start again. Shown here is the appliance end of the flex with the insulation removed from the conductor wires. Ensure each conductor has its strands securely twisted together. Trimming to length to match the original may be required prior to this on some items

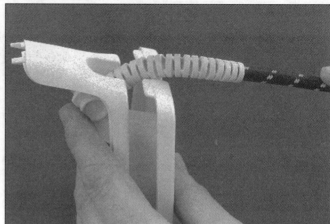

8 The prepared cable is now ready for fitting. Apply a little detergent/soft soap to the grommet to allow the cable to pass through easily

9 Secure the flex by the cord grip within the appliance ensuring that it is gripped firmly on the outer sheath only

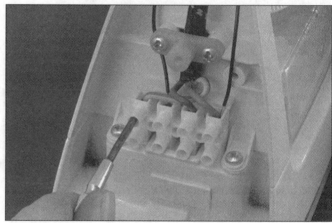

10 The conductor wires can now be fitted to their respective positions ensuring that any sleeving or protection originally used is fitted to the new flex and that each fitting is secure and no stray strands protrude from the terminal

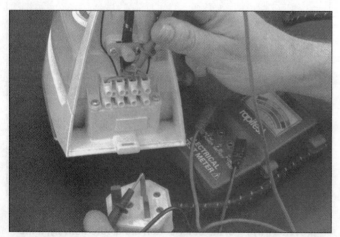

11 Double check all fixings, covers and connections. Check the continuity of each conductor prior to refitting the cover

For the fitting of the plug, follow the instructions given in the *Plugs and Sockets* section. A new plug will be required if the appliance previously had a moulded type fitted. With covers refitted and secured, a functional test can be carried out

Note: *Ensure the socket is part of a circuit protected by an RCD. If not a portable RCD should be used. See* A General Safety Guide, *and* Basics

Area guide to water hardness in the UK

Due to a new grid system for water, hardness may vary considerably in times of shortage. Details shown are therefore only an indication of normally expected hardness.

Area	Authority	Water Hardness
Argyll	Scotland	S
Ashborne	Severn – Trent	MS – H
Ayrshire	Scotland	H
Birmingham	Severn – Trent	S
Bolton	North West	S – VH
Bournemouth	Wessex	S
Cambridge	Anglia	H – VH
Carlisle	North West	SH – H
Cheshire – Mid	North West	MS
Chester	North West	MS – H
Chiltern	Thames	SH – H
Clyde – Lower	Scotland	VH
Colne Valley	North West	S
Corby & District	North West	H – VH
Cumbria South	North West	H
Cumbria West	North West	S – M H
Derbyshire – North	Severn – Trent	S
Derbyshire – South	Severn – Trent	S – H
Derwent Valley	Severn – Trent	MH
Dorset	Wessex	S
East Anglia	Anglia	H – VH
Eastbourne	Southern	SH – VH
Eden	North West	S – M H
Essex	Anglia	S – VH
Exeter	South West	S – H
Fife & Kinross	Scotland	S – VH
Folkestone & District	Southern	S – VH
Fylde	North West	S – SH
Gloucester	Severn – Trent & Thames	MH – VH
Guernsey	-	SH
Hampshire Central	Southern	H
Hampshire North	Southern	H
Hampshire West	Southern	H
Hartlepool	Northumbrian	H – VH
Invernesshire	Scotland	S – M H
Ireland Eastern	-	S – H
Ireland Northern	-	MS
Ireland Southern	-	S – VH
Ireland Western	-	MS
Isle of Wight	-	SH – H
Jersey	-	MH
Kent	Southern	H
Kent East	Southern	H
Kent Mid	Southern	SH – VH
Kent West	Southern	MS – H
Lakes & Lune	North West	S
Lambourne	Thames	SH – VH
Lanarkshire	North West	S – VH
Lancashire	North West	S –VH
Lee Valley	Thames	VH
Leicester	Severn – Trent	M H – VH
Liverpool	North West	S – SH
Loch Lomond	Scotland	S
Loch Turret	Scotland	S
London – Metropolitan	Thames	MH – VH
Lune Valley	North West	S – SH
Macclesfield	North West	MS – H
Makerfield	North West	S – M H
Manchester	North West	S
Mersey Valley	North West	S – VH
Montgomery	Severn – Trent	S – M H
Newcastle & Gateshead	Northumbrian	MH
Nottingham	Severn – Trent	MS – M H
Northumberland & Tyne	Northumbrian	SH
Nuneaton	Severn – Trent	SH – VH
Pennine – West	North West	S – MS
Plymouth	South West	S–SH
Preston & District	North West	S
Rickmansworth & Uxbridge Valley	Thames	H – VH
Salop	Severn – Trent	H
Scilly Isles	-	MH
Scotland – Mid	Scotland	S – M H
Scotland – North	Scotland	S – VH
Scotland – North East	Scotland	S
Scotland – South East	Scotland	S – H
Scotland – South West	Scotland	S – M H
Sherwood	Severn – Trent	M H – VH
Somerset	Wessex	S – VH
Stafford	Severn – Trent	H – VH
Staffordshire – South	Severn – Trent	H – VH
St. Helens	North West	SH
Stockport	North West	S
Sunderland & South Shields	Northumbrian	MS – VH
Surrey East	Thames	MS
Surrey North	Thames	H –VH
Sussex	Southern	H
Sussex East	Southern	MS
Sussex Mid	Southern	S – H
Sussex North West	Southern	MS – VH
Sutton District	Thames	SH
Tees	Northumbrian	S – MS
Tendring Hundred	Anglia	H
Truro	South West	S – SH
Vales	Thames	MS – VH
Warwickshire	Severn – Trent	MH – VH
Wear	Northumbrian	S
Wiltshire	Thames	H
Wolverhampton	Severn – Trent	SH – VH
Worcestershire – North	Severn – Trent	S - VH
Worcestershire – South	Severn – Trent	MS – H
Wrexham & East Wrexham Denbighshire	Welsh	SH
York	Yorkshire	H
Yorkshire North	Yorkshire	S – VH

	Parts per million as $CaCO_3$	Degrees Clark	Degrees French
Soft	0–50	0–3.5	8–5
Moderately soft	50–100	3.5–7.0	5–10
Slightly hard	100–150	7.0–10.5	10–15
Moderately hard	150–200	10.5–14.0	15–20
Hard	200–300	14.0–21.0	20–30
Very hard	over 300	over 21.0	over 30

Fault finding – irons

1 Symptom: Won't work at all

Possible causes
a. Faulty plug or socket
b. Fault in flex

c. Open circuit thermostat

d. Open circuit TOC or overheat protective device

e. Open circuit element

Action
See *Plugs and Sockets*
See *Cables and Cable Faults* and *Electrical Circuit Testing*. Renew as required
Check that the correct setting is being used. Check thermostat. See *Temperature Control and Thermostats*, and *Electrical Circuit Testing*
Check for continuity. See *Temperature Control and Thermostats*, and *Electrical Circuit Testing*
See *Heating Elements, Irons* and *Electrical Circuit Testing*. Ascertain if element is separate from sole plate

2 Symptom: Iron overheats

Possible causes
a. Faulty thermostat. Contacts stuck or bi-metal plate failed

b. Broken selector knob

Action
See *Thermostat Control and Thermostats* and *Electrical Circuit Meter Testing*. Renew as required if preset stat is obtainable, if not, it will require dealer repair
This will give incorrect reading, ie low indicated on knob, high selected by stat. Look closely for cracks on 'D' shaft of knob. Renew as required

3 Symptom: No steam (steam iron only)

Possible causes
a. Incorrect setting of iron

b. Water tank empty
c. Water control valve faulty, blocked or scaled

d. Scale in chamber or steam vents

Action
If the setting is too low, steam cannot be produced. Check that steam setting has been selected
Refill and test, as above
Test by repeated operation of button or arm (dependent on model) Some allow stripdown of this part, but iron must have cooled down first and have been isolated. Renewal may be required
Descale as described in this chapter. May require more than one treatment if regular descaling has not been carried out

4 Symptom: Poor spray/no spray

Possible causes
a. Tank empty

b. Jet/spray nozzle blocked (often called an atomiser)

Action
Refill and try again. Priming may be required for the pump to function correctly. This varies between makes and models. See your instruction book
Most nozzles can be removed easily for cleaning. Some contain filters that require cleaning. See your instruction book

All of the above checks and tests are to be carried out with appliance isolated – switched OFF and plug OUT, unless otherwise stated as in the case of functional testing to verify correct or incorrect operation. When carrying out a functional test, take care to avoid touching the hot sole plate and steam vents and remember to let the iron cool fully before continuing.

Chapter 21
Toasters

The toaster is another appliance that uses heating elements and, in most instances, a bi-metal strip thermostat to control the length of time the bread is exposed to the heating element. This in turn relates to the degree of browning required by varying the position of the bi-metal contact points. When bread is inserted, a latched spring system is actuated holding the bread carrier mechanically in place, at the same time making a switch contact to supply power to the elements. The heat from the elements, as well as toasting the bread, will heat the bi-metal strip causing it to bend. The bending of the strip manually trips the latch system or actuates an electrical contact depending on toaster type. An electrical type control usually involves the use of a coil which, when energised, creates a magnetic attraction to a movable plate. When attracted to the now magnetised coil, the plate trips the latching device which ejects the bread and at the same time switches off the elements. Various methods of damping are used to smooth the eject operation. Calibration between bi-metal movement and the toast indicator is required. The way in which this is done differs from make to make, and adjustment should not be carried out unless all other checks prove satisfactory. As always, any cleaning, adjustment or repair must be carried out on isolated appliances only – Switch off, Plug out.

One of the most common causes of personal injury or damage to equipment is trying to clear a jammed latch mechanism whilst the toaster is still plugged in. It is not an uncommon occurrence for the mechanism to jam through debris or pieces of curling bread being wedged in, but NEVER should it be cleared while the toaster is still plugged in. Neither should it be poked and prodded with knives or similar objects even when it is unplugged.

Toasters use an exposed heating element wound on to an insulating heat-resistant material. Very early toasters used asbestos, but that has since been replaced by more suitable and inert materials. Faults with element windings are not uncommon but with many modern toasters, single elements cannot be obtained, only complete carriage units of latch mechanism and sets of elements. The cost of these can be very high in relation to the price of a new toaster. Some makes still offer individual parts replacement, so enquire first about their availability before discarding your toaster (or before buying it!).

With careful use and regular cleaning, you can extend the useful life of all appliances, and the toaster is no exception. The main problem encountered is damage to the mains lead due to poor storage, eg wrapped around the toaster when it is still cooling down after use, or allowing the lead to trail across cookers or hobs, etc. Simple care and attention will prevent most problems. A list of faults is given below along with an indication of causes that will help in diagnosing the fault.

Fault finding – toasters

Won't work at all

Possible cause	Action
a. Faulty socket or plug	See *Plugs and Sockets*
b. Faulty mains lead	See *Cables and Cable Faults* and *Using a Meter* sections
c. Internal loose connections	Check for continuity. See *Electrical Circuit Testing*
d. Failure of switch on latching mechanism (often double poled)	Check switch contacts for continuity. See *Electrical Circuit Testing*. Also check that mechanism actuates switch. Adjust or renew as required
e. Latch failing to hold – mechanism or switch	Check that the latch points engage correctly and hold the bread carriage in locked position and that switch is actuated
f. One or more elements open circuit. Some toasters have heaters in series ie one open circuit would stop power reaching the others	Test for continuity. See *Electrical Circuit Testing*. Some models have individual elements as spares

Burns toast on any setting

Possible cause

a. Bread carriage or latch mechanism sticking

b. Failure of bi-metal strip/stat

c. Failure or open circuit de-latching coil

d. Contact failure in latch switch, i.e. shorted together

e. One element open circuit (if it is the one that also heats the bi-metal, excessive trip times will occur)

Action

Clean and check carriage and de-latch action, then retest

Ascertain whether NC or NO or mechanical stat operation and test as required. See *Electrical Circuit Testing*, or manually check tripping action. This is dependent on type of appliance. Renew if adjustment fails

Check for continuity, See *Electrical Circuit Testing*. Renew if open circuit

Check switch for correct operation (make and break). See *Electrical Circuit* testing. Renew if found to be faulty

Check continuity. See *Electrical Circuit Testing*. Renew as required

Toast too light

Possible cause

a. Latch mechanism nuisance-tripping, ie failing to hold bread carriage down as toaster warms up: expansion trips the latch

b. Bi-metal strip or stat out of adjustment in relation to indicator

c. Some appliances cannot repeat cycles, ie once hot, subsequent toasting will lighten as bi-metal strip/stat is already warm

d. When toasting one slice only, some toasters will indicate which slot should be used. By using the wrong slot, incorrect tripping of the latch mechanism will occur

Action

Check for secure latching or worn latch edges. Renew if worn, otherwise adjust if possible

Adjust bi-metal strip/stat if all other checks are OK

Do not adjust bi-metal strip. This is not a fault but a design weakness. Leave to cool between repeat toasting or rest gauge/indicator on toaster to compensate. Remember to reset to original setting otherwise, when next used from cold, the higher setting will apply

Read instruction booklet

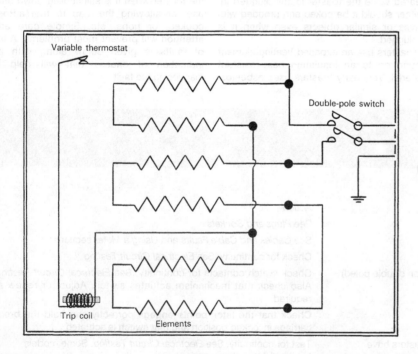

This theoretical diagram shows elements in typical series connection. Note: Live supply to trip coil is via a tap on the heater circuit. It uses the first four elements as resistors to drop the voltage to the coil

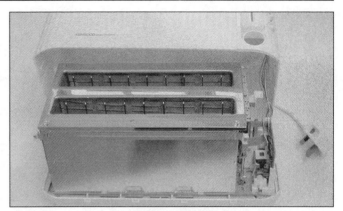

Typical modern toaster

Showing case removed

Toaster – typical repair

1 Continuity testing will identify cable, switch or element faults easily, with the appliance isolated. (This photo shows the toaster casing already removed)

2 Close-up of thermostat

3 Double pole switch can be clearly seen. Check action by latching and de-latching manually

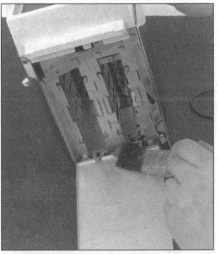

4 Remove crumbs and other debris regularly

5 Some latch mechanisms may require a little lubrication to avoid sticking. This must be done sparingly and only to the moving parts of the slides. Do not use sprays

Individual elements, like the ones shown, can be obtained for some makes, but many are complete inner units

Chapter 22
Kettles

The humble kettle has been given a whole new image in recent years. Simple versions consisting of only a container with a heating element fixed inside are still available, but for many years the trend has been towards the automatic kettle that turns off once boiled.

Some more recent models have been improved even more, with high-speed elements and spout filling. The latest jug version combines all the features of a modern kettle, but has the handle positioned on the side, thus enabling the user to avoid the steam when pouring. As with irons, cable damage through wear and tear and misuse, tend to be a common fault, although cordless kettles are now being produced. The cordless kettles and jug kettles are similar to cordless irons in that they require a power base that has its own mains lead. When the cordless kettle is placed on its base, electrical contact is made to its heating element. The operation from this point is then like any other automatic kettle.

For the purpose of fault finding and repairs, the kettle section will be split into three types – basic, automatic kettle and automatic jug.

The way in which they all work is much the same apart from added refinements and styling. They each have specific problems, though many apply to all three.

Basic kettles – how do they work?

A sealed heating element, which is fixed within the kettle, will start to heat up once the connecting mains lead is plugged into its 13A three-pin socket and switched on. Because the kettle has no isolating switch of its own, it is essential that the element is covered with water before plugging in and switching on. The basic kettle, once boiled, will continue to boil until it is manually switched off. However, most are fitted with a boil dry protector to prevent the element melting. If overheating does occur, whether due to boiling dry or being switched on without containing any water, a mechanical, thermally operated device is activated. The operation of this safety device

releases a powerful spring and rod that ejects the mains lead from its socket at the rear of the kettle. Some kettles can be reset when the element has cooled down, but others, once activated, cannot be reset and have to have a new element fitted. Replacement elements are widely available for these kettles and are supplied with fitting instructions. Make sure that the correct size and shape of element is obtained and renew all seals and washers at the same time, it is not advisable to fit old seals to new elements. Check earth continuity of the kettle and the socket earth path. Fill the kettle with water and leave to stand for a short time to confirm there is no weeping or leaking present before carrying out a functional test. Look closely for poor connections in the socket on the kettle lead and renew at the first signs of any problems. See *Cables and Cable Faults*.

1 Standard kettle (non-auto)

2 Auto kettle

3 Auto jug kettle

Automatic kettles – how do they work?

Heating is similar to the basic kettle with the added bonus of switching off automatically once the water has boiled. This simple operation has many variations but nearly all types use the bi-metal strip. The appliance generally has a biased ON/OFF switch or button which, when turned or pushed to the ON position, supplies power to the element to commence the heating process. Steam produced by the boiling water is directed on to the bi-metal strip which, because of the heat applied to it, bends and the corresponding movement is transferred to the switch button. The movement then trips the biased switch into the OFF position.

Two versions are commonly used: vapour stat and steam stat. The vapour stat operation allows steam vapour to escape through a small

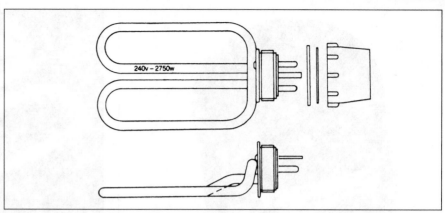

Simple kettle element kit. There are two sizes of boss available; make sure you get the right one

hole at the top of the kettle. The hole directs the steam vapour directly onto the bi-metal strip. The mechanical action of the bi-metal is transferred to the switch by a rod, which keeps water vapour away from the switch device.

Steam stat-controlled kettles have a special element with an open-ended tube fitted to it. The open end of the tube in the kettle is

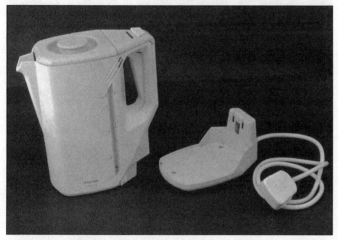

4 Cordless jug kettle with base unit. There are many variations on this style of kettle. A base is used to house the kettle and supply power for the element within the kettle. The kettle does not have a cord (cable) but the base unit does

5 This cordless jug kettle has a central power supply point which allows the jug to revolve through 360°

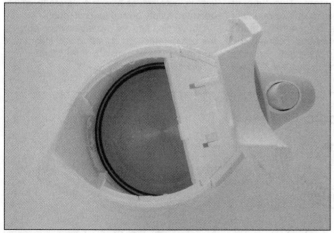

6 This modern jug kettle has a concealed element moulded within the metal base to reduce scaling and create a larger surface area for heating

7 Small internal water filters can be found on some models

Steam stat switch showing bi-metal plate in base

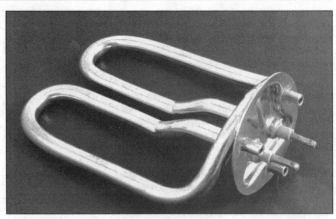

Vapourstat element

Descaler

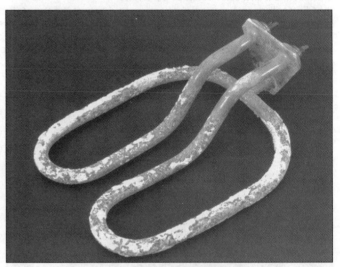

Typical encrusted kettle element

A comprehensive range of replacement elements is available for most makes. This one is used in the later repair sequence

designed to be above the normal fill level so that when boiling occurs, steam is forced down the tube and again on to a bi-metal strip, the mechanical action of which operates the kettle switch as before. This type of control allows for the switch unit to be lower down on the kettle and generally much smaller in size. Problems can occur if the steam tube has water trapped in it, which is caused by incorrect filling or misuse. This will stop or impair the transfer of steam to the bi-metal strip and affect the auto-switching. Allow the kettle to cool, empty contents and invert kettle to drain the tube. As with basic kettles, auto kettles have a separate thermally operated safety device for protection.

Conversion kits are available which convert the basic kettle into an automatic steam stat operation. The kit consists of the element and stat switch.

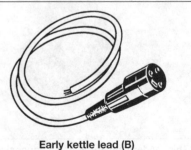

New style coiled lead (A)

Early kettle lead (B)

Kettle lead types

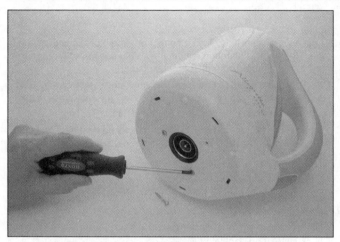

Three screws secure the base cover on this kettle

Removing the base cover exposed a sealed circular element with two bi-metallic disc activated safety switches (arrowed)

Jug kettles – how do they work?

Jug kettles operate in the same way as auto kettles, using both vapour and steam stat operations dependent on make and model. The switch action on the vapour stat version may involve a long, pushrod operation to actuate the switch situated within the handle of the appliance. Again, a thermal safety device is fitted. The element within the kettle obviously has to be much smaller in dimensions, but its wattage is still usually around 2kW enabling it to boil up to three pints of water quickly. Unfortunately, much of the early promotion of jug kettles concentrated mostly on their ability to heat only the amount of water required, thus saving energy by not heating water that was not required. This in itself was admirable, but posed a certain design problem that occurred when the kettle was filled and boiled as normal then emptied of all the water. The residual heat within the smaller and tighter wound element could not be dissipated. This would cause early failure of the jug element if occurring regularly. The effect would also result in repeated tripping of the thermal safety device (resettable on most jug kettles).

The bi-metal strips on most appliances are adjustable to allow for a degree of boiling time prior to 'switch off'. Do not attempt adjustment until all other possibilities have been investigated (see: *Fault Guide*) before considering adjustment. Do not make any adjustments, repairs, descaling or filling of any kettle whilst still plugged in; isolate completely – Switch off, Plug out.

In common with all appliances that heat water, scale will be produced, the degree of which will differ from area to area (see chart – *Chapter 20 Irons*). While some areas are unaffected, others will have a continuous battle against it. Kettles of all designs will highlight water conditions because of their regular use. To avoid premature failure of the element and to improve the efficiency of the kettle, regular descaling is recommended. The frequency of this will obviously depend on the area you are in and the degree of hardness used. Do not chip at the scale within the kettle, but use a descaler designed specifically for kettles. The one shown can be used on all types of kettles from plastic to stainless steel. Read all instructions for the product before descaling.

Fault finding kettles and jugs

Won't heat at all

Possible cause `	*Action*
a. Faulty mains lead or plug/socket	See *Plugs and Sockets, Cables and Cable Faults* and *Electrical Circuit Testing Meter* sections
b. Blown fuse/blown element	See *Plugs and Sockets, Electrical Circuit Testing Meter* and *Low Insulation*
c. Loose connection in kettle lead, socket or not pushed into kettle sufficiently	Check plug for loose connections or loose fit on pins (heat marks) Check for correct fit (push in firmly). Renew if suspect
d. Thermal safety switch activated	Reset if possible and retest. If still faulty, check for scale and descale if necessary. Test see *Electrical Circuit Testing* and *A General Safety Guide*
e. Open circuit heating element	Check continuity. See *Heating Elements, Electrical Circuit Testing*, element renewal and photo sequence
f. Faulty contact/s in kettle switch	Check switch operation and continuity. See *Electrical Circuit Testing* Renewal of complete switch is usually required
g. Bi-metal strip failed in actuated position; this will not allow the main switch to engage 'ON' position	Check for free movement of rods. If free, renew bi-metal strip. This may come as a complete switch assembly

2. Symptom: *Will not switch 'OFF' automatically*

Possible cause	*Action*
a. (i) Steam tube blocked/overfilled (steam stat versions only). a. (ii) Lid not fitted correctly	Reduce water level if too high. See text on tube blockages of steam stats. Refit lid into correct position. If lid is fitted incorrectly, vapour may not be directed onto the bi-metal plate
b. Actuating rod on bi-metal plate stuck	Check for grease and dirt on push rod. If in doubt, renew switch unit
c. Contacts welded together on switch	Usually double-pole switches are fitted, but faults can occur. Check switch action and continuity. See *Electrical Circuit Testing*
d. Bi-metal plate split or corroded	Inspect bi-metal plate closely. Look for cracks on bent section or rust. Renew as required. This may entail a new switch in some instances

3. Symptom: *Cannot re-use shortly after first boiling*

Possible cause	*Action*
a. This may be normal. Bi-metal plate may require cool-down period	Check instruction booklet of kettle Some can recycle quickly, others cannot
b. Bi-metal needs adjusting	Only adjust after checking item a. Use quarter turns only on any adjustments made. Keep a note of all adjustments so that the original position can be reset if necessary

4. Symptom: *Leaking (do not use until fault is rectified)*

Possible cause	*Action*
a. Element fixing screws or nuts loose	Retighten. Fill kettle and leave to stand on kitchen towel and check for further leakage. If OK, before doing functional test, check that all switch parts and mouldings of the kettle are dry
b. Split or perished element washer	If action in item a. fails, renew element seal if it is obtainable separately. Ensure any scale and dirt is removed from area of seal on both sides
c. If steam stat type, check for overfilling and time taken to switch 'OFF' when boiling	Check overfill possibilities and adjust bi-metal plate if required Excessive boiling time may cause dampness at base of switch
d. If leak persists after all the above checks	Possible failure of joint on element to fixing plate. Renew element

5. Symptom: *Switches 'OFF' too soon*

Possible cause	*Action*
a. Leak into switch on the kettle socket area, ie blows fuse or trips RCD	Check for leaks as in Symptom 4. If flash-over/short circuit has occurred, a new switch unit will be required. Test thoroughly. See *Electrical Circuit Testing*, and test with RCD in circuit. See *Low Insulation*
b. Adjustment on bi-metal plate too keen	Adjust bi-metal plate only if all other checks are OK
c. Poor spring pressure on switch bias on kettle; switch not holding 'ON'	Some makes have adjustments for this, others do not. Only adjust if all other checks have been made. Be careful not to over-adjust mechanism – it must have free movement
d. Scale build-up on element; tripping safety device due to overheat within the element	Descale regularly to prevent this problem. Fault may require new element. Scale does not allow element to dissipate the heat generated into the water as it should, hence the tripping of the thermal safety device

Many of the faults shown will also relate to basic kettles. With any stripdown or renewal, it is most important that all seals and wires are refitted in their correct positions. Take care therefore, to make notes and drawings of positions etc during stripdown. If seals are suspect, ie split, perished or worn, they must be renewed. A slight smear of water on new seals will help ease them into position, but only enough water to moisten the seal should be used.

Typical kettle element renewal

1 This automatic kettle had Symptom 1 and tests on the supply outlet and base unit proved OK (refer to later photo sequence for base unit faults)

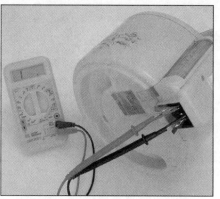

2 When this kettle was tested for continuity it was discovered that the element had simply gone open circuit

3 The two screws at either side of the switch were removed. As always, a note of the position of each item was kept and each part stored carefully

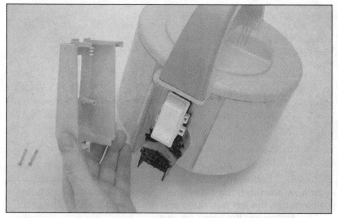

4 With the securing screws removed the cover was eased out of position taking care not to dislodge the switch and the level indicator

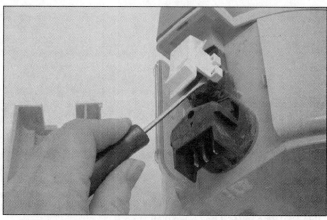

5 The switch rocker can be removed by inserting a small flat bladed screwdriver and carefully releasing the two pivot points

6 Removing the switch rocker allows access to the top element screw. NOTE: It is essential that the replacing of this part is correct so make a note of the order of removal

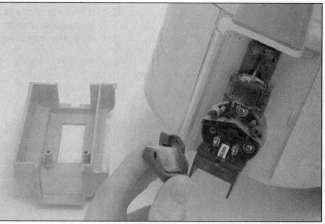

7 This lower cover needs to be removed to gain access to the two lower element screws

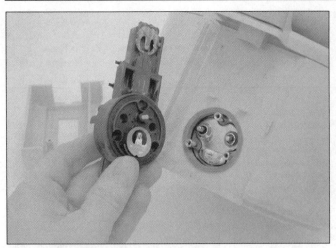

8 Remove the three element/switch fixing screws

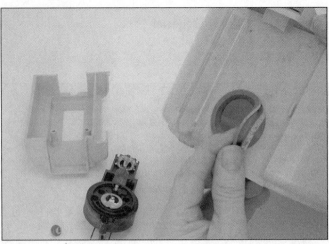

9 When all three screws are removed the switch unit and the element can be removed

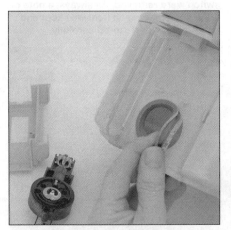

10 Check the lipped seal closely for damage or perishing. It is wise to renew this seal whenever it has been disturbed

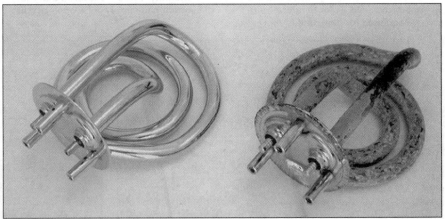

11 This picture shows just how corroded the old element had become prior to it going open circuit. The new element on the left was fitted and positioned correctly prior to tightening the fixing screws

12 A double check of all work carried out was undertaken and a continuity check of the metal outer sheath of the element to the earth pin of the plug was made. In this instance the kettle was placed on the base unit in order that the full earth path of the product was tested

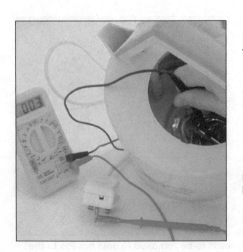

With the kettle fully reassembled and tested, it was filled with water and stood on a paper towel to check for leaks (left for about 15 minutes to verify no leakage or weepage present). As no leaks were found, the next step was a functional test to verify boiling and auto switch off (with RCD in line or on supply socket)

Checking a base unit

Cordless kettles need base units to supply them with power. The constant removal and replacing of the kettle can lead to contact problems in the connecting socket (on the base) and/or the plug (on the kettle). The following sequence shows how they can be tested.

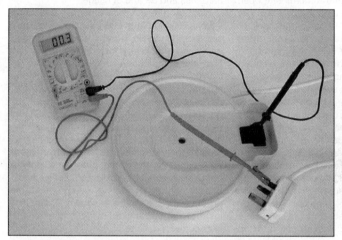

1 After checking that the plug and fuse were OK one probe of the test meter was connected to the 'live' pin of the mains plug and the other was inserted into the base connector socket (ensuring a good contact was made with the connector inside).
A low ohms range was selected to check for continuity. In this instance continuity existed between the two points

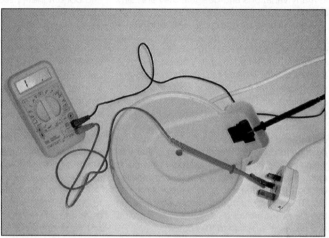

2 The test in step 1 was repeated but in this instance an open circuit fault was found indicating that a fault existed in the neutral connection

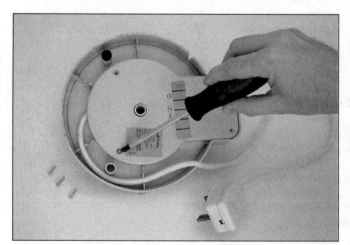

3 To check whether it was the cable or the base connector socket at fault the lower cover was removed

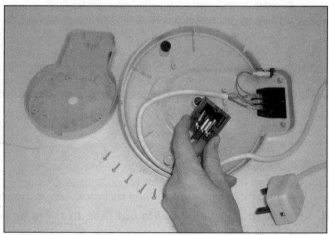

4.The cable was checked for continuity from the mains plug to the base connector and found to be OK on both live and neutral. This meant that the fault lay in the base connector socket and a new unit was obtained and fitted

NOTE: Although not shown in this fault location sequence it is essential that the earth connection is also tested for continuity, see previous sequence for details.

Chapter 23
Filter coffee makers

Filter coffee makers have become extremely popular in recent years. Although they come in many variations and designs, they are fairly straightforward in the way they work.

When water is added to the cold-water compartment, it flows down through a small hole in its base and into a silicone tube containing a non-return valve. The silicone tube feeds water to a metal boiler tube in the metal base plate. The base plate is similar to an iron sole plate and contains a heating element which, when switched on, quickly heats the water in the tube causing it to rise towards the outlet end of the system. The outlet is positioned over a holder containing a filter into which coffee will have been added. Hot water is ejected from the end of the tube and percolates through the coffee and filter on its way to the jug. This is a continuous process as long as there is water in the cold-water compartment and power is supplied to the heater.

When all the cold water has passed through the boiler tube, the temperature of the element and bottom plate rises and a thermostat open circuits the heater and stops the process. The jug containing the filtered coffee will be kept warm by the base plate. If the temperature drops below the preset level, the thermostat will close and supply power to the element once again. This cycling will continue for as long as the appliance is switched on. A safety thermostat, microtemp, TOC or fusible link is included to open circuit the element if, for any reason, an overheat fault should arise. Useful additions are fitted such as float level indicators to show the tank capacity and neon indicators to show when the appliance is switched on and which setting is in use.

Problems encountered are similar to those in the kettle section. Leaks should be attended to immediately and the appliance not used until rectified. Scaling can build up

quickly with this type of heating process, although again, this will depend on water hardness and degree of usage.

Manufacturers recommend descaling intervals varying from every six weeks to every six months, while others will recommend descaling after every forty to fifty uses. The first signs that scale is building up is an increase in the time it takes to complete its normal operation. As this will be a gradual increase and not a sudden change, do not rely on this as an indication that descaling is required. Allowing the scale to build up may result in TOC tripping or failure of the heater. Most appliances have the heating element embedded in the base plate and only a complete unit is obtainable as a spare. Avoid this by regular descaling, using a suitable product like the example shown. Follow the instructions and make sure it is for use with filter coffee machines.

Fault finding – filter coffee makers

1. Symptom: Will not work at all (indicator light/neon not on)

Possible cause	Action
a. Faulty plug or socket	See *Plugs and Sockets*
b. Fault in flex	See *Cables and Cable Faults*, and *Electrical Circuit Testing*. Renew as required
c. Faulty selector switch on appliance	Check for correct switching action and continuity. See *Electrical Circuit Testing*. Renew switch if required

2. Symptom: Light/neon ON (but appliance does not work)

Possible cause	Action
a. Poor connection or open circuit	Check for continuity. See *Electrical Circuit Testing*. Inspect all connections and renew or retighten as required
b. Faulty element/open circuit	Check for continuity. See *Electrical Circuit Testing*. Renew if faulty
c. Faulty thermostat	Check for continuity. See *Electrical Circuit Testing*. Renew if faulty
d. Blown TOC/microtemp/fusible link	Check for continuity. See *Electrical Circuit Testing*. Renew if faulty

NOTE: b, c and d may be due to scale build-up. Descale prior to use after repair has been carried out to prevent damage to new parts fitted.

3. Symptom: Appliance heats but fails to transfer water to filter

Possible cause	Action
a. Scale build-up in system	Descale as mentioned previously
b. Non-return valve sticking or scaled	Descale as mentioned. If no success, renew valve

Note: Water system must be sealed correctly. Ensure all connections are watertight before functional testing, ie fill container and stand appliance on paper to check all the seals are OK. Do not plug in or use until this test is satisfactory.

4. Symptom: Appliance works but light or neon not illuminated

Possible cause	Action
a. Faulty neon or open circuit light	Check light continuity. See *Electrical Circuit Testing*. Renew if required. Neons will require renewal. Combined switch and neon will need complete new switch unit

All of the previous checks and tests are to be carried out with appliance isolated, switch OFF and plug OUT, unless otherwise stated as in the case of functional testing to verify correct or incorrect operation. When carrying out a functional test, take care to avoid touching the hot base plate and remember to let the appliance cool fully before continuing.

Coffee maker typical repair

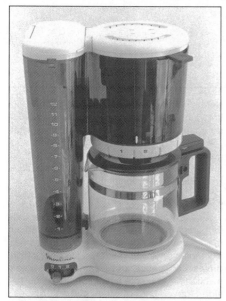

1 This filter coffee maker had Symptom 2. Lead and socket checks proved to be OK

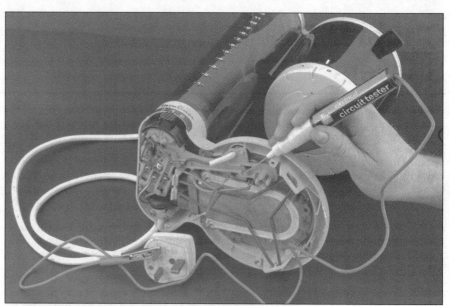

2 (above, right) With the base cover removed, checks can be made to the switch, element, TOC and thermostat. Simple leap-frog continuity testing verified a thermostat fault

3 A replacement thermostat was obtained identical to the original (quote model and make when obtaining spares)

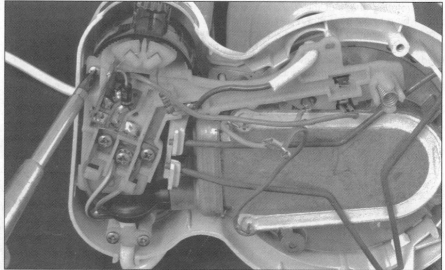

4 Refitting the thermostat was straightforward. All connections and fittings were checked to ensure a secure fit. A double check of all work carried out was done along with continuity check and position of all wiring prior to refitting covers. The unit was tested for leaks (filled and allowed to stand on paper kitchen towel) prior to functional testing. A functional test was carried out on an RCD-protected circuit to verify correct operation of appliance

Chapter 24
Shavers

Shavers fall into two main categories: fully portable (powered by batteries, either dry cell or nickel cadmium rechargeable), and mains powered usually with variable voltage option switch (110–130V or 210–240V to cope with varying supply between countries). Care and correct maintenance of these products is essential if they are to work efficiently and have a long and useful life. Simple care and cleaning will greatly improve their operation and reduce the likelihood of recurrent breakdowns.

The cutting head can be one of two basic types: rotary cutters, and foil cutters. The rotary shaver type has a rotating cutting edge beneath one or more circular slotted cutting heads. The foil shaver type consists of a slotted foil of metal under which a multi-edged cutting bar moves rapidly from side to side. Both types deliver hundreds of cutting actions per second.

The rotating heads of these shavers are driven by a brush gear motor (see *Electric Motors*) via a gearing system directly beneath the cutting heads. Two types of motors are used. For portable battery-powered shavers, a DC-powered motor is used which runs on the low voltage supplied by either dry cell or fixed nickel cadmium batteries. The drawback of this motor is that, should failure occur, it usually has to be replaced with a completely new one. Thorough cleaning and the application of a very small amount of

lubrication to the end bushes/bearings of the motor are a worthwhile maintenance task. When renewing a motor of this type, ensure that the connections are replaced exactly as the originals. If this is not done, the motor will run in reverse. The same applies if fixed nicad batteries are to be renewed. Nicad batteries require care in use, disposal and fitting (see *Batteries*).

For mains powered versions, a larger bush-gear motor is used. Individual components are generally available for this much larger motor. Take care when dismantling and note positions of all relevant parts. The motor brushes are easily removed with care. Each should be clean and free to move within its brush-holder. Renew any brushes less than 5mm in length and any brushes that are burnt or in poor condition. The motor bearings are larger than those of the battery operated shaver. They are pre-oiled and should only need lubricating after a long period of use. A very small amount of light machine oil should be used on the pinion side of the bearing. Do not allow any lubricant on to the field coil or commutator. The cutting heads can be removed for cleaning. Immerse them in surgical spirit or industrial alcohol for two minutes, remove and allow to air dry. Apply a little machine oil with a fingertip to the cutter guard prior to refitting. Squeaking of the rotary cutters is usually caused by use on dry skin.

Normally the natural oils from the skin would help lubricate the rotating heads. If squeaks do occur, apply a little light machine oil with the fingertip to the cutter guard. Cutters and guards are not repairable and are changed as a pair. They are easily damaged so take care when cleaning or repairing the shaver.

Foil shavers

As with rotary shavers, the foil shaver can be battery-powered (dry cell or fixed nicad) or mains-powered. The battery type uses a small DC motor similar to the rotary version, which drives an eccentric cam and crank mechanism to create a reciprocating, side-to-side movement of the cutting blades. Cleaning and maintenance is similar to that of battery rotary shavers. Mains-powered foil shavers, however, differ considerably in the way the vibration/reciprocating movement of the cutting blade is produced.

A much simpler system, using far fewer moving parts, is often used and no recognisable motor as such is present. Movement is generated by a vibrating motor that consists of two stator coils mounted on fixed metal laminate cores. Suspended above this on a pivot and held centrally by two strong springs is a second metal laminate called a yoke. When mains power (AC) is supplied to the coils the two poles of the fixed stator become magnets with alternating poles of north and south due to the alternating

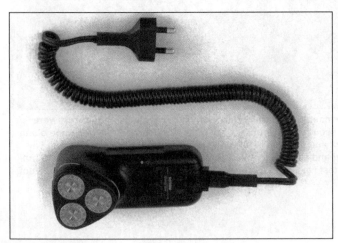

Rotary shaver

Battery type

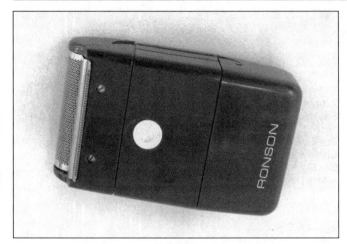

Foil type

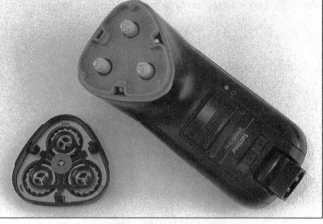

Internal view of a rotary cut shaver

current supplied. The movable yoke is drawn against one spring and then the other as it is attracted to the ever-changing strengths of magnetic field produced. Having two poles, the movement induced is 100 times per second (mains voltage at 50 cycles per second x 2 poles = 100 variations in magnetic attraction per second). The movement made is linked directly to the cutting blades.

Typical worn/damaged foil. Renew as soon as possible to avoid further problems

This type of motor is finely balanced during manufacture and no lubrication or maintenance is necessary other than cleaning. Only dismantle the motor if repair/renewal of parts is required. Instructions for cleaning and lubricating the heads of foil shavers are the same as for rotary types.

Shavers with nicad batteries

Some shavers will contain fixed nicad batteries with the facility to plug in a lead to the shaver for recharging. Such chargers are normally supplied with the shaver and only the one specified for it should be used. The charger is a sealed unit and matched to the specific requirements of each shaver and the size and quantity of batteries it contains. Obtain an exact replacement should the charger become defective. Further details regarding nickel cadmium batteries are given elsewhere in the book and particular attention should be given to that chapter when dealing with appliances containing these batteries.

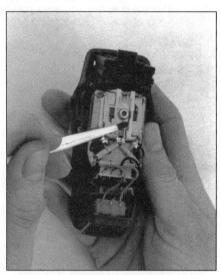

Use a small brush to carefully clean the motor and casing

Battery-powered DC motor. This type would require a complete motor if a fault occurs within it. Only three clips need removing to gain access for cleaning, repair, etc.

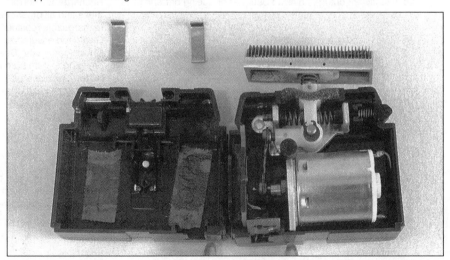

Checking motor brushes for wear and inspecting the commutator for damage. Note: *Mark brushes to ensure they are the correct way around and in the same slide if they are to be refitted*

Fault finding – vibration type motors

1. Symptom: Won't work at all

Possible causes
a. Faulty mains lead or plug/socket

b. On/Off switch faulty
c. Incorrect setting of voltage switch (if fitted)
d. Open circuit stator coils
e. Short circuit stator coils

Action
See *Plugs and Sockets, Cables and Cable Faults*, and *Electrical Circuit Testing*
See *Electrical Circuit Testing*
Check switch setting and supply voltage being supplied
See *Electrical Circuit Testing*
Is fuse blown? See *Electrical Circuit Testing*

2 Symptom: Running slowly/sluggish

Possible causes
a. Incorrectly fitted foil or cutting head
b. Damaged or worn foil
c. Yoke out of position or spring faulty
d. Winding in stator coils short circuit (ie not balanced/ unequal resistance)

Action
Check, and refit if required
Renew parts immediately
Check; adjust or renew as necessary

See *Electrical Circuit Testing*. Renew defective parts.

3. Symptom: Poor shave

Possible causes
a. Foil and blades clogged
b. Damage or wear to foil/blades
c. Sluggish/slow action

Action
Clean thoroughly and regularly
Renew immediately
See: Symptom 2.

Fault finding – brush-type motors

4. Symptom: Won't work at all

Possible cause
a. Faulty mains lead or plug/socket on mains shavers or on adaptor for charger unit for chargeable shavers
b. Is socket adaptor being used?
c. Insufficient charge on nicad batteries or ageing batteries

d. Worn or sticking motor brush
e. Internal wiring open circuit.

f. Cutter jammed

Action
See *Plugs and Sockets, Cables and Cables Faults*, and *Electrical Circuit Testing*
Check fuse in adaptor for continuity
Recharge for correct length of time. Check a. relating to adaptor. If these and all other checks prove OK, renew ALL batteries with correct rechargeable replacements
Clean and ensure free movement or renew
Check continuity. See *Electrical Circuit Testing*. This also applies to charging unit on battery versions
Note: *Many charging units are sealed and, as such, non-repairable. Check that all other tests prove OK and renew if suspect*
Check foil and cutter for damage or clogging. Clean or renew as necessary

5. Symptom: Excessive noise

Possible cause
a. Motor or other parts loose
b. Clogged, damaged or worn foil or blades. Cutters or foil incorrectly positioned

Action
Check all parts are in their correct positions
Inspect closely. Clean thoroughly if required. Renew any incorrectly positioned or defective parts

6. Symptom: Slow action

Possible cause
a. Low battery
b. Worn or sticking motor brush
c. Clogged cutting blade or foil

Action
Recharge. See also 1c
Clean and ensure free movement or renew
Clean thoroughly and lubricate as detailed in text

7. Symptom: Intermittent operation

Possible cause
a. Poor internal connection to battery, motor or switch

b. Check mains lead for wear or intermittent open circuit
c. Sticking motor brush

Action
Check continuity and all joints and wiring. See *Electrical Circuit Testing*
See *Cables and Cable Faults* and *Electrical Circuit Testing*
Remove, clean or renew as required

8. Symptom: Poor shave

Possible cause
a. Low charge
b. Worn cutting blade or foil
c. Clogged cutting head

Action
Recharge and retest
Renew if faulty
Clean thoroughly after each use

9. Symptom: Shaver gets excessively hot

Possible cause
a. Battery short-circuited

b. Motor short circuit/overheat
c. Loose socket on mains shaver

Action
If this happens, correct short circuit and renew batteries, as they will have been damaged
Renew motor
Check socket on shaver body and lead for overheating or poor connection. Renew any defective parts

Many of the above symptoms, possible causes and action relate to both mains power and rechargeable battery shavers. Find the symptom and possible cause applicable to your type of shaver

Chapter 25
Hairdryers

Nearly every household possesses an electric hairdryer of one type or another. Designs vary from hand-held to large hooded models supported on a stand. They all work on the same principle of blowing air over a heating element by means of a fan. The fan is either a simple bladed type or cylindrical version. The air, as it passes over the hot element, is heated and vented from the appliance ready for use. The element is usually a wound exposed wire on a heat resistant mount. A more solid version of element may be found mounted in a zig-zag fashion on a mica former. The element is protected by a thermostat to control the safe working temperature of both heater and appliance, and is usually self-resetting. The motor used can be one of four types: (AC) Brush, Induction Motor (capacitor start), Induction Motor (shaded-pole) and DC Permanent-Magnet Motor. The first three motor types are covered in the *Motors in General* section. The operation of the DC motor is given later in this section.

The main fault areas are:

1 Flex damage due to wear and tear or misuse.

2 Overheating due to clogging or blocking of the air intake either by careless use in holding the appliance or allowing fluff and loose hair to block the intake.

3 Damage to the fan either from rough handling or from fluff or loose hair jamming and slowing the fan.

Special note should be made of the prohibition against using electrical appliances in bathrooms. Many fatal accidents occur every year, simply because people use items like hairdryers in the bathroom or shower room. **Never** use any portable mains-powered electrical equipment in these areas. There are specially designed fixed position dryers available for use in the bathroom which have to be fitted by a competent and qualified electrician to rigorous electrical safety standards.

Flex damage and failure are common in this type of appliance due to continuous movement when in use. Take care to store the flex after use, do not pull or stretch when using the dryer, and inspect regularly for faults such as outer sheath cracks or splits, heat damage, etc. Pay particular attention to the entry point of the lead and also the plug cord grip, and renew any faulty or suspect flex immediately. **Do not** use the appliance until this has been done (see *Cables and Cable Faults*).

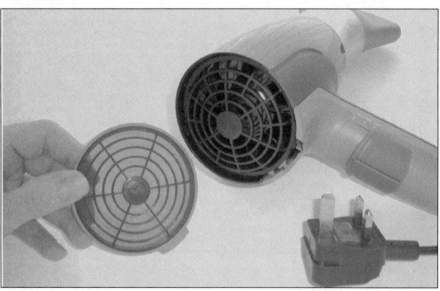

Ensure air intakes are free from blockages, fluff, etc.

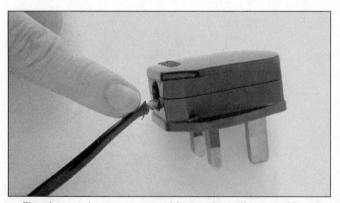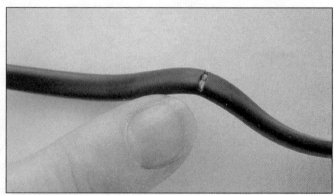

Flex damage is a common problem and usually caused by misuse or lack of care. Store the flex carefully and avoid twists or kinks forming which will weaken it. Check the flex regularly for damage or wear along its whole length. Pay special attention to both ends at or near their fixing points. If in doubt about the flex, renew it

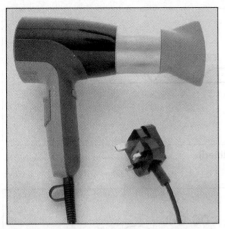

Many modern hair dryers are supplied with a range of attachments. This particular dryer also has two main switches in the handle giving a combination of up to six heat and blow settings. In addition it has a self-setting trigger switch which when pressed turns the heater OFF but still allows the fan motor to run resulting in a quick cooling effect

During periodic checks, ensure the air intake to the fan is clean and clear of fluff and loose hair. If not, it will result in the airflow being reduced which leads to the heater thermostat or TOC tripping repeatedly, eventually resulting in failure of the stat or heater or both.

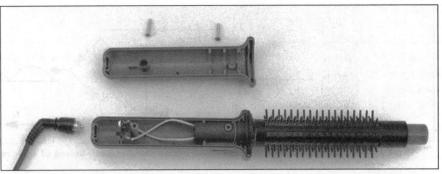

Most hand-held equipment is double insulated. It is therefore essential that all the components and wiring are refitted in their original positions after any repair or maintenance. Make notes during stripdown to ensure this is done

The DC motor

The DC motor, as the name implies, runs only on direct current (rather than on normal household AC). The operation of the motor is similar to the brush gear motor described in 'Electric Motors'. DC power is supplied to a wound armature via a commutator and carbon brush system. A similar field coil system can also be used but more often a permanent magnet field is used requiring no electrical supply. *See below*. Power in the form of direct current is supplied only to the brushes. This

induces rotation of the armature within the permanent magnet poles. Such motors are easily reversed simply by reversing the supply

A small DC motor and rectifier unit. This type of system is now widely used

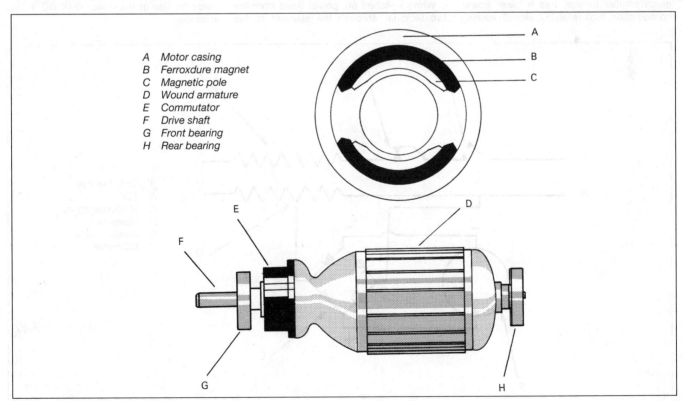

A   Motor casing
B   Ferroxdure magnet
C   Magnetic pole
D   Wound armature
E   Commutator
F   Drive shaft
G   Front bearing
H   Rear bearing

Permanent magnet motor (DC)

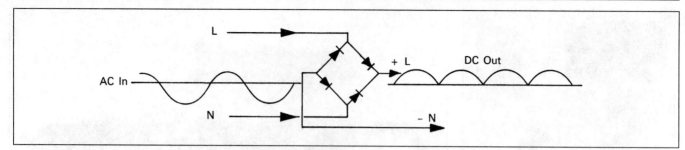

Full-wave bridge rectifier (both halves of wave rectified)

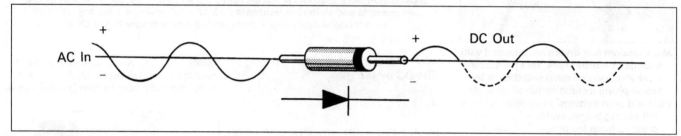

Single-wave rectifier (AC in, single polarity DC out)

voltage to the brushes. Care must be taken when dismantling the appliance because if the terminals are reversed, the fan action of the dryer will be reduced or even rendered non-existent. As always, make notes when stripping down appliance for cleaning or repair.

This type of motor is used because it is much smaller in size, has a lower power consumption, high reliability, smooth running and low cost. Failure of the motor will require complete motor renewal; make sure only the correct replacement is obtained.

A bridge rectifier is mounted within the appliance. This is recognisable as a small printed circuit board arrangement, or a small rectifier unit with four wires leading to it.

When switched on, power flows from the live terminal, through the element to the neutral terminal and heating then takes place. A connection (tap) is made part way through the element to supply power to the bridge rectifier. The element acts as a resistor and so reduces the voltage, usually to 1/10, to the rectifier. The reduced AC voltage supplied to the rectifier is then converted by it to DC ready for use in the motor (24V DC in this instance).

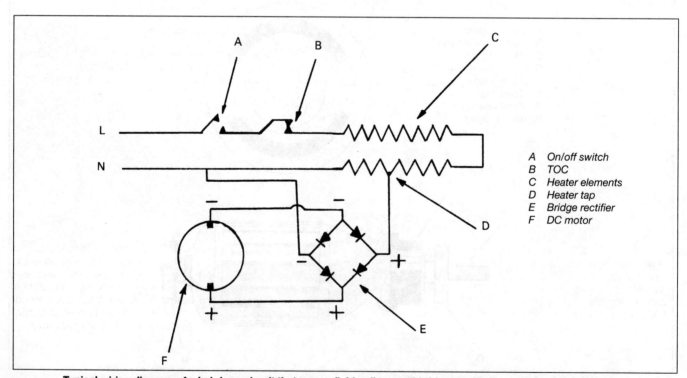

A   On/off switch
B   TOC
C   Heater elements
D   Heater tap
E   Bridge rectifier
F   DC motor

Typical wiring diagram of a hairdryer circuit that uses a field coil tap and bridge rectifier to power a small DC motor

Hair dryer typical repair

1 This dryer had Symptom 4 and overheated to the point of TOC operation. When it had cooled, it was foolishly used again. As the appliance seemed to function correctly when cool, a mechanical problem was suspected although a check on the air intake proved OK

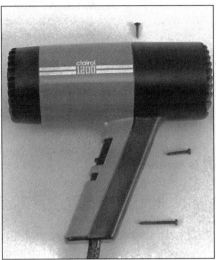

2 With the unit isolated, access was obtained to the internal parts by removing 3 screws, 1 cross head and 2 special anti-tamper

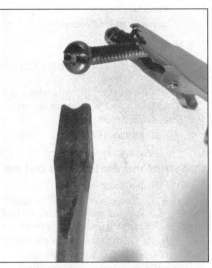

3 Modifying an old flat-bladed driver allowed the 2 special screws to be removed. Various types of special fixings may be encountered. Specialist tool shops may be able to help; if not, modifying existing tools will often be the only answer

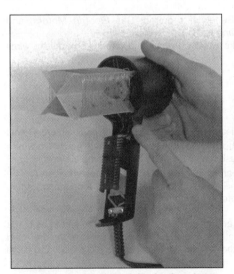

4 A close inspection of the fan bearings showed that a thread was acting as a brake and slowing the fan down. This in turn allowed the element to overheat and trip the TOC due to a reduction in airflow

5 After carefully removing the thread and ensuring free rotation, a check of all other parts, including TOC, motor, heater and all connections was carried out to confirm that no other damage or blockage was present

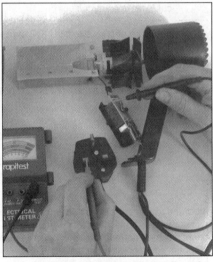

6 A double check was made on all work done to verify that all parts and wires were in their correct positions prior to refitting the casing. A functional test was carried out on an RCD-protected circuit to confirm correct operation of the appliance

Fault finding - hairdryers

1. Symptom: Will not work at all (no heat or motor action)

Possible cause

a. Faulty plug or socket

b. Fault in flex

c. Open circuit thermostat (DC motors with heater tap only)

d. Open circuit TOC or overheat protective device (DC motors with heater tap only)

e. Faulty on/off switch

f. Internal loose connection

Action

See *Plugs and Sockets*

See *Cables and Cable Faults*, and *Electrical Circuit Testing*. Renew as required

Check thermostat. See *Temperature Control and Thermostats,* and *Electrical Circuit Testing*

Check for continuity. See *Temperature Control* and *Electrical Circuit Testing*

Check switch operation and continuity. See *Electrical Circuit Testing*

Check continuity of appliance. See *Electrical Circuit Testing*

2. Symptom: Motor runs but no heat is produced

Possible cause

a (i). Heater element neutral return is open circuit. (This allows neutral return through the rectifier so boosting voltage output) (DC motor version)

a (ii). Open circuit heater element (non-DC motor version)

b. Open circuit TOC/Safety stat

c. Faulty selector switch (if fitted)

d. Internal loose connection.

Action

Check neutral return of heater element for continuity. See *Electrical Circuit Testing*

Check for continuity. See *Electrical Circuit Testing*

Check for continuity. See *Electrical Circuit Testing*

Check for continuity. See *Electrical Circuit Testing*

Check for continuity. See *Electrical Circuit Testing*

3. Symptom: No motor action but element heats up (trips TOC)

Possible cause

a. Moving parts jammed

b. Open circuit internal wiring/connections

c. Motor open circuit

d. Failure of bridge rectifier (DC-powered types only)

Action

Check for blockage of fan or lint/loose hair around motor shaft. Remove and clean. **Do not** over-lubricate

Check all connections and links for continuity. See *Electrical Circuit Testing*

Check continuity. Renew if required. See *Electric Motors*, and *Electrical Circuit Testing*

Verify all other checks are OK. Renew and retest. Look out for wires shorting together

4. Symptom: Motor and fan run slowly

Possible cause

a. Debris on motor or fan shaft

b. Motor brush fault

c. Motor or fan bearings worn. This allows excess sideways movement and slow running of motor due to friction

Action

Check thoroughly. Clean and remove all lint and loose hair, etc. Retest

Check continuity and inspect brushes. Renew if possible. Some makes may allow brush renewal, others require complete new motor

Inspect closely all bearings. Check for sideways movement and excessive play. Some makes may have renewable bearings, others will require a new motor/fan unit

All of the above checks and tests are to be carried out with appliances isolated – switch OFF and plug OUT, unless otherwise stated as in the case of functional testing to verify correct or incorrect operation. When carrying out a functional test, make sure all cables and wiring are fitted back into their correct positions when reassembling. Any parts renewed must be identical to the original specification. Quote model and serial numbers when obtaining spare parts

Chapter 26
Room heaters

This section deals with domestic free-standing portable electric heaters. Three types of heaters are widely used:

1. Radiant heaters

In this type, heat is produced by an element that glows red-hot when power is supplied to it. The heat generated by this action is directed by a highly polished reflector through an open front, protected by a metal grille. The element can be externally wound on a ceramic mount or internally mounted in a heat resistant silica glass tube. Simple switching of the element(s) is included and faults can be easily traced. See *Electrical Circuit Testing*, for continuity testing of the heater elements.

2. Convector heaters

Heating in a convector appliance is by an open spiral/spring element supported on mica or ceramic plates at the base of the unit. No moving parts are used to distribute heat from the appliance, only normal convection air current created by warm air rising from a heater. A simple on/off switch is usually included and often a variable thermostat of the bi-metal type is used to maintain a pre-set temperature by switching the element on or off as required. A TOC is often fitted to prevent overheating. Circuit testing can be carried out to ascertain faults. See *Electrical Circuit Testing* and *Temperature Control and Thermostats*.

3. Fan heaters

The fan heater is the most popular of all portable heaters, largely because of its compact size and its capability to heat a large room quickly. This is done in a similar way to the hairdryer described in Chapter 25. In this instance a much larger element is used (up to 3kW) which can have a variable heat output, typically 700W, 1300W and 3000W by using a switchable combination of elements. A cold blow facility is often included for summer use; this simply allows the motor and fan to run without any of the elements in circuit. The motor used is normally a shaded-pole version. Large fans or barrel fans are attached directly to the rotor to blow air over the element

Radiant heater

Convector heater

Fan heater with thermostatic control

assembly. This creates a powerful airflow that rapidly heats (or helps cool) the room. These versions can be found with a variable thermostat to switch the heater on and off automatically to a pre-selected temperature, keeping the room at a constant level.

The fan heater is a more complex heater than the other two types and, as such, has mechanical problems as well as electrical. A safety thermostat/TOC is incorporated to switch off the element should motor failure occur.

All three types of heaters must have the correct rated cable fitted and care must be exercised, not only in repair or servicing, but in the use and positioning of all heating appliances.

DO NOT use them for drying or airing clothes.

DO NOT restrict airflow around them or place them in close proximity to other items.

DO NOT use an appliance without the safety guard or with covers removed or when damaged.

DO NOT use an unsuitable extension lead or out of doors. See *Cables and Cable Faults*.

Most heating appliances require three-core earthed flex, but some modern fan heaters may be double insulated and have only two-core flex fitted. Ensure the correct cable is fitted when renewing and check the rating plate to verify if double insulated or not. See *A General Safety Guide*.

It is essential that all wiring and covers are refitted in their correct positions after servicing or repair. Make a note of each item and its position during stripdown.

Combinations of heater type can be found in

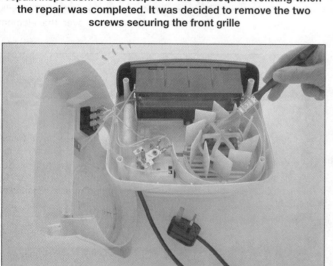

1 This fan heater had symptoms similar to 3 and 4 alternating between the two. With the appliance isolated, a note was made of the fixing screws and position of grilles, etc. This helped in deciding how best to gain entry to the heater for repair/inspection. It also helped in the subsequent refitting when the repair was completed. It was decided to remove the two screws securing the front grille

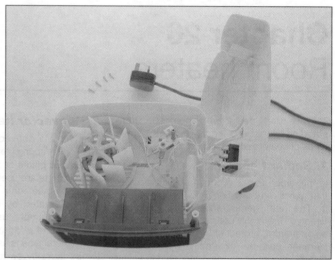

2 Removing the four recessed screws allowed the casing to split into two halves

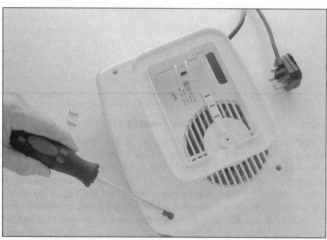

3 The heater was in relatively good condition. A thorough cleaning of motor, fans and grilles, etc., was carried out as a standard measure

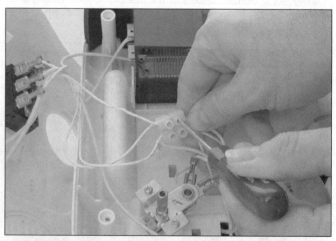

4 During cleaning, a loose motor connection was found at this terminal block. This had been the cause of an intermittent motor fault, which in turn resulted in the heater tripping it's TOC. To correct the fault the motor connection was reconnected and all other connections were checked

5 To gain access to the top motor bearing the fan was carefully eased from the motor shaft. The fan was a tollerance fit (push on) and was carefully removed by inserting a large flat bladed screwdriver between the motor and frame and the fan centre. Take care not to damage the plastic fan, motor end frame and motor coils.

6 A little light machine oil was applied to the motor bearings prior to reassembly. Before refitting the covers, a double check was made to ensure that all parts were back in their original positions. When reassembled, checks on the cable and plug were also carried out as a matter of routine

With all panels fitted back into place and all tests proving OK, the heater was ready for a functional test with an RCD in circuit. If in doubt as to the electrical safety of the produce have the appliance PAT tested by a competent person, refer to Chapter 2

some appliances, eg a convector plus radiant bar, and each will be switched independently. Both convector and radiant appliances will require little maintenance. Periodically, check the mains lead for damage or wear and tear along its whole length. Inspect cable sleeves and terminal block connections, making sure they are tight and no overheating is present. Regularly check the air inlet grills on the base of a convector heater for fluff and debris, cleaning as necessary. On radiant heaters, keep the reflector clean and bright, but take care not to damage the ceramic or glass mounts of the elements when cleaning. Check the radiant bar ends, making sure they are tight and a good electrical connection is being made. When cleaning or inspecting these items, ensure a correct earth path exists between all linked metal parts and the earth pin of the plug (unless it is a double insulated appliance).

Fault finding - fan heaters

1. Symptom: Won't work at all

Possible cause	*Action*
a. Faulty mains lead or plug/socket	See *Plugs and Sockets*, *Cable and Cable Faults* and *Electrical Circuit Testing*
b. Variable thermostat (if fitted) incorrectly set or faulty	Check variable thermostat for correct setting and continuity. See *Temperature Control and Thermostats*, and *Electrical Circuit Testing*. Do not adjust. Faults in thermostat require fitting of new compatible thermostat
c. TOC tripped or failed. (Some appliances may have self-setting TOCs, others may have manual reset	Check for continuity. See *Electrical Circuit Testing*. Check for blockage of fan/motor seizure. Reset TOC if applicable and retest. Renew auto reset TOC if suspect
d. Internal wiring fault	Check all connections. Retighten or renew if suspect. See *Electrical Circuit Testing*
e. Switch failure	Check switch action (audible clicks) and verify continuity. Inspect closely for overheating and renew if suspect

Note: Models with multi-select switch banks require renewal of complete switch unit even if only one switch has failed.

2. Symptom: Motor runs but no heat produced

Possible cause	Action
a. TOC tripped or failed. (Some appliances may have self-resetting TOCs, others may need manual reset)	Check for continuity. See *Electrical Circuit Testing*. Check for blockage or fan/motor seizure. Reset TOC if applicable and retest. Renew auto reset TOC if suspect
b. Open circuit heater	Check continuity of heater element. See *Electrical Circuit Testing*
c. Internal wiring fault	Check all connections, retighten or renew if suspect. See *Electrical Circuit Testing*
d. Switch failure	Check switch action (audible clicks) and verify continuity. Inspect closely for overheating and renew if suspect

Note: *Models with multi-select switch banks usually require a complete renewal even if only one switch has failed.*

3. Symptom: Element heats but no motor action

Possible cause	Action
a. Open circuit motor	Check continuity. See *Electrical Circuit Testing*. Failure of coil or internal TOC will require renewal of motor
b. Fan or motor jammed	Check all moving parts and bearings. Clean or renew as required
c. Switch failure	Check switch action (audible clicks) and verify continuity. Inspect closely for overheating and renew if suspect.

Note: *Models with multi-select switch banks usually require complete renewal of switch unit even if only one switch has failed.*

Note: *All of the faults in Symptom 3 can cause damage to the heater TOC by tripping on and off as heating and cooling takes place due to no airflow over the elements. TOC renewal may be required if cycling has happened over a long period of time. Failure to do so may cause nuisance tripping after the original fault has been rectified. This is due to the TOC becoming weakened and tripping at a much lower temperature than normal. This type of fault is often called temperamental TOC and can occur in any appliance that uses a self-setting TOC.*

4. Symptom: Noisy

Possible cause	Action
a. Debris on fan assembly	Clean fan and inlet grilles and check for free rotation
b. Damaged or bent fan	Misuse or accidental dropping of appliance often causes this problem. Check for free rotation of fan. Check housing position **Note:** *This fault will cause slow running and subsequently reduced airflow. See* **Note** *at end of symptom 3.*
c. Bearing fault on motor or fan.	Check for excessive movement on bearings. On motor, check closely that rotor does not foul the stator due to worn bearings. This would cause the rotor to be pulled on to the stator only when power creates the powerful magnetic field. Check for this kind of fault on all shaded-pole motors.

All of the above checks and tests are to be carried out with the appliance isolated – switch OFF and plug OUT, unless otherwise stated as in the case of functional testing to verify correct or incorrect operation. When carrying out a functional test, take care to avoid parts of the appliance that remain hot.

Fan heaters – tips

1. Ensure all air grilles and inlets are free from fluff, etc.
2. The life of the motor and fan bearings will be extended if a drop of light machine oil is applied every six months. A small amount only is required; excess will cause a build-up of fluff. Do not use aerosol spray oil on this appliance. The indiscriminate use of spray lubrication is to be avoided on all electrical items.
3. Some heaters have bladed fans fitted on each side of the motor. If these are removed for any reason, it is important that they are refitted in the correct position, as they are handed (ie left-handed and right-handed). All fans are easily damaged so great care should be taken in removal and storage during repair and servicing.

Chapter 27
Food mixers

The electric food mixer can truly be called a labour-saving appliance. Many variations can be found from the simple hand-held type to the large table-top version with additional attachments available such as juice extractor, liquidiser, potato peeler, can opener and wheat mill. At the heart of all mains-powered mixers will be a series-wound brush gear motor. This type of motor is used because of its good power output (up to 1/3hp on large table-top models) combined with the capacity to have variable-speed control. These two advantages are used to their full extent in this most versatile appliance.

Hand-held mixers

This type of mixer, as the name denotes, is designed to be hand-held, although most have the provision for a stand if required. Most, if not all, versions will have variable speed control to suit the varying conditions when in use. Some may have set speeds (usually three) whilst others have the capacity for variation of speed over a wide range

(similar in principle to a volume control on a radio or TV).

The power from the motor is transferred to the beater attachment points via helically cut gearwheels driven by a wormshaft cut into the end of the motor armature. Nylon gearwheels are used to keep weight down, and much of the appliance is made of moulded plastic for the same reason. Unlike table-top mixers, hand-held mixers are unable to power a wide range of attachments. Dough mixing and shredding attachments can be used, but because of the compact size and power output, continuous use of these is often

Hand-held mixer with three preset speeds

View of gear drive on hand-held version

limited to no more than 6 to 10 minutes. It is wise to take this into consideration when using the appliance because, if the mixer is not allowed to cool after the prescribed length of time, the motor or ancillary parts could become overheated and fail.

It is possible to obtain spare parts for some makes, whereas for others only items like the motor can be obtained as a complete unit, regardless of the fault. Motor brushes are generally available separately for all makes, wear being one of the most common faults. Renew any brush that is less than 5mm in length or shows signs of sticking. Burnt or dirty brushes also need to be renewed. Always ensure that the brush is free to slide within the holder and that the commutator is clean, bright and free from grease and dirt.

Drive gears are best renewed as a set. Look for missing teeth and make sure to mark and note the meshing positions prior to removal. Often an aligning mark is moulded onto each gear and it is imperative that these marks are matched up for correct meshing of attachments such as beater bars and dough hooks. When renewing or servicing the gear assembly, lubricate only the wormshaft and gear spacers. Do not over grease and take care that the grease does not come into contact with any motor parts. As with any service or repair, ensure that all parts, wiring, screws and covers are refitted in their original positions during reassembly. Verify the correct earth path if required or check if double insulated.

Preset speed control – how does it work?

As the term implies, speed control is the ability to select a preset speed. In the case of hand-held mixers, three presets are usually available via a selector switch, ie 1, 2, 3 or low, medium, high. Each corresponds to a set motor speed, in turn directly proportional to the beater speed via the drive gear. The switch position selects the size of field coil to be used for that particular setting. The field coil is wound in such a way that it can be split into three (this is called field tapping). Position A requires power to flow through all three windings resulting in low speed (but high torque). Position B allows power to flow through two windings resulting in medium speed (and medium torque). Position C selects just the single field winding, which results in high speed (but low torque). Continuity testing as detailed in *Using a Meter* will assist in fault finding although failure of one coil will result in a complete field coil if available, or if not, a complete replacement motor. Selector switch faults can be traced in the same way.

Variable speed control

Unlike the preset speed control, variable control allows a greater variation in motor speeds. The motor itself is a plain AC series-wound brush motor and, as such, it is incapable of speed variation on its own.

Control of speed is gained by the use of a separate speed control unit, which consists of a printed circuit board with a number of solid-state components, often called the speed module or motor control module. In simple terms, this device interrupts the power supply to the motor at regular intervals. In effect, it pulses the motor. If the pulsing is increased, the motor will run faster and if pulsing is slowed, the motor will run slower. This pulsing is carried out many times per second by a thyristor or triac which in turn is controlled by various other components, one being a variable resistor connected to the speed control knob or slide. When the control is set to the required speed, the resistance allows the thyristor to pulse the motor at a given rate resulting in the required speed. Such pulsing would create uneven running of the brush motor so the module carries out a smoothing technique. When the motor is without power during the pulse cycle it will still be rotating. The rotation of the brush motor creates a voltage, the motor being now, in effect, a generator (such voltage is called back-EMF – electro motive force). The back-EMF produced is used by the module through a diode to smooth the pulses. The utilisation of the back-EMF also helps keep the speed of the motor constant even under load. All this occurs many times a second and is undetectable during normal operation. Modules are not repairable and are normally only available as a complete replacement unit.

If speed problems are encountered, look for burnt components or loose connections, etc. Check all other parts before suspecting or changing the module. The motor should be checked for any shorting insulation, loose wires, worn/damaged brushes, etc. See *Electric Motors* and *Electrical Circuit Testing*. Only when all other possible faults have been eliminated should the module be replaced. Ensure the correct replacement is obtained and a note of all wires and connections made prior to repair.

Table-top mixers

The table-top or worktop mixer is a far more robust appliance capable of more continuous use than the hand-held mixers described

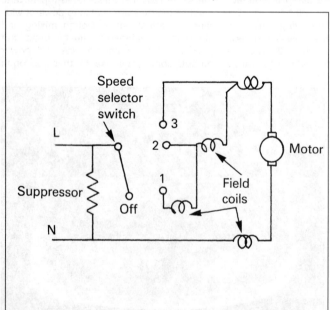

Typical preset speed control circuit

Table-top mixer with infinitely variable speed control

Much larger gear box unit of the table-top mixer. Note the damage to crown wheel (of large gear) on this degreased gearbox

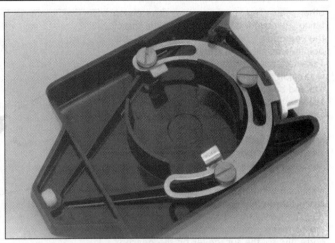

Top cover with dog clutch actuating pin

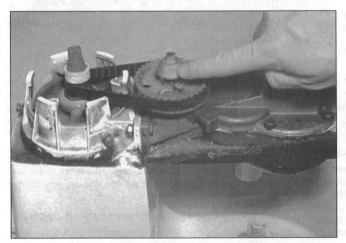

Wear on dog clutch threads is common

Internal drive gear from clutch prone to splitting

earlier. It has a much larger motor, to cope with a wider range of tasks and attachments. The motor can drive high-speed attachments like liquidisers by a power take-off point on the armature shaft. The motor also drives a large gearbox via a toothed belt (on early mixers a dog clutch was used to disengage the gearbox when the direct motor take-off was in use). The gearbox forms the top arm of the mixer and has three power take-off points designed to take a variety of attachments. The lower drive is a planet gear drive and is used for mixing, beating and making dough, etc. The front take-off is a slow-speed drive used for mincing, slicing and shredding, etc. The top gearbox drive is a medium-speed outlet for use with a juice extractor. The attachments mentioned are only a few from the wide selection available for this type of mixer.

Altering the drive motor speed can vary the speed of each power and take-off point. The motor is a series-wound AC brush-type motor and all parts are available separately or as a factory-assembled service replacement. When parts are required, it is essential that all

available information be supplied, ie model number, serial number and date of purchase. Components are upgraded continuously and failure to give full information may lead to incompatible parts being obtained. Owing to the high speed of the motor and the long periods that the mixer is in use, motor brush wear and belt wear are the most common causes of failure. When inspecting motor brushes, remember to mark the existing brushes to ensure that they can be refitted the correct way round. They will have a leading and a trailing edge as the motor only rotates in one direction.

Closely inspect for the following:

1 The fan on the armature must be securely crimped on to the shaft.
2 The armature bearing (lateral movement or noise).
3 Damage to armature windings or field coil windings.
4 Overheated field coil. This may be apparent by charring or discoloration. Coils or

armatures that have short circuit faults will be discoloured and the commutator segments will be pitted or loose. Such faults will require both field coil and armature renewal (a complete unit may be more cost-effective).

Gearbox problems are not too common because this assembly is of a robust construction. A common problem with early mixers was the failure of the dog clutch assembly, which transfers drive from the external pulley driven by the belt to gears within the gearbox housing. Several faults can occur:

1 Failure of the dog clutch to engage, ie cannot be pressed down far enough by the actuating pin situated on the cover. This is caused by wear of the pin. Renewal of cover and pin is usually all that is required.
2 Threads within the aluminium top of the dog clutch strip off and no drive is transferred to the shaft. Renew dog on shaft.
3 Internal gear at the other end of the driveshaft to the dog clutch splits. This allows all external parts to function correctly and the shaft to turn but fails to transfer drive to the

other gears. This requires a new drive pinion fitting. Remove the dog clutch and the top of the gearbox, remembering to note the position of all items during the stripdown. Take care not to cross thread bolts or screws in the soft aluminium casing. The joint of the top and bottom halves of the gearbox can be sealed with a smear of silastic or silastoseal (on early models, red Hermetite was used).

All parts of the gearbox are available separately or as a complete unit. Make sure when inspecting or servicing that all the gears mesh correctly and that no teeth are damaged or missing. Renew any suspect items. Before regreasing during a service or repair, first clean thoroughly with paraffin and allow to dry. After checking that all shims and gears are correctly positioned and the gears mesh correctly, fix the top cover on the gearbox using the sealant mentioned earlier. On the underside of the gearbox there is a large screw with a fibre washer. Remove this screw and insert 135 grams of Shell LGP1 through the hole, using a grease gun. Having done this, refit the screw and washer and reassemble the rest of the appliance and refit all covers. Double check all the work carried out and run the mixer to distribute the grease within the gearbox. Some grease may be seen to escape from the top drive outlet, this is normal as it acts as an overflow for any excess grease within the gearbox.

All of the above checks and tests are to be carried out with appliances isolated – switch OFF and plug OUT – unless otherwise stated as in the case of functional testing to verify correct or incorrect operation. When carrying out a functional test, make sure all cables and wiring have been fitted back into their correct positions when reassembling. Any parts renewed must be identical to the original specification. Quote model and serial numbers when obtaining spare parts.

Variable speed control on table-top mixers

The speed control on this type of mixer is a combination of mechanical action and electronic control interacting with one another. Two variations of electrical control can be found but each use the same mechanical action.

The mechanical action

Fixed to the cooling fan on the lower end of the armature shaft are two small spring steel plates, slightly bowed and joined at either end by a small weight. The top plate only is secured to the fan and shaft. When the motor rotates, the weights on each end of the joined plates are forced outwards by centrifugal force. As they are formed in a bowed configuration and joined at either end the outward movement of the weights causes the lower plate to be forced downwards. The

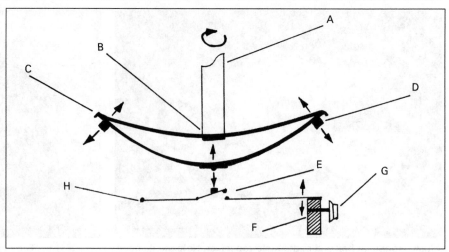

Motor mechanical speed control

A	Armature shaft	D	Weights	G	Speed selector knob
B	Fixing point to shaft (normally part of cooling fan)	E	Normally 'open' switch	H	Pivot point of mounting plate (adjustable for speed calibration)
		F	Cam to vary position of switch 'E' by moving mounting plate		
C	Spring steel plates				

degree of movement is proportional to the rotational speed of the armature. This movement is used to actuate a switch on the speed control panel; detailed in the next section.

The electrical action

There are two types of electrical motor control. The first one, used on early machines, quite simply uses the movement of the governor (the centrifugal device described above) to actuate a switch. The switch is mounted on a movable plate beneath the armature and governor, and is usually closed, thus allowing the motor to receive full power. As the speed of the motor increases, the governor will distort and actuate the switch, which in turn open-circuits the direct supply to the motor. Supply is now via a large resistor that slows the motor. As the motor slows, the governor reacts, the switch resets and the motor speeds up. This is a continuous process as long as power is supplied to the motor. If left like this, the motor would run at only one speed. Variation in speed is achieved by moving the speed control plate containing the switch further away from the governor. The motor then needs to run faster to create sufficient centrifugal force to activate the switch and the resistor. A greater speed is therefore maintained during cycling of the governor and switch. The distance between the governor and the speed control plate is increased or decreased by a cam linked directly to the speed indicator knob. An on/off switch is also included on the speed control plate and operates at the zero position. Later models may also include a manually resettable overload switch. Look for a button on the motor cover base with the head of the mixer raised.

Speed control on later mixers use a similar governor and switch system, but the simple, large resistor has been replaced by an electronic control which uses a smaller resistor and triac control similar to that described in the hand-held mixer section. Although similar in some respects, the parts are not interchangeable, therefore make sure that model and serial numbers are quoted when obtaining spare parts.

Checking correct speed control

After service or repair, the calibration of the speed control should be checked. The speed control plate is mounted on two spring-loaded screws that act as a pivot, and adjustment of speed control is gained by the turning in or out of these screws. It is important to adjust the screws evenly, only half a turn at a time. Clockwise (tightening) reduces the speed of the motor and anti-clockwise (slackening) increases the speed. Do not adjust with the mixer running – as always, switch OFF and plug OUT.

Access to the adjusting screw is through a hole in the base cover of the motor through which is passed a long, insulated screwdriver, with the head of the mixer in the raised position. The only tools required are the screwdriver and a stop watch or watch with a second hand or read-out.

Proceed as follows:

1 Ensure all parts and covers are fitted to the machine correctly. **Note:** *Do not fit any attachments to the mixer for the test.*
2 Raise the head of the mixer and leave it in this position.
3 Run the mixer at full speed (ie the maximum setting on the dial) for no less than three minutes.

4 After the three minutes' warm-up period, turn the speed control knob to the minimum setting.

5 With the mixer running on minimum, count the rotations of the planet hub drive (this must be done within fifteen seconds of turning from maximum setting to minimum to obtain a correct reading). Use the stop-watch to count rotations for exactly one minute or equal parts thereof. The correct setting is between 60 and 68 revolutions per minute of the planet hub.

6 If a figure outside that stated in 5 is counted, switch off and unplug. Adjust as required, clockwise to reduce speed and anti-clockwise to increase speed. Remember, adjust both screws evenly and only one half turn at a time.

7 Remove screwdriver. Plug in and switch on. If less than 15 seconds have elapsed since last test, run on minimum and repeat count. If more than 15 seconds have passed, run again at maximum and reduce to minimum for the count.

8 Repeat until correct setting is achieved. If difficulty is encountered in setting the speed, repeat the whole test procedure.

Hand-held mixer typical repair

1 This mixer would work only when medium or high speeds were selected. Although power was obviously getting to the appliance, a thorough check of both plug and cable were made as a matter of course to verify they were OK

2 The next step was to identify the fixing screws or clips that needed to be removed for access to the interior. A note of all fixing points and positions were made prior to removing them from the isolated appliance. Only four fixings needed to be removed. Half the outer casing could then be removed, allowing access

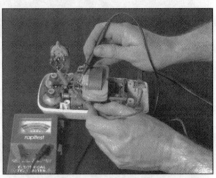

3 Continuity testing with a meter was carried out using a leap-frog method. See *Electrical Circuit Testing*

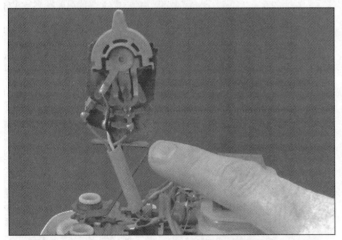

4 As suspected, a simple open circuit fault was found in the low speed circuit. A connection had broken between the selector switch and low speed coil. This was easily corrected but if the fault had been in the field coil itself a new motor would have been the only answer

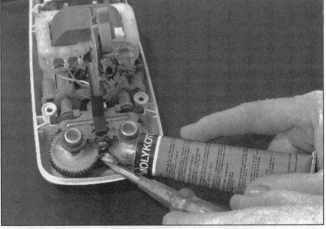

5 Although the open circuit was the obvious fault, a thorough check of all other parts was made. All checks proved OK. The motor bearings in this instance did not need lubricating but a little Molykote grease was placed at the drive point of worm and gears

A double check of all parts was made prior to refitting the casing. In this instance it was found that moving the selector switch to the middle setting made locating the casing much easier. All the fixing screws were fitted carefully back in their original places. Fully assembled, the mixer was ready for a functional test

Table-top mixer brush renewal

1 The problem with this mixer was that it ran unevenly. As all other tests proved OK, it was decided to check the motor brushes. This required the removal of the motor unit. First, remove the top and front covers

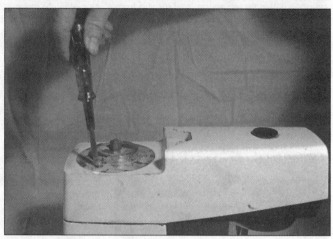

2 After noting the correct position of the fixing plate, the securing screws were removed

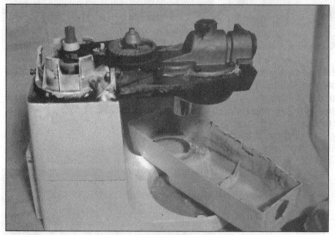

3 By lifting the rear of the cover first, the top cover was removed

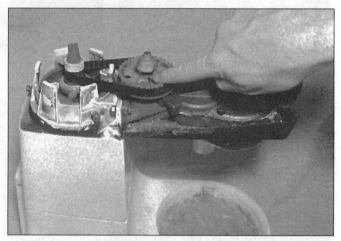

4 With the cover removed the belt can be eased off by moving it up off the large pulley

5 Slacken off the motor centralising screw just a little

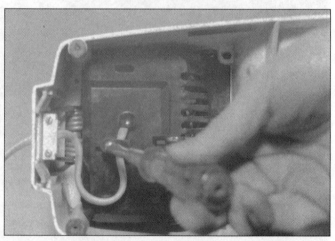

6 At the base of the machine, the terminal cover was removed and connections were noted prior to removal

7 Four screws allow for the removal of the motor cover and access to the two screws holding the latch bar system. Note: *In this shot, this has already been removed for photographic purposes*

8 With the cover removed and terminal board allowed to drop into the motor area, access was gained to the four motor fixing screws

9 When all four screws are free, the unit can be manoeuvred out. Note: *It is essential that the small washers be refitted to both sides of the rubber motor mounts. If they are loose, gluing them onto the rubber will help*

10 With the motor out, access to both motor brush screws is possible

11 When removed, the brushes showed severe wear resulting in intermittent motor action. On the left is the old motor brush and on the right the new replacement highlighting the degree of wear. Always renew if shorter than 10mm (3/8in). Checking the commutator showed no damage so a new motor brush was fitted. It is essential that brushes be fitted as pairs before reassembly. The other brush was also fitted

Refitting was a careful reversal of the stripdown procedure, ensuring that all parts and cables were replaced as they were originally. It is essential that the motor be central upon completion. Normally a special tool would be used for this purpose but if this is not available use the top securing/adjusting screws to centralise the small drive shaft of the motor in relation to the chrome fixing plate. When central, use the locking nuts to secure their positions. Double check position when top cover is refitted with fixing plate. Carry out a functional test on an RCD-protected circuit and check speed as detailed in text.

Belt tension adjustment

More recent table-top mixers have adjustable drive belts. To maintain optimum efficiency and avoid wear, the belt tension should be checked as shown. Adjustment is made by loosening the three motor mounting bolts and turning the small adjusting bush to the rear of the mixer, thus allowing the motor to slide as required to achieve the optimum tension. Ensure all bolts are re-tightened and re-check tension.

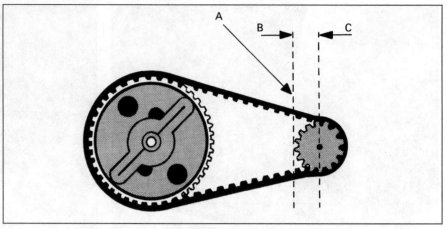

Belt tension adjustment

Squeeze the belt with thumb and forefinger at point A. If tension is correct belt should be parallel between B and C. Adjust as required

Chapter 28
Microwave ovens

In recent years, the microwave oven has become a very popular and much used kitchen appliance. Many misunderstandings have arisen regarding the safety aspects of cooking with microwaves. Perhaps by understanding how this appliance works and the need for certain rules to be followed, these fears and misconceptions will be dispelled.

The purpose of this chapter is not to instruct or invite the DIY repair of microwave ovens as we feel this product should be left to the experience of the professional engineer. There are several reasons why this advice is given, the main ones being the danger of high voltages present within the appliance, the requirements of the intricate fail-safe door interlock system and the possibility of microwave leakage if parts are not correctly fitted or aligned according to manufacturers' instructions.

Many criticisms are levelled at the microwave oven but most are unlikely to be as a direct result of a faulty product. A high proportion of problems, both mechanical and during cooking, results from misunderstanding, misuse or neglect by the user. It is in this area that the following text will concentrate.

Even with care and attention being exercised, faults may still occur and it is then that a suitably qualified microwave engineer should be called. The main danger that exists in relation to microwave ovens is **not** microwave leakage (this type of fault is extremely rare), but concerns the extremely high voltages used in producing the microwaves themselves. A large transformer (which accounts for most of the weight of an oven) combined with a high voltage capacitor (that may hold a high charge even with the appliance turned off and isolated) increases the supply of voltage of 240V around tenfold to about 2400V. For this reason, these appliances should **never** be stripped down by anyone other than a qualified engineer. The requirement of an earth path is most important for this appliance and the mains lead and earth continuity of the exposed metal parts to the earth pin of the plug should be checked regularly. Also make sure that the correct earth is present in the socket. See *A General Safety Guide, Plugs and Sockets* and *Electrical Circuit Testing*.

The microwaves used within the oven are a form of electromagnetic energy which flows in waves from an aerial within the oven called a magnetron. The waves are similar to radio or TV waves but have a much higher frequency of 2450mHz (megahertz). The length of radio waves from a transmitter is in the region of 100-600m whereas a magnetron emits waves of only 12cm. The waves from the magnetron are, therefore, much smaller – hence the term microwaves.

Like infrared radiation, microwave radiation only increases the temperature of food and does not produce chemical changes within it (often classed as non-ionising radiation as opposed to ionising radiation). Materials react to microwaves in different ways. Metal cannot absorb microwave energy, nor will it allow waves to pass through it; it can only reflect it, in a similar way as a mirror reflects light. As the metal is unable to absorb microwaves it will not heat up, thus allowing metal to be used in the construction of the oven to guide the waves from the magnetron into the oven and keep them there. Items made of pottery, plastic, paper and glass will allow microwaves to pass through and absorb little or no energy in doing so, therefore they remain unheated and only the food within them is heated (take care, the container will heat up a certain amount by conduction). Utensils that absorb water will heat up and care should be taken not to use vessels made from thermosetting plastics or pottery with gold edging, etc. Use only microwave proof cookware. Any item that contains water, sugar or fat will absorb microwave energy and as a result, heat up. This is of course most, if not all, foodstuffs.

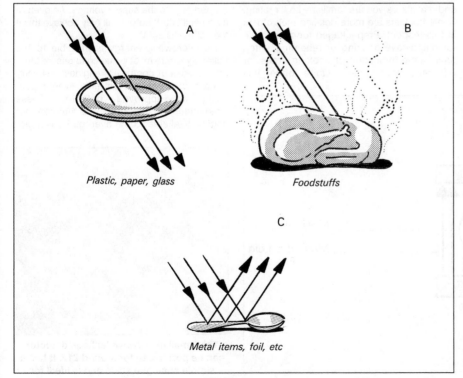

Plastic, paper, glass

Foodstuffs

Metal items, foil, etc

Microwaves

How do foodstuffs heat up?

The food placed in the microwave consists of any one or a combination of substances, each of which have one thing in common: they are made up of electrically charged molecules of water, fat, protein, etc. In the same way that a magnet can affect the needle of a compass, the microwaves acting upon these atoms and molecules change their orientation from north to south 2450 million times per second. The molecules try to line up with the ever-changing field and as a result generate friction, in turn generating heat. This occurs to a depth of around 2.5cm in the food. With thicker foods conduction transmits the heat deeper into the item; that is why standing time is important after the microwave has stopped as the cooking continues for a period after. For even cooking, the microwaves must be spread evenly over the whole of the oven and its contents. There are three systems which help in the distribution of microwaves within the oven: a simple turntable to rotate the food; a rotating antenna; and a microwave stirrer that has metal fins to reflect the microwaves and direct them within the oven. Rotation in the first two is created by the movement of a fan that also cools the magnetron.

If glass allows microwaves through, why do most ovens have glass doors? This is possible due to the doors' being of a sandwich construction, the inner section being a specially perforated metal gauze with holes, designed so as not to let microwaves out but to reflect them safely back into the oven.

If metal items are not to be placed in the microwave oven, why do some have metal shelves or inners? Metal items supplied with your microwave oven will have been specifically designed, the dimensions and shape being matched carefully to the ovens waveform. Only items supplied with your

This combination oven also has a conventional fan assisted cooking element behind the rear wall of the oven cavity

particular oven should be used and reference to the instruction booklet should be made as to their correct use.

The power of a microwave oven is different from model to model. It is indicated on the rating plate of the appliance in watts. It is this difference in power output that can lead to specific cooking instructions to cover the multitude of variations. What can be said, however, is that it is most important to read the instruction book applicable to your oven and make sure you are familiar with its rating. Some booklets are more detailed than others in this respect. Prepackaged foods suitable for microwave cooking or reheating, often have some indication of cooking times for different rated ovens. Quite often this

information can be vague. Remember that food cooked in a microwave oven continues to cook for a period after the oven is switched off (standing time), so make sure you allow for this. If the booklet that accompanied your microwave is lost or of little use, there are many good cookery books specifically for microwave cooking. Look for a book that gives comprehensive information with reference on conversion tables for various wattages. The wattage output of an oven is proportional to the supply voltage. An oven of a nominal 500W output will only achieve this if the voltage is 240V.

As microwave energy is invisible to the naked eye, care must be taken to ensure there are no leaks. A competent engineer will carry out a microwave leak test after every repair, using an approved detector. These instruments are expensive and therefore not usually available to the average household.

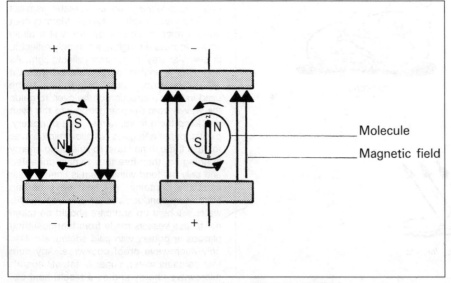

Molecule

Magnetic field

Action of very strong alternating magnetic field

This small microwave leakage detector can be purchased for around £12. It has a simple analogue scale and is ideal for home use.

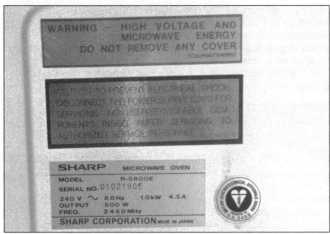

Typical rating plate

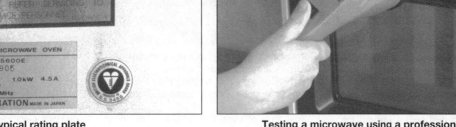

Testing a microwave using a professional meter

Small test meters are available from electrical and DIY stores at a reasonable price and they will give an indication of leakage. If a leak is indicated or suspected and all door sections are clean and free from food particles, etc., the oven must not be used until it has been checked/repaired by a qualified microwave engineer. **Do not** attempt any servicing other than cleaning.

A decrease in power output, possibly resulting in the need to extend the cooking time to compensate, may be the first indication that something is wrong within the oven.

Checking power output

If a drop in power output is suspected, the following simple check can be carried out. You will need two containers of more than 500ml capacity suitable for use in a microwave oven, ie glass or plastic, and a thermometer capable of readings between 10°C and 50°C. (The thermometer should not be used in the microwave, it is for external readings.) A pen and paper will be required for writing down the results and a stopwatch facility for timing (unless seconds can be set on the oven itself). With this basic equipment the actual power output of the magnetron can be assessed in watts.

Proceed as follows:

1 Mark the containers A and B so that they can be easily identified. Fill them each with 500mls of water and stir them. Measure the temperature. Ideally, this should be 15°C but not above 20°C, otherwise the results will not be accurate. Write down the temperature of each container and record it as T1 (temperature at start).
2 Place the containers each side of the centre line of the oven, (either on the turntable if fitted, otherwise the base).
3 Set the oven to maximum microwave setting, ie full power, and switch on.
4 Allow the oven to operate for 87 seconds and then switch off.
5 Remove the containers and stir well. Read the increased temperature and write it down as T2 (temperature after 87 seconds).
6 Armed with this information, take T1 from T2 in both columns and calculate the average rise in temperature from both readings. The average temperature rise figure is then multiplied by 50 (this being the power supply cycle in the UK of 50Hz. The result is the output of the magnetron displayed as a wattage figure reaching the oven and contents. Check the rating plate to confirm that it matches the manufacturer's rating figure.

An example of a typical test on a 700W oven might be as follows:

	Container A	Container B
T1	15°C	15°C
T2	27°C	29°C
Rise in temperature		
T2-T1	12°C	14°C

Average temperature increase

$\frac{12 + 14}{2} = 13°C$

Wattage = 13 °C x 50 Hz = 650W

If results are found, as here, to be much lower than the nominal rating, the indication is that there is a fault developing within the circuitry of the appliance. Check that the oven is clean and dry and double-check all readings. If the reading is still low, have the microwave circuitry checked by a qualified engineer. To continue using the oven when a fault is suspected is false economy as further damage may result.

Cleaning

Although there is little that can be done with regard to self repair of microwave ovens, there is a lot that can be done in relation to the correct use and care of the product which will help reduce faults. It is much easier to clean than a conventional oven but even so, failure to do so is a common source of problems. A build-up of fats or sugars will absorb

The simple equipment required to test for correct power output

microwaves and heat up and burn. The carbon formed on such burnt particles attracts even more microwave energy and the concentration of this energy can damage the interior of the oven and drastically shorten the working life of the magnetron. Such problems result in expensive parts replacement. Any spillages during cooking should be mopped up immediately and thoroughly (some ovens have removable bottoms to the compartment where liquids can seep into the cavity and cause severe damage).

If cleaning is done regularly, wiping the interior with a paper towel or slightly damp cloth is all that should be necessary. Grease spots may need a little detergent but abrasive cleaning liquids or pads must not be used. Ensure the surfaces are clean and dry, paying attention to corners and grilles. For stubborn deposits, place a small container (suitable for microwave use) full of water in the centre of the oven and switch on to full power. Allow the water to boil (but not boil dry) for a short period. The steam produced should loosen the stubborn deposits enough to be wiped away with a cloth. The outer surfaces of the oven should be cleaned with a slightly damp cloth or sponge moistened with a little detergent. Do not allow any droplets to run into vents or panels. This applies also to the door inner and outer. Avoid using wet cloths or aerosol sprays on the touch control pads of electronic ovens as the liquid may seep into poorly sealed panels and cause damage or render the appliance inoperable until at best dry, or possibly resulting in a new switch panel being fitted. Similar problems may arise from poor siting of the appliance, eg being too close to an open cooking area, a kettle and above normal oven vents, etc. Steam produced from these areas may seep between touch control membranes or condense as water droplets on components within the casing. This type of problem can cause low insulation or corrosion resulting in eventual failure. Often the first signs of a problem of this nature are intermittent faults

like being unable to set the oven or start it even though it worked fine when last used. After leaving it for a while and then resetting it, everything is seemingly working properly again. Watch out for this type of problem occurring and try to prevent it by placing the oven in a more suitable position.

Combination ovens

Combination ovens utilise conventional heating elements in addition to microwave energy. Conventional heating may be of the fan-assisted type or comprise of grill elements.

This type of oven makes use of the best characteristics of each type of cooking process. Defrosting and cooking to a set temperature is usually faster and more efficient using microwave energy, but food appearance can normally be made much more attractive using conventional heating. In a typical oven, the following programme selections will normally be available:

Grill
Fan assisted
Microwave
Microwave and fan assisted
Defrosting

It is important to remember not to place metal objects in the oven, as the induction created can cause arcing and shorten the life of the magnetron significantly. However, a grid is usually used on which food is positioned, and although it can be of metal construction, it is designed to avoid microwave interference.

Many microwave manufacturers also give instructions on the use of foil to cover food in microwave operation to enhance the cooking process and this requires close adherence to the procedures indicated to avoid the problems mentioned above.

Multi-ovens are usually provided with a tray

for convenience in conventional cooking, but it must not be used for microwave or combined programmes.

The conventional heating elements are normally of the standard tubular type, and if a fault is suspected then the element should be resistance and insulation tested. Remember to isolate the element when conducting tests.

If the element has shorted to earth, the internal fuse will normally be found to have blown.

Do's and Don'ts

• DO ensure that the appliance has a good earth path, lead, plug and socket.
• DO check the cable of the appliance for damage and avoid routing near hot or sharp areas.
• DO make sure that the oven is cleaned regularly.
• DO use the correct setting and times for the type of food being cooked.
• DO remember that standing time is important.
• DO, if in any doubt, have the appliance checked by a qualified microwave engineer.
• DO make sure that all parts are in place when using the oven, ie all seals and panels, door shut and seated correctly.
Note: The door is not a sealed fit when closed. As it is designed to prevent microwave leakage only, it is quite normal for steam to leak from the door edges during the cooking of certain foods.
• DO NOT allow the oven to operate when empty.
• DO NOT attempt to use a microwave oven if the door is damaged, if the hinges are bent, broken or loose or is difficult to close. Seek qualified help.
• DO NOT interfere with or poke items into the door latch holes under any circumstances. A series of interconnected switches and interlocks are housed behind them and must

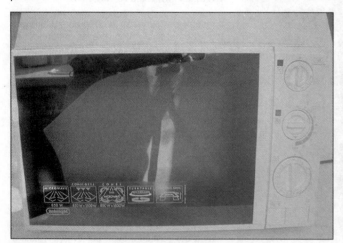

Typical combination oven

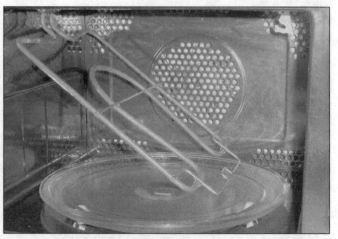

The grill element in this combination oven drops down for ease of cleaning

not be tampered with. The setting up of these require information that is normally available only to qualified service technicians.

•DO NOT use domestic ovens for commercial applications, ie in cafes or restaurants, etc. Only commercial grade units should be used in such situations.

•DO NOT allow food particles or debris to build up within the oven cabinet, door seals or lip, etc.

•DO NOT block air intake vents for the cooling fan or situate the oven in damp or humid (steamy) conditions.

•DO NOT use metal cooking containers, metal bag ties, metal meat skewers, porcelain with metal design for edging (painted or otherwise), food completely wrapped in aluminium foil although **small** amounts are sometimes recommended to shield items in certain recipes.

•DO NOT remove the outer cover of a microwave oven. As mentioned earlier, this will expose parts that work at extremely high voltage, which can still be present, even with the appliance isolated. Consult a microwave service agent for such work.

•DO NOT use a microwave oven if the inner oven compartment is cracked or corroded in any way. Do not paint over, cover or ignore these defects. Consult a qualified engineer.

In the most unlikely event of a fire occurring within the oven,

•DO NOT open the oven door. If possible, switch the appliance off at the socket and remove the plug. On some microwave ovens, by switching off the oven, the door automatically opens. In this instance this must be avoided, as air will be allowed into the oven area.

Fault finding – microwave ovens

1. Symptom: Will not work at all

Possible cause

a. Faulty mains lead or plug/socket

b. Door open or not closed properly
c. Is display lit? (electronic ovens)

d. Faulty timer or on/off switch. Manual and electronic control versions
e. Damp/condensation on touch control pad on front of appliance or internal components

Action

See *Plugs and Sockets, Cable and Cable Faults* and *Electrical Circuit Testing*

Open and relatch properly
If not, see a. if it is make sure the clock is set. On some ovens the clock must be set before the oven can be used. If the oven has been unplugged or the power has been turned off, the clock may need resetting

Qualified technician required
Move oven to more favourable position and retest after a period of time to see if fault has gone. If fault persists, damage has possibly been done to internal parts or touch panel. Consult a qualified engineer

2. Symptom: Arcing, sparking or burning in oven compartment

Possible cause

a. Unsuitable cookware being used

b. Too much metal foil being used
c. Build-up of food particles

Action

Switch off immediately. Use microwave safe items only. No metal-edged plates, foil containers, etc.
Restrict the use of this material to a minimum for use in the microwave
Clean thoroughly and regularly as mentioned

3. Symptom: Under-cooking food

Possible cause

a. Incorrect cooking time set

b. Incorrect power setting
c. Low voltage supply

d. Fault on magnetron or internal circuitry

Action

Check content and weight of food and adjust times accordingly (remember standing time)
Check at which heat level the food should be cooked or heated
Unusual occurrence, but check other appliances – main oven, washer, tumbledrier, etc., are not all on the same circuit. If so, this could reduce the voltage level and ultimately the power output of the oven. See graph
Check power output as detailed earlier

4. Symptom: Over cooking food

Possible cause

a. Incorrect cooking time set

b. Failure to allow for standing time
c. Air vents blocked or covered; either internal or external

Action

Check content and weight of food and adjust times accordingly (remember standing time)
As above
Ensure all vents are clear of blockages and leave a space between oven and wall. If built-in, make sure the correct fitting kit was used and that the oven was suitable for being built in

5. Symptom: Door steams up, steam from door space or from rear vent

Steam is a normal part of any cooking process; the amount produced depending on the moisture content of the food being cooked. Air is blown over the magnetron to keep it cool and then passes on into the oven and is vented through apertures in the rear of the oven. This air movement often carries with it the steam produced during cooking and any excess steam may find its way out via the edges of the door or condense on the glass surfaces of the door, often between the double glazed section. This is normal as the door is not airtight when closed but it will still prevent any leakage of microwaves.

6. Symptom: Television/radio interference caused by oven

Possible cause
No Earth path **Note**: *This is a serious fault*, **do not** *use the appliance or supply until the fault is identified and rectified.*

Action
Check the earth bonding of the oven and the socket/supply earth See *Basics Chapter 2*. A faulty internal mains filter unit could cause the interference and if this is suspected then the appliance should be checked and repaired by trained personnel.

7. Symptom: Electric shocks from oven cabinet

Possible cause
No earth path **Note**: *This is a serious fault* **do not** *use the appliance or supply until the fault is identified and rectified.*

Action
This fault would indicate poor, or worse still a non-existent earth connection. Check the earth bonding of the oven and the socket/supply earth. See *Basics Chapter 2*

8. Symptom: Oven starts immediately when door is closed

This would indicate that the main control unit/timer has failed in the ON position
Some ovens incorporate a start switch, which is simply an additional micro-switch; this may also have failed in the ON position

9. Symptom: Oven shuts down randomly

The fault in this case would indicate a faulty magnetron, controller/timer or cooling fan. If the cooling fan ceases to function then the magnetron may overheat and cause operation of its thermal cut-out (TOC). After a period of time the cut-out will reset and if the oven has a mechanical timer the oven operation may recommence. A blockage in the ventilation grilles may cause a restriction of airflow and, again the thermal cut-out may operate. After shutting down randomly, some ovens may recommence cooking when the thermal cut-out resets. If the food had been removed during the inoperative period, serious damage to the magnetron could result when power is restored. The mechanical or electronic controller may develop symptoms, which cause random shutdowns. In all such instances the appliance should be checked by trained personnel.

10. Symptom: Interlock switch failure

This is a common problem, possibly accounting for up to 75% of all failures, and usually results in a blown internal fuse. After many years of use and opening and closing of the oven door, misalignment or simply wear and tear of the latch or the series of safety switches within the door latch mechanism may occur. This results in the fail safe interlock system blowing a special internal fuse. This along with any fault/problem that requires the removal of the outer cover must be left to trained personnel who possess the correct safety and test equipment. **Due to the possibility of high voltages remaining within certain components even when the appliance is unplugged DO NOT attempt to remove the outer cover under any circumstances.**

11. Symptom: Damaged oven interiors

If the oven has not been regularly cleaned then food deposits will eventually carbonise leading to arcing and damaged paintwork. Removal of such deposits may require scraping with a blunt knife. Once damage has occurred then fine sandpaper should be used to smooth the metal and feather the edges of the paintwork. Special microwave cavity paint is available for recoating small imperfections, however, care must be exercised in its use and severe damage should not be treated in this way.

Chapter 29
Video CD, Audio and TV

Most households will have one, if not all of these items. Although a high degree of technical knowledge combined with expensive equipment and detailed service manuals would be required to tackle faults within such appliances, there is much the user can do to prevent problems occurring and to extend the life of the product and keep it in peak condition. It is to this aim that this section is dedicated. The intricate nature of several internal mechanical and electronic components, and the high voltages make it unwise to remove panels or outer covers oneself. It is more advisable to leave this to the skills of the specialist. Do not however jump to the conclusion that all the causes of faults on electronic equipment are complex. Poor connections, lack of care, little or no maintenance from new, the plain misunderstanding of the correct way in which to operate the appliance count for a very large proportion of faults. With a little thought and the correct safe approach, they are also the easiest to overcome often with little or no cost.

Video

Over the years the number of households that have video cassette recorders (VCRs) has increased enormously. Along with the increased popularity of the video, product reliability has also improved. This is good news for the owner but can be bad news for the equipment! With the reliability of the machine and the consequential reduction of visits from the service engineer, apathy on the part of the owner is common, often proved by

the lack of maintenance afforded it. Dirt from the atmosphere, dust from carpets and oxide dust from tape wear all build up within and upon the components of the machine. Over a period of time the picture and sound quality will drop but, because it is a gradual process and not a sudden loss of quality, it is accepted as the norm until the build up of deposits begin to damage the tapes when used in the machine. Serious damage to the video head and other parts of the mechanism can also result from the lack of cleaning. A

very expensive repair requiring several new parts will then be necessary. All this can be alleviated quite simply by regular use (depending on how often the video is used) of a high quality cleaning system like the one shown. This is an effective head cleaning system that is easy to use and cleans the whole of the tape path.

Note: *Thorough cleaning of internal electronic components, electronic boards, etc. cannot be achieved using this cassette-based system and is better carried out by a qualified*

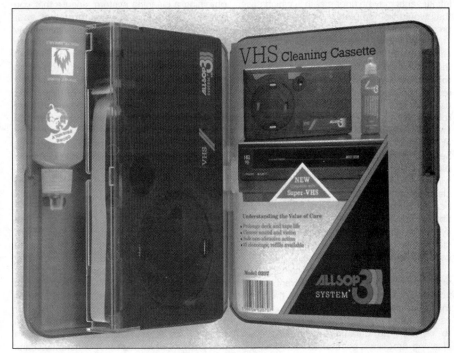

Video cleaner system

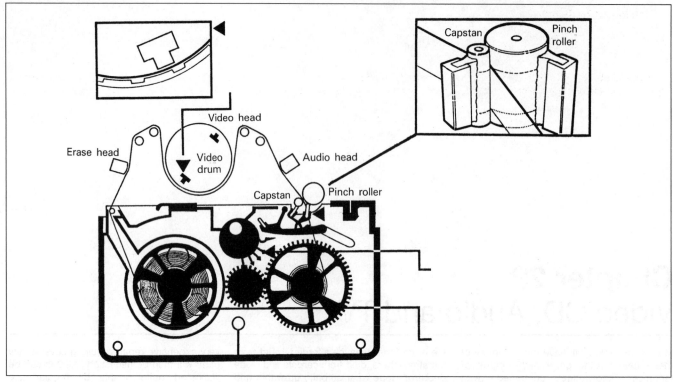

Video cleaning system

engineer at a time when internal adjustments or parts renewal is required.

Avoid standing video recorders directly on the carpet beneath the television set. Fluff and dust is more readily drawn in by cooling fans within the unit and on some machines the air intake vents may be underneath in which case they would be completely blocked. Use of a proper video stand will alleviate this problem.

When a video tape or cleaner is inserted into the video (and set to play or record) it is then drawn into the tape mechanism. A large rotating head is used to scan the tape during record and playback and two static heads are used for erase and audio respectively. The rotating video head is easily damaged. Dirt and oxide shed from the tape are unwelcome at any point along the tape path, but the video head is at most risk from even the smallest particles. If this head becomes scratched, dirt will adhere more readily to it. Poor quality tape cleaning systems can add to the problem by being too abrasive and possibly shedding fibres during the cleaning process on a dry system, or on wet systems leave a residue of cleaning fluid. Ensure only a high quality kit is used that protects as well as cleans.

The kit shown mimics the original tape path and uses a wet system (liquid solvent) that is fibre-free with pads that also clean the pinch roller. The system is automatic and extremely easy to use. The main cassette has the ability to perform 50 cleaning cycles. At each cleaning process a section of fresh cleaning tape is used. Another good feature is that

after the 50 cycles have been used, a refill kit is available to replenish the cassette with pads, tape and fluid. A further bonus is that the cleaning solution no longer contains Freon, which is a CFC, and the removal of this from the product is most welcome. When obtaining a cleaning system, ensure that you get the one that suits the format of your machine (VHS, BETA, U-MATIC, etc.). Follow the instructions that come with the kit and do not be tempted to use more than the stated amount of cleaning fluid per cycle, as an excess could create further problems.

Not all problems are a result of dirty video heads; so if there is no improvement after three cleaning cycles, try another tape on playback (perhaps a fault exists on the original tape). If the fault persists, check all connections to and from the video as detailed further on in this section, and if the fault still remains, then an internal mechanical or electrical fault is likely and this will require the expertise of a video engineer.

When purchasing tapes, select a high quality named brand. Beware of cheap tapes of dubious origin, which are more likely to break and get trapped in the tape run. They can also shed the oxide coating causing wear of the heads and, if excessive on the pinch roller, can cause the video to eat a tape. A sure way to increase the chances of tape or video head wear is to over-use the pause/still facility. This is due to the tape being held in one position whilst the head constantly scans (rotates) across it. Also avoid excessive use of

the stop-start control because this can stretch the tape and cause picture problems. Store tapes in the vertical position to help prevent stretching or loops forming, and always put them in their cases with the tape facing inwards. Do not store them near other magnetic sources, eg loudspeakers, motors, etc. As the signal is recorded on the tape in a magnetic format by the video, other sources of magnetism can distort or blank the tape. Avoid storing tapes in sunlight or where temperatures may be too high or too low.

When hiring tapes from video clubs, it is wise to check that the tape and cassette are in good condition. Do not touch the tape because grease from fingers will damage both tape and video head, but inspect the entry points for dust or flaking of the oxide from the tape, (fine brownish powder or flakes). Other users may not have been as careful as they should or their video recorder may have caused tape damage. One run of a faulty tape can be enough to cause serious head damage for the future. When bringing in a tape from a cold environment, it is advisable to let the cassette acclimatise before playing owing to the possibility of condensation forming on the tape which could cause it to stick to the video head when played. The same also applies to a video machine if brought into a warm room from a cold environment, but a longer period should be allowed.

Note: *Some machines have dew protection sensors and will not operate until they are clear.*

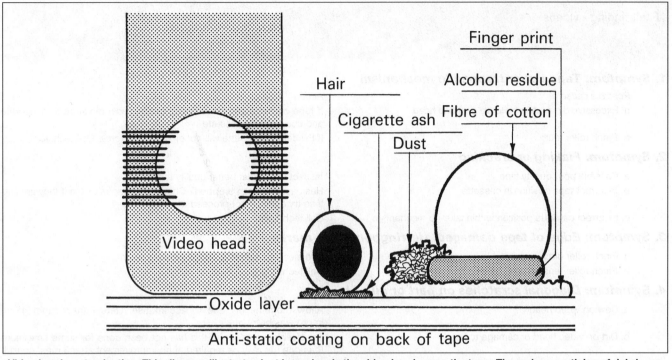

Video head contamination. This diagram illustrates just how closely the video head scans the tape. The various particles of debris are to the same scale

Tapes

Except for a couple of exotic formulations, the actual recording material on a cassette tape is what chemists call ferric oxide and what we call rust. Ferric oxide is used because it can be magnetised easily. Magnetism is what recording is all about.

When you make a recording, an electromagnet in the tape head pulses with an electrical current that originates at the microphone, record, TV, camera or whatever source you are taping. This current arranges the magnetic polarity of the tiny particles of oxide, creating an electrical analogue tapestry of the music or image.

Play the tape back and those magnetised particles now induce an electrical current in the tape head that sends the signal to be amplified and then sent to your speakers or TV.

The other part of the tape is the backing and is the medium to which the rust adheres. It is plastic similar to clear kitchen cling film or sandwich bags but treated so that it is anti-static. The trick is to keep the rust (oxide) stuck to the plastic. Tape manufacturers concerned with quality go to great lengths to improve the process of binding and polishing the oxide and backing. They call it calendering. If it is not done properly, or missed out to cut costs, two problems result which makes the customer unhappy. The first of these is called dropout; when the oxide material falls off the backing it cannot be magnetised by the head, creating silence where there should be sound on audio tapes and break up of picture on video tapes. The second occurs when tape sheds oxide and it goes onto the cassette mechanism. Recording tape is unique in that it works best when it is rusty.

Pre-recorded tapes are a different story. Often these tapes are made with inexpensive materials that lack the important polishing steps of the better quality tapes. These tapes are therefore much more likely to leave small particles in your machine each time you play them.

Inspecting the tape itself can help diagnose certain faults. Again, avoid touching the tape surface with fingers. If blemishes or damage is found do not use the tape again. A list of common tape faults is shown below along with their possible cause.

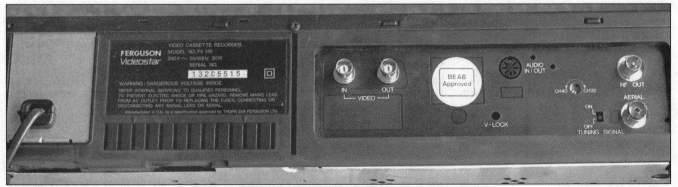

Typical sockets

Fault finding - videos

1. Symptom: Tape cut or trapped in mechanism

Possible cause	*Action*
a. Excessive dirt or dew build up on video head	If tape cassette can be removed easily, allow moisture to evaporate and use cleaning cassette
b. Pinch roller fault	If this fails or cassette will not eject, do not force. Call technician

2. Symptom: Flaking or cracking

a. Possible poor quality tape	Inspect your other better quality tapes
b. Incorrect tape position in cassette	Has cassette been dropped? Check other tapes to see if they are OK. If so try again, if not proceed to c.
c. Incorrect cassette position within take-up mechanism	Call technician

3. Symptom: Edge of tape damaged. Herringbone type marks

a. Pinch roller dirty	Use cleaning cassette. If fault persists see b.
b. Pinch roller tension/position incorrect	Call technician

4. Symptom: Diagonal scratches on part or all of tape

a. Dew on video head	Allow machine or tape to acclimatise. Retest (new tape). If no improvement try b.
b. Dirt on video head or damage to head	Try cleaning cassette. If this has not been done for some time more than one run may be required. If no improvement after 3 runs, consult technician

5. Symptom: Horizontal marks with regular spacing

a. Dirt or defect on tape guide roller within the machine	Use cleaning cassette. If no improvement call technician as roller may be scratched

6. Symptom: Continuous line near edges of tape

a. Tape carriage mechanism misaligned	Call technician

7. Symptom: Continuous line on centre of tape

a. Dirt or mark on tape guide on tape mechanism	Use cleaning cassette. If fault persists there is possible damage to the roller – call technician
b. Dirt or mark on erase/audio head	Use cleaning cassette. If fault persists there is possible damage to the erase/audio head. Call technician

Note: *As mentioned, the tape mechanism is mechanical as well as electrical. There are several moving parts within the machine, which will require lubricating occasionally to keep the unit operating correctly. As only small amounts of lubrication are required at specific areas, this task is best left to a qualified technician. Several adjustments may also be required to compensate for deterioration and use. Such settings and types of lubrication differ between makes and models and it is unwise to attempt any such maintenance yourself.*

The faults detailed so far are linked directly to care in use and the type of video or tape being used. Before we move on to cable and connection problems, one thing must be made clear. To get the best from your video recorder (or any appliance for that matter), it is an advantage if you fully understand the way in which your particular machine should be used. This book cannot give details on the myriad of different makes, models and styles. Each new model will be different from its predecessor, mechanically as well as cosmetically. Take time to read your instruction booklet thoroughly, it is the only way to get the most from your machine and it will help you to understand problems that may occur. Sometimes the problem is nothing more than an obscure, but correct, function of the unit.

Cables and connectors

When linking your video to your TV or other equipment, numerous combinations of different connections may be encountered. They will all have one thing in common: the need to pass an interference-free signal between video and TV or video, TV and audio. If interference is present on an audio system, the human ear can readily compensate and will often accept quite poor quality. Vision, however, is more acute in all of us and even a very small drop in vision quality will not be easily tolerated. Poor connections are the most common faults due to the stress on the connecting plug or socket. Route cables carefully avoiding stretching and kinking. Dirt on the pins or socket can seriously impair the signal transmitted by the cable. Keep all cables stored in coils, not bent or twisted together, and out of reach of children and pets. Don't leave them lying where people or pieces of furniture can stand on them. If a connector or socket is damaged, or pins bent, do not try to force a connection between them. Some cables carry several small wires to multi-pin sockets or plugs, which must be connected to the correct pins within the fitting, and a high quality secure joint must also be made. This applies equally to co-axial cable with only an inner and an outer connection. If in doubt, ready-made cables are available to fit all situations, and be advised to go for a high quality one. Cutting

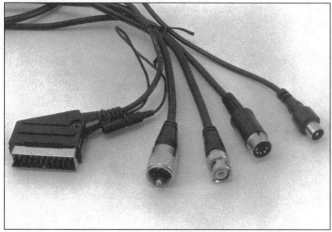

Variations of cable connectors used

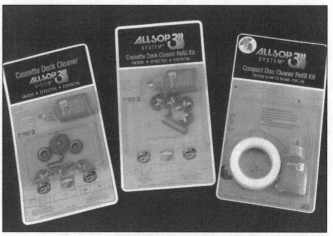

Audio kit and refill

corners and going for cheap cables and connectors may prove to be false economy in the long run.

With the ever-greater sophistication of electronics, video, CD, etc., the area behind the units can become a conglomeration of cables and connectors. Much time will have been spent on setting up the equipment, albeit gradually in some instances, as the systems are added to, but the resulting mass of (usually black) wires can cause quite a headache when a fault arises. Which wire belongs where? Similarly, if the equipment is moved and a connection dislodged – which one is it? It is far easier to take a little time to keep all wires and connectors tidy. When adding to your equipment, a little forward planning when installing it will help. Mark each cable with coloured tape or stickers from and to. Use a code that suits you best eg V for video, A for audio, C for CD, etc. Don't just

rely on the stickers; use a belt-and-braces approach (children and animals enjoy removing stickers). Keep a log of all new equipment and how you connected the equipment up originally, and store it in a safe place. Although this approach may take a little extra time in the beginning, it can save hours of work later on and reduce the chance of damage caused by incorrect connection.

Audio

The way in which the audio tape system works is very similar to the video system described earlier. The main difference is that the tape is not scanned by a revolving head. In an audio tape player, the tape is fed in front of a fixed head, and information is either laid

down or picked up by it. A similar pinch wheel/roller system is used to transport the tape across the head. On units with auto reverse facility, two pinch wheels will be present on each side of the head to pull the tape in the direction required.

The tape itself, though smaller than the video tape, is much the same in that it uses ferric oxide to store the audio track magnetically. Problems of dust, dirt and oxide shedding are the same as that for video recorders. Most of us have experienced the 'eating of the tape' phenomenon, often caused by dirt or deposits on the pinch roller/wheel and capstan. The sticky deposit makes the tape stick to the pinch roller and is subsequently wrapped around it. Usually the tape can be removed quite easily although it is by now rendered useless, but the problem will recur if thorough cleaning is not carried out. The system shown works in the same

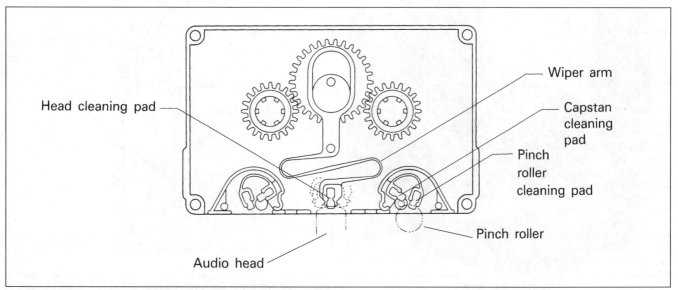

Head cleaning pad

Wiper arm

Capstan cleaning pad

Pinch roller cleaning pad

Pinch roller

Audio head

Tape cleaner cassette. Note the two pinch roller cleaning pads for use on auto reverse decks

Tape trouble, often caused by dirt

Tape deck showing pinch roller drive, record head and erase head. On auto reverse decks a second pinch roller would be present on the right in this instance

way as that described in the video section. The audio version shown is capable of cleaning both pinch rollers simultaneously on auto reverse systems as well as the head. Tape damage is similar to that shown for video tapes. In severe cases, the pinch roller/wheel if worn or damaged will need replacing. Damage can be seen by looking into the tape compartment. A new pinch roller/wheel is a dull black colour. Worn or dirty pinch rollers/wheels are rust-coloured (due to the oxide deposits), shiny and sticky. If cleaning does not improve the condition, a new part will be necessary and, as with the video, this is best left to a qualified technician. **Remember:** *Regular cleaning can prevent this problem.*

Compact discs

There are no faults or parts within CD players that are within the capabilities of the DIY repairer. Only care of the unit and consideration to positioning and environment can be advised. Do not place a CD unit in strong sunlight, near heat or in damp/humid conditions. The CD system requires very close tolerances to be maintained for accurate disc reading. Do not attempt adjustment or servicing to any internal components; leave it to a trained service engineer. However, the aim of this book is to

help understand such equipment, and if unable to advise DIY repairs, we can at least offer advice on how to look after your equipment thereby minimising the possibility of faults occurring.

Much is made of the fact that the CD disc makes no physical contact with the pick-up system. Many have been led to believe that because of this the disc can be handled freely and requires little protection or cleaning. This is not so. Even a fingerprint on the disc can cause the reading light beam to be deflected or misread, resulting in jumping or skipping of tracks similar to a crack in a vinyl record. The skipping is often mistakenly blamed on a fault within the player when in fact it is a user fault. To avoid this problem, respect the disc and

CD cleaner system

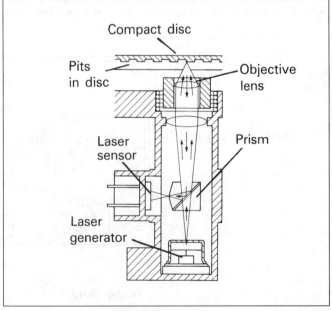

Simplified system of disc reading operation carried out by the CD player

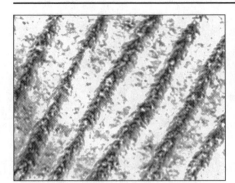

This magnified section of a vinyl record shows severe contamination

This photograph shows what the surface should look like. Regular use of a cleaning system like the one shown will keep the tracks in this condition

Use a high quality cleaning system to maintain both sound and equipment

use a proper disc cleaner. The one shown uses a radial cleaning action to avoid damaging the surface of the CD.

CD systems have the ability to reproduce sounds across an extremely wide range with little or no distortion (about 1/100 of that found on a perfect LP). As there is no physical contact between the disc or the pick-up there is no noise or distortion added to the signal, which is amplified for us to listen to or view. The sound (or vision) is not stored by a series of ridges along a groove like the vinyl record, but in a sequence of pits etched into the flat surface of the disc. It is then read by a laser beam of light that is tuned to detect each pit as it passes. Sound is transmitted in a waveform and picked up by our ears using a diaphragm (the eardrum) that resonates in response to those waves. The disc rotates at between 200 and 500rpm, when data is being read. A scratch in a straight line from inner to outer would, therefore, only be seen by the laser for the smallest fraction of a second and could be filtered out by the error correction circuitry incorporated in the equipment. However, should the scratch or debris, such as a hair, run in line to the laid down track, much more data would be lost and, because this cannot be corrected, audible distortion or skipping would be the result.

Record decks

Record decks are made up of three main parts:
1 A driven turntable on which the record is placed.
2 A stylus (needle) device to follow the contours of the record groove.
3 A drive for the turntable and amplification circuitry to boost the signal picked up by the stylus.

There are numerous variations on this theme ranging from the cheap and simple to extremely complex systems with stroboscopic control of the turntable speed, balance systems for stylus contact weight and very sophisticated amplification systems. Again, this diversity and complexity of internal components means that DIY repairs and maintenance are generally restricted to the accessible exterior parts of the deck only. Having said that, some decks use belt driven turntables and belt renewal is possible provided care is exercised to avoid damaging other items and altering adjustment settings. As always, isolate the machine before any repairs are made. Even though belt renewal may be possible, obtaining the correct size belt replacement could prove more difficult. Remember that only the correct size belt should be obtained and ensure that it matches the original to avoid any further damage. Problems with amplification and control circuitry are better left to qualified technicians. Your efforts are best employed in preventing problems.

From the simplest and cheapest to the most expensive deck, the one basic thing they all have in common is their aversion to dirt and debris which is statically attracted to the vinyl record and in turn damages the stylus resulting in the all too familiar click, pop and jumping of the track. Sound is stored on the vinyl record on a continuous groove starting at the outer and finishing at the inner of the disc. The groove has microscopic ridges that are proportional in size to the sound wave that created them. When the record is rotated, the stylus is deflected by the microscopic ridges as it runs in the groove. These minute deflections are then amplified. For the stylus to track correctly, two requirements must be met. The first is that the arm holding the stylus must apply just enough weight to hold the point within the groove (usually 1 to 2 grams) but not so much as to create excessive wearing of the groove. The second requirement is that the groove of the record is free from blemishes and foreign matter that the stylus would react to.

During the playing of only one side of a record, the stylus will have to travel along a groove of as much as 426m (1400ft). The point of the stylus is moved extremely quickly as it reacts to the thousands of ridges it continually encounters (such movement increasing the higher the frequency of the music). All this movement and contact pressure results in friction, which in turn creates heat. This can, surprisingly, be as high as 500°C at the tip of the stylus. If dirt and grease left on a record come into contact with the hot stylus, a hard crystalline deposit forms on the stylus which not only reduces the playback quality but also tends to wear away the higher frequency ridges on the record resulting in permanent damage. Correct cleaning is therefore essential to maintain sound quality and record life, and also to reduce the frequency of stylus renewal. Make sure a high-quality cleaner is used. The picture shown highlights degrees of contamination that can be present. Debris within the grooves and surface of the record can include cigarette ash, household dust, chemicals like tobacco tar, aerosol sprays ('fresh air' sprays, etc.) and grease and acid from finger prints and mildew.

The stylus

There are many different types of stylus in use today (over fifteen hundred variations, and rising). All, however, have several things in common. To operate correctly they need to be cleaned regularly and handled with care when in use, thus avoiding damage to the stylus tip. Remember that a build-up of dirt or a damaged stylus will not only give poor sound reproduction when playing a record, but will eventually cause permanent damage to the groove of the record. In order to prevent this, cleaning of the stylus should be carried out at least once every twenty LPs. Like the cleaning aids shown for tape and CDs, a stylus cleaning kit is available which contains cleaning fluid and a specially designed brush. Each kit comes with detailed instructions, which must be followed to eliminate the possibility of damage to this delicate piece of equipment.

At some point, whether due to wear or damage (see photos), the stylus will need to be replaced. To put off or ignore the need for replacement is false economy in the long run as permanent damage to your records would be inevitable. Due to the vast selection of available styli, you will need to be armed with all possible information about your player and type of stylus it uses to ensure that you obtain the correct replacement.

A check-list follows:

1 Ensure you have the brand name of your product.

2 Most makes also have a model number.

3 Look closely at the old stylus, it should have a unique number.

4 Make a note also of the colour of the stylus body (this often helps to locate the correct type).

As with any repair, make a note of the correct position of the stylus before removal and take care when removing and refitting. Fixings differ greatly from simple clip-in types to those which require a fine watchmaker's screwdriver to remove and refit them. Some may come in a cartridge form, which click in and out of position. Ensure that connections or contacts are correctly positioned prior to refitting and do not use excessive force for removal or refitting. Often the angle at which the cartridge is removed and refitted is critical, so take care and avoid rough handling.

Television

The television is another appliance with internal functions that are best left to those with the relevant skills, tools and in depth knowledge and manuals. Even though it is quite easy to do, don't be tempted to remove the cover, which would expose parts that are not only easily damaged, but may carry high voltages. Leave all internal faults, service and repair to qualified engineers. As with all the items in this chapter, however, many things can point to a fault within the appliance which turns out to be something external to it and within the realms of DIY. This **does not** extend to roof mounted aerials. Although the fitting and adjustment of aerials is essentially a simple task, the correct equipment for gaining access to the roof – a good set of ladders, including proper roof ladders – combined with a good head for heights is called for. This work is better left to the specialist! In good reception areas, aerials can be mounted in the loft space and thus alleviate all external problems of damage due to weather conditions, corrosion or poor connections caused by the elements.

Picture problems can be a result of a poor/weak signal being received by the set. This can happen with both indoor and outdoor located aerials. The cause can be:

1 Adverse weather conditions (only a temporary fault).

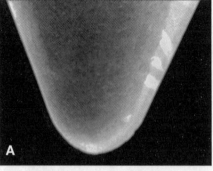
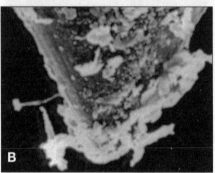
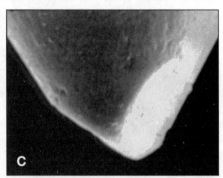
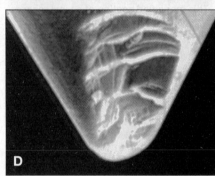

Shown here is a series of magnified pictures which highlight various stylus conditions

A = stylus in good condition
B = contaminated stylus

C= worn stylus
D = damaged stylus

2 An incorrectly tuned set (one channel poor, others OK).

3 Poor reception area (house situated in a valley).

4 Incorrect aerial direction.

5 Faulty cable or connection.

A simple process of elimination can be employed to ascertain if the problem is an external fault or if the set itself has a fault.

Remedies are:

1 Check with neighbours to see if they are having the same picture problem.

2 Check tuning of faulty channel. This will require reference to the instruction booklet for your particular set as tuning differs between makes and models.

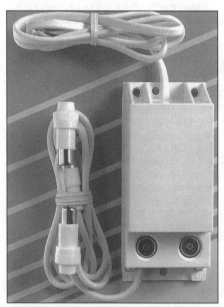

This unit allows for two sets to use the same aerial without loss in signal

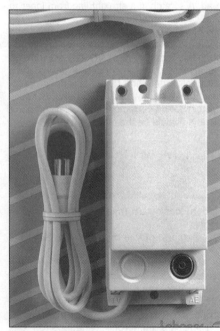

This unit boosts a poor signal by a factor of three. Ideal for areas with low signal strength

A high quality indoor aerial may be adequate for good reception areas. This model can also be purchased with a signal amplifier

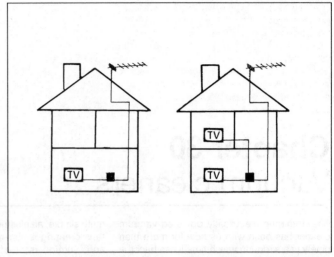

Aerial/signal sharing. Amplifier for two sets. Signal amplifier for poor reception areas

3 Again, check with your neighbours. This fault will not be intermittent but a continual one and might be alleviated by using a signal amplifier like the one shown. As its name implies, the signal is amplified before the video or TV receives it.

4 This can be checked by observing other aerials in the street and comparing their direction. This is not so simple in a loft, so utilise a compass to obtain direction. When in the loft, keep the compass at arm's length and away from other objects (cables and metal items) otherwise a faulty reading may be given. External aerials may be moved by high winds and correction is best done by an aerial fitter.

5 When a cable or connection fault is suspected, check each cable (there may be several if a video is linked) by slowly flexing them whilst watching the screen and looking for an intermittent good/bad picture to appear as you move along the cable. In this way the fault should be pinpointed. A common problem with cables and connectors is oxidisation (corrosion). If this can be cleaned

off easily do so, but fitting a new cable complete with ends may be wiser. Such cables are readily available for DIY fitting. Take your old cable along to ensure that you obtain the correct replacement as there are several variations. If after obtaining a new cable the fault still persists, the socket or internal connection may be at fault on the set and this will require the services of a trained TV engineer.

Do's and Don'ts

•DO ensure the correct rating of fuse is used.
•DO make sure that you fully understand the operating instructions by reading the accompanying booklet.
•DO take care to keep children from playing with mains appliances, TV, video, etc.
•DO watch out for glass panels and doors on some hi-fi equipment. These may be easily damaged by careless adults or inquisitive children.
•DO NOT remove fixed panels. Keep all repair work on this equipment to external faults only.
•DO NOT continue to use equipment that you

suspect may have a fault. Switch it off and remove the mains plug.
•DO NOT cover or allow the ventilation apertures on equipment to be blocked by curtains, loose covers, etc. Heat is generated by electronic components, overheating will shorten their working life or worse!
•DO NOT leave equipment switched on when unattended unless you are certain it is safe to do so. This would mean that it has been designed for unattended operation or has a standby mode.
•DO NOT place equipment on makeshift stands. TVs and other audio items can be very heavy and easily damaged. Injury could also be caused. It is advisable to use a stand approved by the manufacturer. NEVER should DIY legs be fitted to an appliance using wood screws!
•DO NOT use headphones with volume turned up too high. This could permanently damage hearing. This warning applies especially to the use of portable tape players used by children and teenagers.

Chapter 30
Vacuum cleaners

The domestic electrically powered vacuum cleaner has been with us now for more than ninety years, during which time it has become the most popular labour saving appliance in the home. The basic principle of operation is

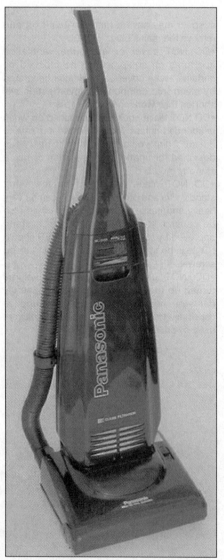

Upright vacuum cleaner

quite simple; an electric motor is used to drive fans creating a fast-moving airflow. At one end, suction is created as air is drawn in whilst at the opposite end the air is exhausted. If the air is moved quickly enough at the inlet (suction) end it will carry with it any debris that enters the airflow. Obviously a means of removing the debris from the airflow is required to prevent redistribution of the debris as the air is expelled from the exhaust. This action is the basic principle by which any vacuum cleaner works.

Over the years there have been several operational variations. In the early years, two styles emerged – one was the upright vacuum cleaner, the other a cylinder type vacuum. The upright cleaner was designed to drive a rotating brush as well as to create a suction action. The cylinder model cleaned purely by suction using a flexible hose and a range of attachments. For many years, manufacturers of vacuums stayed with these two basic styles adding to the design by increasing the suction power, automatic cord rewinds and variable power and height settings, etc. The amount of variations in design were astonishing,

however, in more recent years a change has been made to the humble vacuum cleaner. Models have been designed that combine the functions of both the upright and cylinder cleaners. Some upright models have even had power drive take-offs from the motor, not only for driving the revolving brush, but also to drive a clutch and gear system that powers the vacuum cleaner wheels, driving it back and forth at the touch of a button.

The most recent innovation for both cylinder and upright cleaners is the use of cyclone/vortex particle removal and the use of electrostatic/micron filtration, the details of which appear later in this chapter. Cylinder cleaners have undergone a complete rethink and are now split into three categories:

1 Redesigned suction vacuum cleaners ranging from simple suction only to electronic control, variable power settings and even cleaners that are self-diagnostic (a display indicates what fault has occurred within the appliance). There is even a version with a speech processor chip that actually 'tells' you the fault!

2 Canister or bin cleaners are a domestic

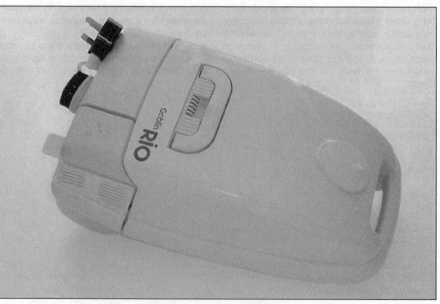

Cylinder vacuum cleaner

Three-in-one canister vacuum cleaner (with wet and dry facility and carpet cleaning

version of what were normally regarded as commercial machines. The greatest change has been to include the facility to vacuum up liquids: something that would in the past have damaged the appliance and created a safety hazard. With the advent of this design, the wet and dry operation, as it is known, has now become an option. Not all bin/canister cleaners have this option. Make sure that if a cleaner is to be used for sucking up liquids, it is designed for that purpose. Ordinary vacuum cleaners must not be used in wet conditions. The wet and dry machine must be prepared for liquid pick-up, ie on most models

specific items must be removed first to avoid damage to the appliance.

3 A further variation of the cleaner described above combine a carpet cleaning facility with the wet and dry bin-type vacuum. This combination is commonly known as a 3-in-1 wet and dry. In addition to wet and dry vacuuming, a system is incorporated in which a detergent solution from a tank is forced into the carpet or fabric and removed by suction into the main body of the vacuum. This is a fairly efficient cleaning operation that won't leave the carpet or fabric excessively damp, unlike earlier carpet shampoo machines that could not extract the soiled liquid. This function can only be carried out by a machine fitted with this feature and in most cases will require extra attachments and specialised cleaning fluids to avoid excess foaming within the tanks.

Hand-held versions of both 1 and 2 are now available and can be mains powered, rechargeable (nicad battery) or 12V-powered for use from a car battery.

Despite the variety of shapes, sizes and makes of vacuum cleaner, they all function in much the same way and therefore are prone to similar faults and user-handling problems. At the heart of a vacuum cleaner, either upright, cylinder, bin or hand-held models, there is a powerful high-speed motor. In most cases the motor will be a series-wound brush gear motor (see *Electric Motors*), because this is the most versatile motor and fits this type of appliance well. It is adaptable in shape and size and capable of high speeds. Induction motors have been used in upright cleaners but their application has been restricted to one or two makes only. Small portable hand-held versions will have motors to suit, ie mains-powered versions will have series-wound brush motors, rechargeable (nicad battery) cleaners will have a DC-powered permanent magnet motor and car battery types will have a DC-powered series motor or a permanent magnet type motor.

This chapter will not only deal with the repair of all types of vacuum cleaners, but will also advise on regular maintenance procedures necessary to keep them in good working order, avoiding serious problems that are often caused by incorrect usage and neglect. However, even with care and attention, faults will occur from time to time due to the heavy demands placed upon these appliances. Faults fall into three categories: electrical, mechanical and misuse. The latter category has a strong link with the first two in many cases.

For a more detailed explanation on how they work and the problems encountered with them, the vacuum cleaners have been split into two sections, the upright models and cylinder/bin types.

Note: *For some models references to both sections will be required.*

Upright cleaners

The upright style of vacuum cleaner is perhaps the best for large areas of carpet. It is especially good at removing dirt embedded within the carpet pile and animal hairs, etc. from the carpet surface, even on sculptured carpets! A drawback with the basic upright cleaner is its difficulty in coping with stairs. The problem has been overcome with the modern combination of upright and cylinder cleaner. This type may be the best option if large areas of fitted carpet and staircases are to be considered. The motor within the upright cleaner creates the airflow (suction) and drives a rotating brush roll (often called an agitator barrel).

The airflow can be produced in two ways as described here. The first system relies on a single fan mounted directly on the armature shaft usually by an elongated metal pulley used to drive the brush roll via a rubber belt.

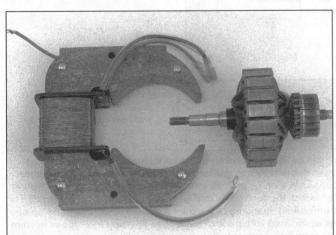

This field coil and armature are from a large Hoover upright cleaner. Individual motor parts are available for many Hoover cleaners

Chipped/broken fans are common with this type of system

Many manufacturers now use plastic fans in place of metal. They are thought to be less prone to blade damage. Check that they are fitted securely to the shaft to prevent them working loose

Early upright vacuum cleaner motor with belt drive pulley

The fan is mounted in a housing (fan chamber) and when rotated at high speed by the motor, creates a fast moving airflow.

The inlet, which is positioned in such a way as to form an area of suction around the rotating brush roll, is often referred to as the mask plate. As the fan rotates the dirt that is picked up or loosened by the brush roll is sucked into the fan chamber and blown into a disposable paper filter bag (on earlier models, reusable cloth bags were used, but more on bags later). Although effective and used for many years, this action has a major disadvantage. All of the dirt and debris picked up by the airflow comes into contact with the moving fan resulting in chipping or wearing of the fan blades. If a large item is picked up a blade could be completely broken off the fan. Uneven wear or just slight chipping will cause severe vibration and noise resulting in poor performance (pick-up) or, even worse, motor bearing or motor case failure caused by excessive vibration. Do not continue to use a noisy machine because this could make the fault worse.

Another style of upright cleaner avoids this kind of problem by using the second suction method. One end of the motor's armature is

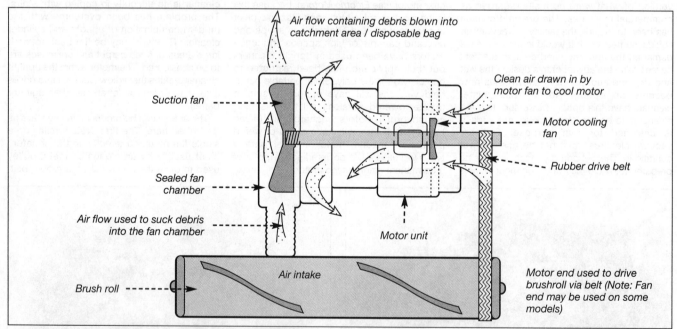

Air flow containing debris blown into catchment area / disposable bag

Clean air drawn in by motor fan to cool motor

Suction fan

Motor cooling fan

Sealed fan chamber

Rubber drive belt

Air flow used to suck debris into the fan chamber

Motor unit

Brush roll

Air intake

Motor end used to drive brushroll via belt (Note: Fan end may be used on some models)

This diagram depicts a system used mainly in upright cleaners but can be found in powered head attachments of some cylinder models. This system is referred to as a 'dirty fan' system. The airflow is created by a single large fan and the dirt and debris comes directly into contact with the fan as it passes through the fan chamber and is then pushed on into the catchment area where filtration occurs. No filtration occurs prior to the air making contact with the fan hence the term 'dirty fan' and often the only level of filtration is the disposable paper bag. Restriction in the airflow (poor quality or infrequent changing of the bag) will often result in a build-up of debris in the lower sections of the system. In addition to the problems associated with poor or ineffective filtration this type of system can easily be damaged by large particles picked-up by the airflow coming into contact with the revolving fan. This often results in chipping the fan which in turn reduces efficiency and causes excessive noise and vibration of the appliance during use. Do not continue to use an appliance that exhibits this type of fault. To avoid the problem care should be exercised during use to avoid picking up large solid items such as stone chips and especially coins

This motor is of the type described. One end is for the belt drive, the other end a series of fans for suction only

This Hoover turbo motor has belt drive at one end and single fan and chamber system at the other

extended and used to drive a brush roll via a rubber belt as before. The main body of the motor is housed in a sealed casing and the opposite end to the drive pulley has a series of specially shaped chambers and fans attached. When turned at high speed by the motor, they create an extremely fast movement of air.

The inlet (suction) connection of the unit is connected via a flexible tube or ducting to a sealed container or body of the vacuum cleaner. This creates a vacuum within the chamber when the motor runs. From the container, a duct runs to the brush roll housing (mask plate). Air is drawn in as before carrying any dirt and debris with it. At the entry point to the container, a disposable paper bag or cyclone/vortex system may be positioned which removes the dust, etc., from the airflow and therefore prevents it from coming into direct contact with the fan, and avoiding damage no matter what is picked up in the airflow. Nevertheless, systems that use disposable paper bags also have a drawback.

The air that flows through the sealed motor casing also cools the motor but if the disposable bag or internal dust filters are not renewed regularly, the airflow through the system will slow down or stop altogether causing not only poor pick up, but overheating of the motor. It is essential that disposable bags are renewed regularly (more about bags later). Filters should also be changed regularly to prevent further problems developing. The advent of the cyclone/vortex

systems has greatly reduced this potential problem area but they still have filters that at some point will need cleaning or renewal. Details of the cyclone/vortex system are given later in this chapter.

Repairs to faulty motors will depend upon the manufacturer of the appliance. Some supply only complete units, whereas others will supply individual items as replacement spares. As a rough guide, the cleaners that fit into the first category generally have individual parts available, or at least split into smaller

units, while those that fit into the second category usually have complete motor and fan assemblies with possibly only motor brushes available as a separate item.

The brush roll

The other main component of the upright cleaner is the brush roll. As mentioned earlier, a drive from the end of the motor is provided for turning the brush roll, creating a sweeping and beating action. The rotating barrel of the brush roll also lifts the carpet pile resulting in

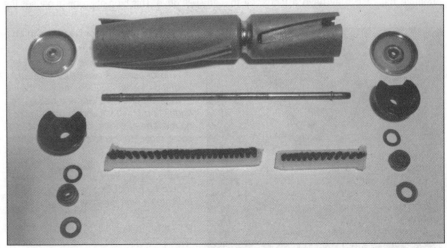

Typical brush roll components. Each part of this roll is available separately or as a complete unit

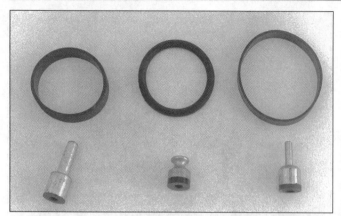

This small selection highlights the many variations of belts and pulleys available. It is essential that only the correct size and type is used

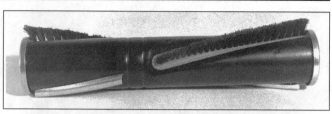

Many brush rolls can now be obtained as complete items

This Hoover turbo brush roll has fixed bristles, not the usual slides found on earlier machines

thorough cleaning action. If a beating action is incorporated (there will be a bar on the barrel in place of one brush row) it will help vibrate grit from the pile base to the surface which will then be sucked up by the airflow and removed. To some, this may seem a rough operation, but this is not really so. The suction of the mask plate lifts the carpet slightly away from the floor and the beater bar on the brush roll taps the carpet to free the embedded grit within the pile.

The removal of grit particles is extremely beneficial to the carpet. If left in place, the movement on the surface of the carpet (when being walked upon) causes the grit to wear through the base of the pile. Likely areas for this particular problem are doorways and passageways. Any resulting loss of pile is often blamed on poor carpet when in fact poor cleaning by an inefficient or unsuitable vacuum cleaner is the main cause.

The brush roll belt can be round or flat depending on the style of cleaner. Numerous sizes of belts are available but it is essential that only the belt for your particular model be used. Belts of various qualities are available, but cheap copies may prove to be less cost effective because they have a tendency to

break frequently or, due to overheating, will shed black residue on to your carpets. Using incorrect size belts will also cause damage to motor and brush roll bearings. The brush roll is supported on bearings at each end allowing the barrel to rotate freely. Several types of bearings, barrels and brushes can be found as the styles differ so much between models as well as manufacturers. Some manufacturers do supply individual parts for the brush roll, such as brush strips, bearings and barrel, but others supply only complete assemblies. The brush roll on some models may have removable brush strips; others may have a solid brush roll of wood or plastic with fixed brushes. A small selection is shown to highlight the differences.

The end bearings can be one of two types, small ball race or simple sleeve bearing. The first is prone to dust penetration causing noise or seizure of the brush roll. Cleaning and regreasing regularly will alleviate any serious problems. Sleeve bearings are prone to dirt penetration also, but although regular lubrication does help, often the shaft of the brush roll wears or the sleeve bearing hole becomes elongated by the constant pull of the belt drive. This type of problem causes the

brush roll to stall (stop rotating). The result would be poor pick-up and frequent belt renewal. In this instance the belt acts like a fuse or weak link. If the brush roll is jammed or slow running, the motor will continue to turn (though in a laboured way), the belt will be unable to transfer all or any movement to the brush roll and the drive pulley rotation will cause the belt to heat up due to friction. In a severe stall situation, the belt will burn through in one position. With slightly impaired rotation the whole of the belt will become worn and often tacky to the touch before finally breaking.

Stalling is common to all brush roll types. Carpet threads, hair and cotton threads are easily wrapped around the rotating barrel. If this occurs between the barrel end and the bearing plate (often called the thread guard), the resulting build-up will act as a brake and slow the rotation down by creating friction. In severe cases the barrel will stop rotating and the belt will burn through as described. Regular cleaning of this area will keep the barrel rotating freely. Avoid any loose edges from cut carpet as the barrel rotating at high speed can unravel loose threads. For cleaning

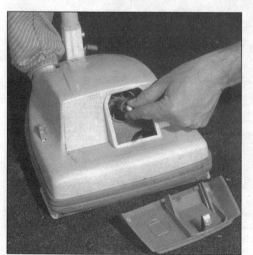

Checking the motor bearings in an upright vacuum cleaner

On this type of cleaner, a simple test of the motor bearings can be carried out. With the cleaner isolated, remove the front cover and belt. Grip the pulley tightly and pull back and forth; little or no movement should be discernible. If some movement is felt, the large front bearing is suspect. Next, try to move the pulley up and down pivoting on the front bearing. Again, little or no movement should be found. Excessive movement indicates a worn sleeve bearing (rear bearing). This works with any motor similar to the one shown. As with any repair, maintenance or cleaning should only be carried out with the appliance isolated – switch OFF, plug OUT

Ball race bearing

Sleeve bearing

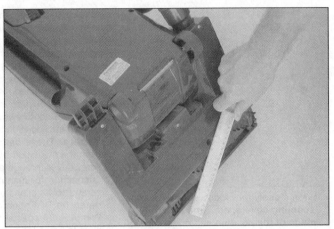

Checking for adequate brush length on the roll

to be efficient, the brushes must be the correct length to work effectively.

To ascertain if the brush roll brushes are worn and need replacing, simply place a straight edge across the mask plate and slide it slowly from one side to the other. Contact along the whole length of the brush strip should be felt, but if the brushes are below this level they need to be renewed.

Some machines allow the brush roll to be disengaged enabling the machine to be used on floor coverings other than carpet, such as vinyl, parquet, etc., by using only the suction without the rotating brushes. This procedure is easily done by moving the drive belt across onto an idler pulley by a moving arm and is held there until the user selects the carpet setting. Some models automatically disengage the brush roll when the cleaner is placed in the upright position. This prevents the brush roll rotating if the cleaner is left running in one position, for instance when using the hose attachment to clean stairs etc. Like the brush roll bearing, the idler pulley may jam or seize due to a build-up of thread, etc. Ensure the free movement of this pulley if fitted.

Note: *Remember if your model has a manually set lever ensure you reset it and check its position if poor carpet cleaning is experienced.*

Repair and maintenance (upright vacuum cleaners)

Regular servicing of your vacuum cleaner will not only keep it working at peak efficiency but will also help you to understand the aspects peculiar to your machine. For instance, it will be of great help if you know the normal noise level when in use or how efficient it is at cleaning. Such information will be invaluable in determining where a fault lies and assessing the success of the subsequent repair. If a working knowledge of the machine is built up prior to its breaking down, a lot of time and patience will be saved.

Most modern machines are double insulated, though earthed versions can be found particularly on older models. Ensure that a close inspection is made to ascertain which version you have and that any earthed appliance is correctly checked (see *A General Safety Guide* and *Electrical Circuit Testing*). Remember to note all stripdown procedures so

that all parts are refitted in their original positions. This is essential on double insulated appliances for they must conform to the double insulated standards met during manufacture. Do not cut corners or rush a repair or service, take time to do a thorough job. References to other sections will be necessary when relating to faults with motors, cables, plugs, etc. It is advisable, therefore, that all sections are read and understood before undertaking any repairs or servicing. As always, ensure that the appliance is isolated during any repair and that all covers are fitted before functional testing of the appliance. Remember a thorough and methodical approach to all work will pay dividends in safety and satisfactory repairs.

Individual parts within upright cleaners are rarely complex although the way in which they are connected and the casings they are fitted into can be somewhat difficult.

Where possible during the photo sequences various types of hidden fixings and clips will be highlighted. Unfortunately, not all variations can be included, as each new model that comes out seems to incorporate another type of fixing. The use of complex

Just two of the many versions of connecting hose (often referred to as bellows hose). Carefully inspect the convoluted hose/s found on many upright cleaners. These bellows (as they are often called) are prone to wear or splitting

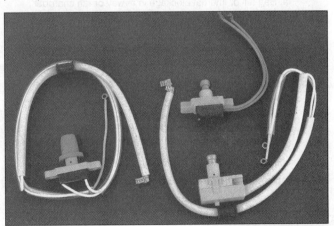

Just a small selection of the many variations of ON/OFF switches. Simple continuity testing will identify problems. Make and model numbers are essential for obtaining the correct replacement

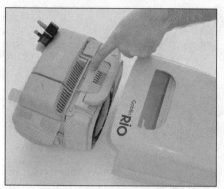

Look closely for hidden screws or clips securing covers, etc. Ensure a note is made of the position and orientation of parts prior to their removal

plastic moulded bodies, handles and covers has increased the use of hidden fixings, some of which are in fact designed as safety features. The way in which some parts are fitted together can sometimes make one think that it is impossible to gain access, but this is not really so. Therefore, do not blindly remove screws in a haphazard fashion, just stop and take time to study the appliance; look for joints or moulding marks or inserts that may have been pushed in to cover screw heads etc. Often no screws are used, a cover being clipped into position and held by small plastic catches. These catches need to be eased from their position by inserting a flat-bladed screwdriver through a slot or recess. It is not uncommon for manufacturers to use special screws to fix cases or mouldings together to deter the DIY person from gaining access. Without that special tool, their engineers will have to be called out, even for the simplest of faults! If such a fixing is found, it is worth contacting a good specialist tool shop (most towns have them, consult Yellow Pages). One widely used type of fixing is the TORX end and screwdrivers can be obtained easily from a specialist tool shop. Do not be defeated – the use of a little lateral thinking is often all that is required.

The use of plastic has become widespread in vacuums of all designs, but because of their heavy workload and everyday knocks and bumps, the casings are often broken or damaged in some way. The cost of replacing some of these plastic parts can be very expensive, and perhaps if the machine is still working you might think it is not an urgent matter to put right. It is unwise, however, to use any appliance that is known to be damaged. Although it can appear to be cosmetic, the damaged area can form part of the overall safety of the appliance, ie, covering cables or exposed internal connections. It is therefore wise to repair ALL faults quickly and thoroughly to check any appliance that has been dropped or banged about prior to its being used again.

Fault finding - vacuum cleaners

The following is a compilation of the most common faults. General symptoms are listed with the possible causes in the most likely failure order printed beneath. Alongside the likely causes are notes on action to be taken. Regular checks and maintenance of equipment will make you more aware of the operation and workings of your particular machine. This in turn will be a great help in diagnosing and isolating any faults that occur. **Do not** jump to conclusions and commence work in a haphazard way. Calmly sit down and start to work out what the problem may be and form the plan of attack in a logical manner.

1. Symptom: Won't work at all

Possible cause	*Action*
a. Faulty plug or socket	See *Plugs and Sockets*
b. Fault in flex	See *Cables and Cable Faults* and *Electrical Circuit Testing*
c. Fault in cord rewind (if fitted)	See *Photo sequence Cables and Cable Faults* and *Electrical Circuit Testing*
d. Motor brush worn/sticking or open circuit field coil	See *Photo sequence, Electric Motors* and *Electrical Circuit Testing*
e. Faulty on/off switch	See *Electrical Circuit Testing*
f. Open circuit TOC or overheat protective device in motor	Check for continuity. See *Thermostat Temperature Control* and *Electrical Circuit Testing*

2. Symptom: Motor runs but little or no suction

a. Bag full or internal blockage in airway or fan chamber	Renew disposable bag and check all airways. See *Photo sequence*
b. Blocked secondary filter (suction vacuum system)	Renew secondary filters. See *Photo sequence* and retest
c. Leak on sealed system (suction system machines)	Check for cracks or poor/ill-fitting seals which allow air to be sucked in other than at the brush roll cavity. Repair or renew as required. On combined machines, check extension hose

Note: *For poor cleaning/performance refer also to section on disposable bags.*

3. Symptom: Brush roll/agitator fails to rotate

a. Broken belt	Renew belt with identical replacement and check for free rotation of brush roll
b. Non-carpet mode selected (barrel disengaged)	Reset to carpet mode and retest
c. Build-up of debris on end bearings	Check for build-up and renew suspect parts or lubricate. See *Photo sequence*
d. Incorrect belt or belt stretched	Renew ensuring correct replacement is fitted and retest

4. Symptom: Excessive noise or vibration

a. Broken or chipped fan (fan and chamber type machines)	Renew fan and check front and rear motor bearings. See *Photo sequence*
b. Dust build-up on motor fans (suction type machines)	Clean thoroughly fans and housing. Check disposable bag and secondary filters for poor fit or holes. Renew as required
c. Brush roll bearings worn or loose in fixing positions	Inspect bearings and fixing position in casing. Renew if suspect. See *Photo sequence*
d. Loose brushes or beater bars on brush roll	Check thoroughly for loose or poorly positioned bars or brushes, as they will cause vibration. Renew as required

5. Symptom: Motor runs slowly

a. Carbon brushes worn or sticking in slides

Check length of brushes and for free movement within holders. Mark brush position prior to removal to ensure they are refitted the same way round. Renew springs and brushes if worn. Check commutator for wear or damage. See *Photo sequence*

b. Faulty commutator or armature windings

Inspect commutator for signs of excessive wear, overheating, loose segments, short circuited windings or catching on field coil when rotated. See *Photo sequence*. If faulty, renew armature and brushes or complete motor as obtainable

c. Build up of dirt and grease on fan (fan and chamber type machines)

Build-up of dirt in fan chamber is often caused by vacuuming damp carpets. Build-up may appear on rear of fan and act like a brake. Remove and clean fan and housing thoroughly

Note: *This fault may damage the motor if not corrected quickly. Do not use this type of vacuum in damp conditions or soon after carpet shampooing.*

d. Worn armature bearings

Check armature for sideways movement. This movement allows the armature to be pulled onto the field coil when motor runs. See *Photo sequence*

e. Loose or defective field coil catching on armature

Check field coil securing screws or clips. Reposition and retighten if possible. Some early Hoover motors susceptible to this fault

All of the above checks and tests are to be carried out with appliances isolated – switch OFF and plug OUT, unless otherwise stated in the case of functional testing to verify correct operation. When carrying out a functional test, make sure all cables and wiring are fitted back into their correct positions when reassembling. Any parts renewed must be identical to the original specification. Quote model and serial numbers when obtaining spare parts.

Plastic casings – tips

1 Do not use excess force on clips or fixings. Before refitting self-tapping screws into plastic casings, ensure all debris/plastic swarf is removed from their threads, otherwise the plastic thread in the casing will be damaged

2 Do not use mineral oil to lubricate moulded plastic because this can damage the structure of the plastic and make it brittle and crack

3 Do not clean plastic mouldings with petroleum because the surface and make up of the plastic will be damaged

4 Avoid heat exposure of all plastic parts. Do not lean them on radiators or stand them close to heating appliances.

UPRIGHT VACUUM CLEANER TYPICAL REPAIR

1 This cleaner displayed symptoms similar to No.4 and was extremely noisy although still operative. With the appliance isolated, the front cover was removed to disengage the belt (on some models securing screws may have to be removed, this model has a push-fit cover)

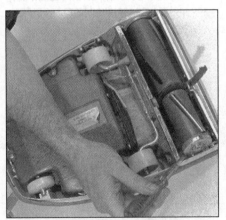

2 With the belt disengaged from the motor pulley, the cleaner was inverted and the agitator (brush roll) removed by first easing one end free. Note keyed end on brush roll

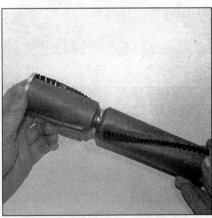

3 Once removed the brush roll was checked for free rotation and noise. Although it was not the source of the original fault, it would be necessary to overhaul it prior to refitting

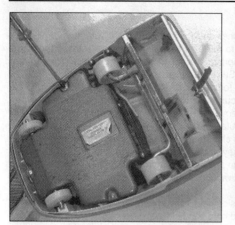

4 Access to the fan and motor bearings started with the removal of the bottom cover and mains lead connections at the terminal block and switch, ensuring a note was made of the relevant positions and fixing points

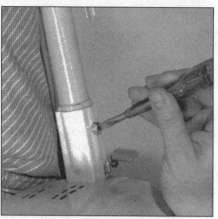

5 To gain access to the lower motor securing screws the handle support socket (often called the handle bail) had to be removed. First step was to remove the securing bolt, which allowed the handle shaft to be removed. The foot pedal was removed (one screw)

6 Four larger self tapping screws securing the socket base. This then allowed the socket unit to be manoeuvred from its position

7 Once the handle socket unit was removed, access to the lower two securing screws was much easier, although a long cross point driver was needed to reach the lower two

8 With all four securing screws taken out, the motor was removed from the outer casing

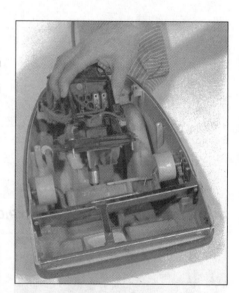

9 All the parts removed were laid out neatly to ensure correct refitting. Notes were made of specific items and positions where necessary

10 Cleaning was required before further stripdown

11 With the motor out of the casing, the cause of the noise problem could be seen. One blade of the fan had broken off. This caused severe imbalance and vibration

12 The fan was removed by grasping it and turning the belt pulley clockwise (LH thread in this instance)

13 A new fan was to be fitted. Take care to refit all the spacing washers that may be found behind the fan

14 At this point, it is advisable to check the motor internally for brush or bearing wear or fluff build up, etc. This requires the screws with captive nuts to be removed. Take care to make a note of the correct screw positions because lengths differ. The large circular motor gasket (seal) was removed and the motor cover was also removed

Note: *A new seal would be required due to wear*

15 Cleaning both halves of the casing with a soft brush was called for before continuing

16 The motor brushes were then removed for checking. The best way to do this is by removing the securing plate holding the housing. This is the simplest way as the spring and brush are easily compressed. Each brush was marked to ensure correct refitting

17 Six screws had to be taken out before the armature could be removed. two holding the front bearing plate, two holding the rear plate and two on the outer of the casing, holding the field coil and suppressor

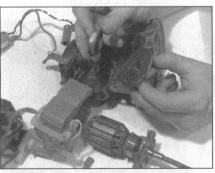

18 With fixings removed, the armature and bearings could now be removed. Note the small front seal and the 'D' shape of the rear bearing – both essential points when refitting. Only the front bearing can be regreased although in this instance, both bearings were renewed

19 As mentioned in Photo 3 of this sequence, an overhaul of the brush roll was needed. With this version of brush roll the metal thread guards (ends) can be unscrewed by holding both ends. One end will then unscrew but the shaft will need to be gripped with pliers before the other can be removed

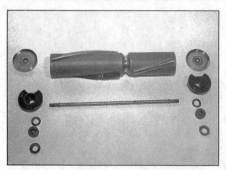

20 Take note of the position and condition of any seals or washers. Renew suspect or worn parts

21 Slide out the old brushes from the barrel and clean all parts thoroughly

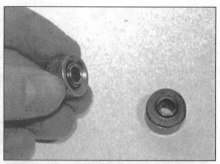

22 When clean, inspect all parts closely for wear. The end bearings in this instance can be regreased or renewed

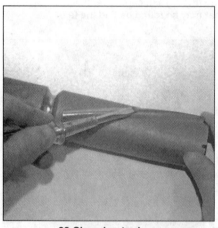

23 Clean beater bars

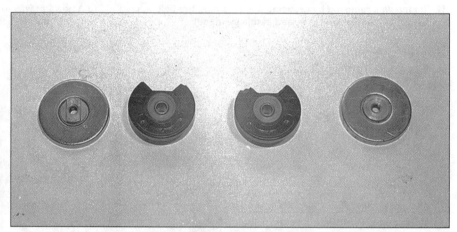

24 New ends ready to be fitted

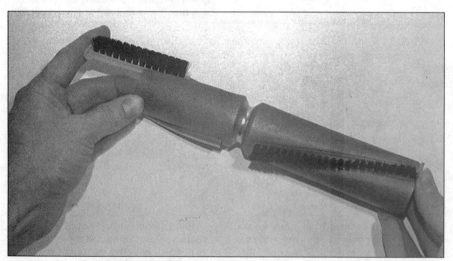

25 Renew brushes by sliding in the new brush strips and reassembling the brush roll in reverse order, taking care to fit all parts back in original positions

26 The square or keyed thread guard must be on the correct end and must fit snugly into position in the casing. If loose, excessive noise will be created and the recess damaged. On plastic casings on this model, an 'H' spring can be fitted as shown to hold it firmly in position

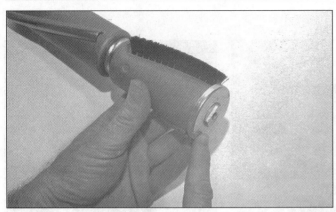

27 Keyed end of thread guard and 'H' spring ready for fitting

28 Fit 'H' spring if brush roll is loose in its fitting by locating one side into the grooved recess first. Next ease the opposite side into position

Sleeve bearing type brush roll renewal

Although all similar in design, there are several variations of brush roll. The one shown earlier uses ball race bearings, whereas the brush roll shown below uses sleeve bearings. These types are from two of the most popular UK cleaners.

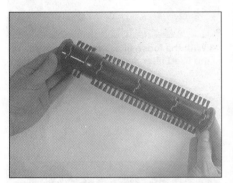

1 This type of brush roll can have fixed or removable brush inserts

2 The sleeve bearing comes complete. Check that old bearings are not oval (worn) or loose. Renew if suspect; smear the shaft with just a little light machine oil prior to fitting

3 Often the shaft of the brush roll works loose and causes binding. Check that it is firmly fixed. If loose, renew barrel. Feel the shaft with the fingers – it should be smooth. If it feels rough, renew barrel. Fitting new bearings to a worn shaft will not make a lasting repair

4 Some later brush rolls may have small ball race bearings fitted to the shaft in place of the usual sleeve bearings. These cannot be greased but can be obtained as spare parts in most instances

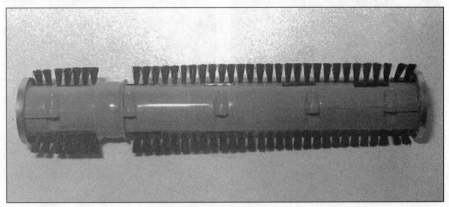

5 It is often preferable to fit a complete brush roll if the bearings have been faulty for some time

Check for free rotation. Fit belt to motor pulley first on this type of cleaner and then fix brush roll into position. Make sure that the brush roll end fits correctly into position in order to prevent binding and belt wear

UPRIGHT CLEANER (SUCTION TYPE) TYPICAL FAULT

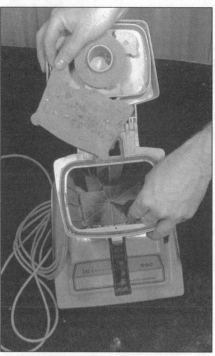

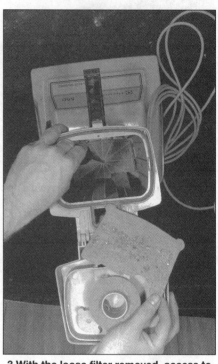

1 This vacuum cleaner had the classic symptom No.2. It appeared to be running correctly but did not pick up any dirt even after user had fitted a new disposable bag. The fault was one of the most common. Although disposable bags had been changed on a fairly regular basis, the two secondary filters had not

2 This model has two secondary filters in the base of the bag compartment – one loose and one fixed by a self tapping screw

3 With the loose filter removed, access to the fixed filter securing screw was easy

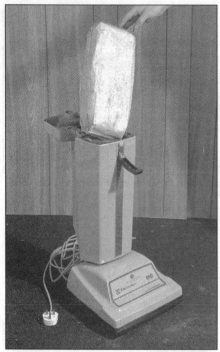

4 Both filters need to be replaced regularly. These had never been changed and had become solidly blocked thus allowing little or no air to pass therefore no suction

5 Due to the restriction of airflow, all the ducting was checked for blockages. Removing the two mask plate screws gave access to the lower section

6 Owing to the reduced suction, the tube at the base was badly restricted/blocked. This had to be cleared before functional testing. Note on this machine the mask plate itself was faulty and a new part would need fitting to complete the job correctly

As the fault had built up over a long period of time, the user had accepted the poor performance of the cleaner as normal. When used after the simple overhaul, the owner was amazed by the increased cleaning power

Cylinder cleaners (including canister/bin types)

This type of cleaner which cleans purely by suction, is better suited for situations other than just large carpeted areas, eg, rugs, car interiors, large areas of hard flooring, walls, curtains and furniture. Carpeted stairs are also much easier to vacuum with a cylinder cleaner. Suction-only carpet cleaning will not remove dirt and grit from the pile base in the same way that the beating and sweeping action of the upright models will.

However, a machine has been developed that combines the cylinder model with the powered brush roll of the upright vacuum. This type of cylinder appliance has the option of a powered cleaning head attachment that can be connected when required for large carpeted areas. This attachment has a revolving brush roll, which is similar to that of the upright cleaner, and the suction is supplied by the motor of the cylinder cleaner. There are two ways in which the brush roll can be rotated. This first is by means of a fan system mounted in the suction head of the tool. The flow of air rotates the fans that in turn rotate the brush roll. This type is not very effective for several reasons. Very little power is produced to turn the brush roll so stalling is common; also the fans within the airflow are easily choked by debris. The second, and by far the best, method of powering the brush roll

is by a second smaller motor which is mounted in the attachment itself and supplied with power via a cable moulded into the flexible hose. This system is very efficient because two motors are used; one of which is purely for suction leaving the other motor to power the brush roll. The drawbacks are that fitting can be somewhat fiddly and cable connections can cause problems due to

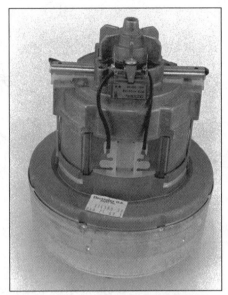

Typical cylinder motors are available as complete items only, apart from motor brushes

constant movement during use. Problems with brush rolls; belts and motors are the same as those listed for the upright cleaner detailed in the previous section.

Suction in cylinder and canister machines is created by a very high-revving series wound brush motor. A series of fans are attached directly onto one end of the motor armature and rotate within a housing. The housing is a series of baffle plates and fixed fans that act upon the airflow in such a way as to increase the airflow substantially. The motors used in cylinder and canister type appliances range in power from 800W to in excess of 1000W. As a result, a great deal of heat is produced when in use. The design of such machines is that the airflow created for suction is drawn over

Motor unit in situ in an Electrolux machine held in place by a large plastic moulding secured by four screws

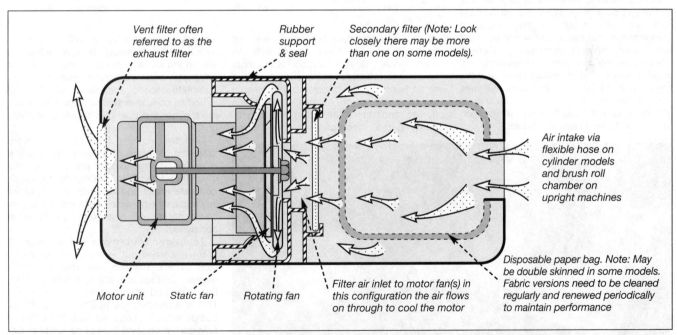

This diagram depicts a typical 'through flow' system of airflow. Variations of the through flow system can be found on cylinder, canister (not wet and dry versions) and upright version. After passing through the various filter medium the air then continues through the motor to keep it cool, hence the term 'through flow'. With this type of system, restriction of the airflow for whatever reason will lead to a rise in the motor temperature leading ultimately to premature failure of the motor. Poor quality, incorrectly fitted bags or filters can allow dirt to pass into the moving parts of the motor and cause considerable damage to this most vital component

Some motors can have individual parts replaced. It is always advisable to find out from the supplier if this is possible. This field coil is for a Hoover cylinder cleaner motor and is available separately along with all the other motor parts if required

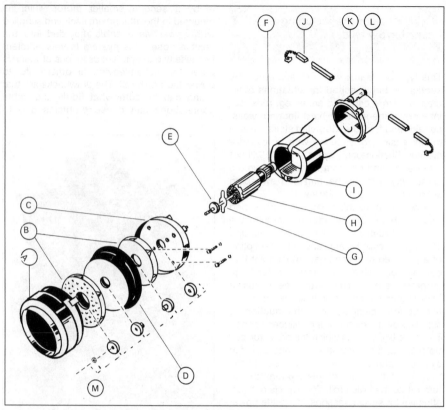

A typical cylinder/canister motor and fan assembly

A	Fan housing	F	Rear bearing	J	Motor brush and slide
B	Moving fans	G	Bearing securing plate	K	Suppressor
C	Motor end frame (front)	H	Armature	L	Motor end frame (rear)
D	Static fan	I	Field coil	M	Spacers and nut
E	Front bearing				

and through the motor to keep it cool during normal operation, which is why the air being expelled from the exhaust/outlet vent is often quite warm. The airflow is normally slowed during use and even over long periods of use will not normally result in any problems. If, however, the disposable bag is not changed regularly or incorrect bags are used, the airflow will become impaired (see *Disposable Bags*).

Infrequent secondary filter cleaning and renewal will add to this problem, therefore it is most important to renew these items regularly. Failure to clean or renew secondary filters or the use of poor or incorrect disposable bags will not only result in poor cleaning performance, but motor damage or burn out will occur through overheating. General cleaning of the dust container compartment, regular renewal of disposable bag and the cleaning or fitting of new secondary filters should be part of a regular maintenance routine to keep the machine in peak condition and prevent serious motor problems.

Both double insulated and earthed appliances can be found, but as with the upright models, double insulation is the most popular. As always, make sure that the correct flex is used and remember to make a note of all wiring, connections and fixings prior to and during servicing and repair. Shown in the accompanying figure is an exploded view of a typical cylinder/canister motor and fan assembly. Though each part is shown individually, many manufacturers do not supply separate parts as spares – only a complete motor and fan unit. To buy individual components often works out much more expensive than purchasing a complete unit.

With the modern, high revving motors, problems, unless spotted early, can result in extensive damage to other parts of the motor unit, therefore it is preferable to obtain complete motor and fan units, thus avoiding any imbalance by worn or chipped fans, poor commutators or heat damage to other components.

If stripdown of the motor and fan assembly is to be carried out, ensure that the motor casings are marked and that the fans, washers and spacers are all placed neatly in the order and position they were removed. This is essential; the positioning of all the components is critical as fans can often be reversed, producing little or no suction. See *Photo sequence*.

A popular feature on cylinder cleaners is the optional variable power settings which controls motor and fan speeds. A reduction in fan speed gives direct reduction in suction

Small speed control module

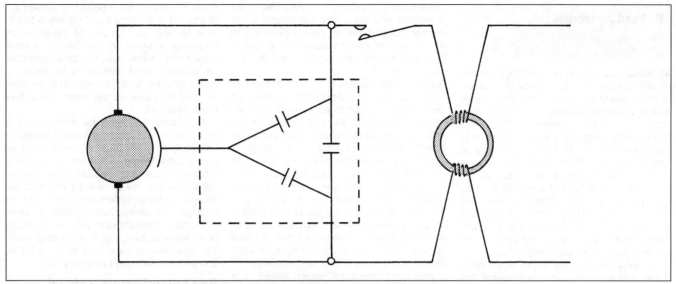

Typical cylinder cleaner circuit, showing motor and twin suppressors

The ends of this modern crush proof hose can be removed by unscrewing them from the threaded coil of the hose

Threaded hose allows easy access to blockages or hose renewal

power which is useful on loose fabrics that would otherwise be sucked into the attachment if the suction was too powerful. Variable speed control is achieved using a special electronic circuit based on a thyristor or triac and a printed circuit board. The circuit achieves control by interrupting or pulsing the

Ball valve system of wet and dry machine

power supply to the motor. The speed control module is not repairable and is available only as a complete replacement unit.

If speed problems are encountered, look for burnt components or loose connections, etc. Check all other parts before suspecting or changing the speed module.

The motor should be checked for any shorting insulation, loose wires, worn/damaged brushes etc. See *Electric Motors* and *Electrical Circuit Testing*. Only when all other possible faults have been eliminated should the module be replaced. Ensure the correct replacement is obtained and a note of all wires and connections is made prior to repair.

Some appliances may have an automatic mode that alters the motor speed to suit cleaning conditions. This is done by a pressure-sensitive switch detecting a change in pressure of the air flowing in the suction hose. Alterations in pressure are countered by increasing or decreasing the motor speed accordingly.

The use of plastic for casings and components, both internal and external, is popular with all manufacturers and reference should be made to the upright vacuum section, which gives assistance and general tips in this area.

Common faults

For fault symptoms, possible causes and action relating to cylinder vacuums refer to the fault finding section of the upright vacuums. Unless the appliance has a power head attachment, references to the brush rolls can be omitted. Checking a long hose for blockages can be done simply by dropping a coin down one end, gradually lifting it whilst listening to the movement of the coin. If a blockage is present, the point at which the coin stops will indicate the location. If the blockage is near either end of the hose, it may be necessary to remove the actual hose end if possible. In most instances, reversing the airflow through the hose should help to free the blockage.

Wet and dry models

Appliances suitable for wet and dry operation have the outward appearance of ordinary cylinder/canister cleaners, but the internal design, which incorporates a ball-type floating valve, is quite different. The valve mechanically closes the inlet (suction) point to the motor from the dirt/liquid container if an excess of water is drawn into it. The operation of this valve is simple yet effective, the increase in water level lifts the ball from its normal position and closer to the inlet (suction) duct. When close enough, the suction will lift the ball into the inlet and effectively seal it to prevent water from being drawn into the motor compartment. This action also prevents any further liquid being drawn into the container. It is essential that the ball moves freely within its housing at all times. Both earthed and double insulated versions of this appliance can be found. It is most important to follow the manufacturer's requirements and reposition all parts correctly.

Three-in-one machines

The basic operation of this machine is identical to the wet and dry type, but with the addition of a tank in which a water and detergent mixture can be put and fed as required to a special cleaning head combining carpet shampooing with soiled water extraction. An explanation of this action is as follows. The tank which holds the detergent and water is pressurised by a feed from the motor exhaust. A tube runs from below the liquid level of the tank to a control valve on the end of the vacuum hose. When cleaning solution is required, the valve is opened and solution from the tank is forced along the tube to the cleaning head. The solution is then fed into the pile of the carpet and as the head is moved over the surface, the now soiled liquid is sucked into the lower container via the normal suction hose. An alternative to this is the jet system which supplies the cleaning head with solution at a higher pressure via a small pump unit.

Note: *To use appliances for wet and dry or shampooing requires the fitting or removing of certain parts peculiar to each model. It is not possible to list all the variations here, so reference should be made to your appliance handbook before carrying out any of these operations. Specialised cleaning fluids are required for use with these products. They usually have anti-foaming agents to prevent foam/water penetration of the motor unit. It is advisable to use only the products approved for use in these appliances, because failure to do so could cause damage or create a safety hazard. Ensure that the machine is cleaned thoroughly after wet and dry operation or shampooing, because soiled liquids and detergent, etc. could cause build-ups or blockages during normal use.*

Cord rewinds (all models)

Cord rewinds are now found on all types of cleaners, from simple hand-operated versions to the fully automatic rewind at the touch of a button. It is the latter type that we deal with here although much of the text will also relate to the hand operated models. Many auto cord rewind systems use open coil springs and great care should be exercised if a stripdown of these systems is called for. Protection for the eyes is recommended. The use of goggles (though by the end of the job these may have seemed to have been unnecessary) will afford protection from the spring itself or any item that it may throw out in the event of its slipping from position.

Operation of the cord rewind relies on tensioning of the rewind spring as the cord is pulled out for use. A small brake pad prevents the immediate return of the spring and cord drum to its original position. When the rewind button or lever is pressed, the brake is released and the drum is rotated by the spring, pulling in the cord as it does so. To ensure that all the cord is returned to the drum, the spring has a degree of tension left at the end of the cord travel (usually 4 turns). This is why care must be taken when removing or servicing this item. The main reason why you will need to gain access to or remove the cord rewind is to renew a damaged cable, which is common at the entry point of the cable on the drum centre. See *Photo sequence.*

A suitable flex must be obtained as a replacement. It must be sufficiently flexible to coil easily on to the drum. The new flex must be the same length as the one that is being replaced. Care must be taken to ensure all cord grips are fitted correctly and that the moving contact points are not bent or damaged. Renew any burnt or damaged rings or contacts. Remember to note the positions of all items at each stage of the stripdown. The operation of each item may not be so apparent if committed to memory only.

Bag full indicators – visual

Found mainly on cylinder models, the 'Bag Full' indicator should be a useful device. Unfortunately, all too often it is ignored. By repeatedly ignoring this device, it eventually fails, sticking and giving an inaccurate indication. The visual indicator operates by moving a coloured piston/slide against a spring. The bag indicator unit has a small bleed hole or slot that allows air into the compartment via the slide/piston. In normal circumstances, air is easily drawn in through the bag and hose, but when these are choked or blocked thus producing a greater vacuum in the compartment, more air is pulled through the indicator inlet. The increase in air movement will progressively push on the piston/slide overcoming the resistance of the spring. An indication of the degree of blockage or bag fullness is then given. Problems arise if dirt is drawn into the bleed hole or slot and jams the piston or slide resulting in a false reading. With care, most can be easily removed for cleaning.

Ensure that all parts are free to move. Testing is quite simple; with the machine in its normal state and ready for use (hose connected, no attachments fitted), turn the

A cord rewind like the one shown can be found on many machines, both cylinder and upright

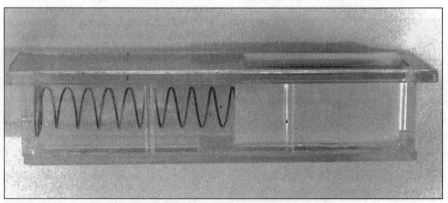

Bag full indicator (spring and slide type)

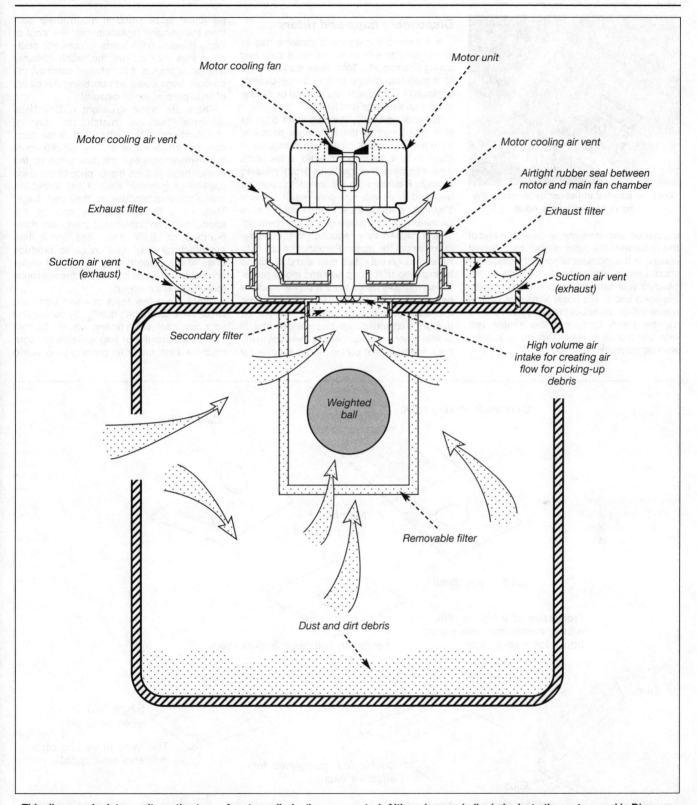

Motor cooling fan

Motor unit

Motor cooling air vent

Motor cooling air vent

Airtight rubber seal between motor and main fan chamber

Exhaust filter

Exhaust filter

Suction air vent (exhaust)

Suction air vent (exhaust)

Secondary filter

High volume air intake for creating air flow for picking-up debris

Weighted ball

Removable filter

Dust and dirt debris

This diagram depicts an alternative type of motor called a 'by pass motor'. Although very similar in looks to the motor used in Diagram (A) there is a major difference – the main airflow is not used to cool the motor. Motor cooling is by a separate much smaller fan mounted on the opposite end of the motor and the air flow in both sections are not allowed to mix, therefore they are vented from different points of the appliance. This type of motor is mainly used in 'wet and dry' models to prevent moisture being passed through the motor. Although the possibility of the motor overheating due to filter blocking is reduced, infrequent filter changing will reduce cleaning efficiency

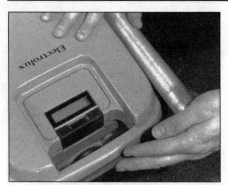

Test the bag full indicator by blocking the hose end with your hand

cleaner on and intermittently cover the end of the hose with the palm of your hand whilst observing the indicator window. The indicator should move across from one side to the other as your hand first covers then uncovers the open end of the hose. Variations on this theme will be found but the basic principle will be the same. Carry out this simple test regularly in order to check that the indicator is working correctly.

Disposable bags and filters

It is easy to dismiss the disposable bag as just a receptacle in which the dirt is collected during cleaning. However, there is a little more to it than that. Many faults can be directly attributed to infrequent bag renewal or the use of poor quality bags and filters.

To work correctly, the bag must offer as little resistance to the airflow as possible, even as the content of the bag increases. It also has to resist clogging while at the same time stopping fine particles from passing through. Restriction to the airflow through the bag and filter will not only result in poor cleaning performance, but could cause premature motor failure due to overheating. This is caused by a reduction in the airflow used to cool the motor. Porosity (the ability to let air through but retain dust and dirt), has to be matched to the bag size and motor power for each model. Because the bag is made of paper (or non-woven fabric as some manufacturers like to call it), it might be thought that any paper bag will do. This is definitely not so. Unfortunately there are many bags available that purport to be suitable for

particular models and at much lower cost than the genuine replacements. The cost of many genuine bags tends to push the cost-conscious into buying the much cheaper alternative brands. If not chosen carefully, the cheaper bags could end up being the cause of an expensive motor renewal!

There are some excellent quality bags available that do match the original specifications. With a little effort, these bags can be identified and they usually cost somewhere between the low price of the inferior bags and the higher price of the bags marked as genuine. Few, if any appliance manufacturers produce all their own bags. They have them made by one of the specialised companies and then have them branded as their own. The same bag manufacturer may then go on to produce bags of the same quality to be sold under another brand name but without the appliance manufacturer's mark-up.

There are a few tests you can carry out which will indicate bag quality. By conducting your own small-scale testing, you will be able to find the quality of bag suitable for your machine. First, check for porosity by covering

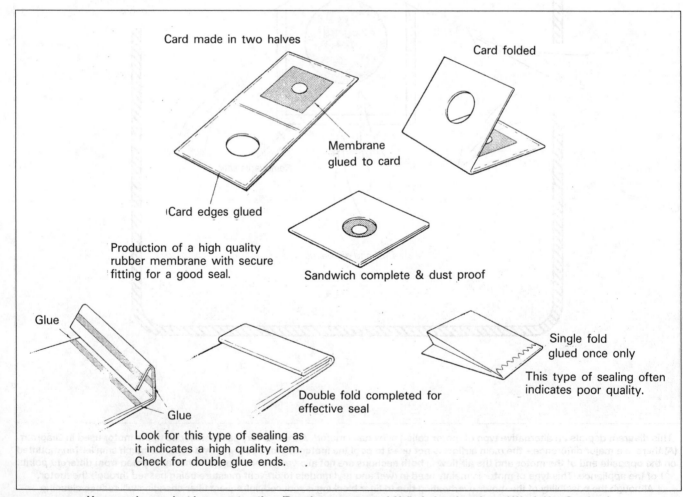

Card made in two halves

Card folded

Membrane glued to card

Card edges glued

Production of a high quality rubber membrane with secure fitting for a good seal.

Sandwich complete & dust proof

Glue

Glue

Look for this type of sealing as it indicates a high quality item. Check for double glue ends.

Double fold completed for effective seal

Single fold glued once only

This type of sealing often indicates poor quality.

Vacuum cleaner dust bag construction. (Drawings courtesy of Airflo Industries plc and Wash-Vac Services)

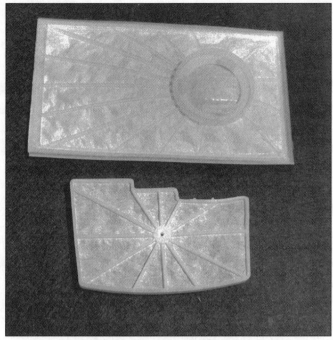

Plastic framed secondary filters. Many variations are found. Regular renewal is essential

This cleaner has three types of filter – disposable bag, secondary filter and exhaust filter

your mouth with a section of the new paper bag and exhale. Little resistance should be felt through easily. Next check the seams and sealed ends of the bag. Look for secure double folding and strong gluing; bags coming apart when full cause many problems. **Note:** *Some bags are designed to have an open end, which is secured by a clip, allowing the bag to be emptied and reused. It is advisable to reuse a bag only once as fine dust blocks the pores of the filter paper. Better still,*

avoid the mess and inconvenience of emptying the bag, and use a fresh one each time. This will also help keep the cleaning action at peak performance. Reusable cloth bags are available, but are not recommended for the same reasons. Fine dust is difficult to remove from the weave, suction and airflow is impaired and they tend to smell if not thoroughly cleaned and washed regularly. Inspect the inner of the bag for many cylinder cleaners use double-wall bags (two layers of filter) to increase filtration

and remove tiny dust particles often missed with cheap poor quality bags. Ensure that bags with cardboard apertures fit correctly. Some use a rubber membrane, so if the original had one, the replacement bag must also have one. The bag must be a secure fit otherwise dust and dirt will bypass the bag and clog secondary filters or, worse still, enter the motor. Bags that are poorly fitted are often only spotted once the damage has been done, so check first to avoid problems.

CYLINDER CLEANER TYPICAL FAULT

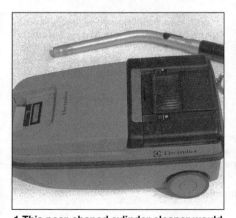

1 This pear-shaped cylinder cleaner would not work at all (Symptom 1). Fault 1. Checked OK so a cable or internal fault was suspected. With the cleaner isolated, checking could commence

2 All the functional parts of this type of cleaner are housed in the rear compartment switch, motor, cord rewind, etc. At first sight the fixing screws, etc., are not visible

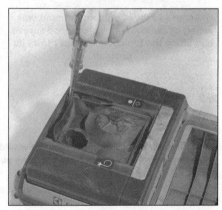

3 However, after lifting and removing the exhaust cover and filter, two hidden screws were found towards the rear. By removing them, the rear panel could then be taken off

4 There were no obvious fixing screws to the front section. It was decided that some form of fixing lay beneath the metal trim in the centre. This was eased carefully from its position (double sided tape held it on).
This particular one had been removed before as it showed signs of slight damage

5 When removed, two special fixing screws were found. To remove them, an old flat-bladed screwdriver was modified

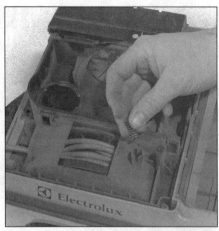

6 The cord rewind pedal and the switch pedal could now be removed. They both have loose return springs and plastic retaining clips

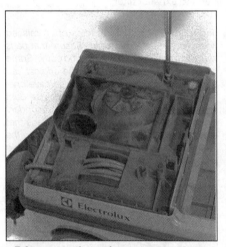

7 Access to the main compartment was gained by removing five crosshead screws and lifting the top cover carefully from its position

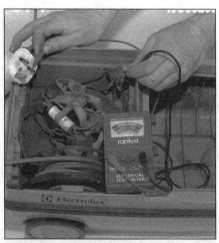

8 Continuity testing of all the circuit could then be carried out to find the cause of the problem

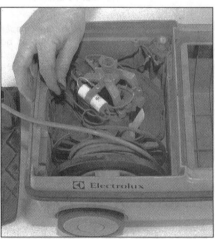

9 With leap-frog testing the problem was traced to a loose connection on the motor. Tightening and refitting was all that was required in this case. The compartment and motor were thoroughly cleaned prior to being reassembled. A complete check of all connections was made

Had the fault been within the motor it would have required the fitting of a complete motor and fan unit because individual motor parts are not available. After double checking all work carried out, reassembly was a straightforward reversal of the stripdown sequence. Care was taken to fit all fixings correctly

A new inner and exhaust filter were also fitted prior to the functional test

CORD REWIND FAULT

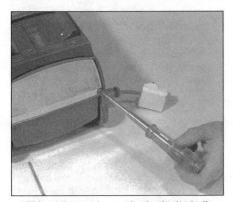

1 This cylinder cleaner had a fault similar to the previous vacuum (Symptom 1). Having isolated the machine, checking could then begin. As before, plug and socket proved OK. Access to this conventional looking cylinder cleaner was much easier

2 The removal of two recessed crosshead screws allowed the cord rewind unit to be removed

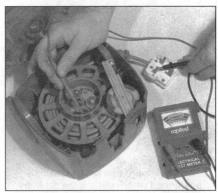

3 From this point, continuity testing could be done. An open circuit was found between the plug and the rewind contact on the neutral side. Note: on this type of cleaner with a neon indicator light, the neon may still light or flicker even with an open circuit neutral return which prevents the motor from running

4 Checks on the plug end proved OK

5 Open circuit faults near to the centre entry point are common on rewinds. This is due to constant movement. At first sight, the fault may not be apparent

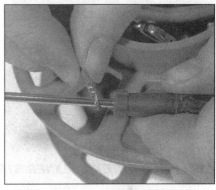

6 Trim the new end of the cable to the original lengths and test for continuity prior to refitting. Make a new circular fixing by forming the conductor around a small screwdriver shaft as shown

If the rest of the flex is in good condition all that may be required is to remove the first section of flex just in front of the fault and reconnect to the rewind assembly

In most instances, however, it is best to fit a new length of flex. Ensure that a cable of suitable quality is obtained which is identical to the original specification, ie, in flexibility, length and diameter (but it is quite possible that the colour may not match)

Note: Some cable may not be flexible enough for use on rewind systems such as these, check when purchasing. The fitting of a new cable was required in this instance as there was a possibility of fatigue problems in other sections of the cable. Fitting of a new length of cable is best carried out by removing the whole unit to enable a new cable to be wound on to it. Procedure is as follows:

7 To remove the cable drum, take care to protect yourself from the coiled spring. With plug removed, allow the rewind to fully coil and spring back before removal. Wear goggles to protect eyes in case of accident

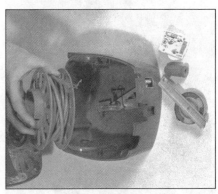

8 With spring removed, press the cord release lever and ease the drum out of its position

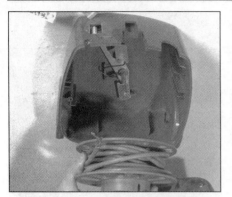

9 This will expose the braking system below. Ensure that this is correctly positioned when refitting the drum by pressing the brake release to allow the drum to seat correctly

10 With new flex fitted to drum, ensure that it is fitted in exactly the same way as the original and that all cable clamps and covers are fitted correctly

11 With drum and new cable positioned correctly, fit the cord stop to the cable. The spring can be refitted with care. Run four turns around the drum centre prior to securing the spring on its mount. (This allows a good return on the whole length of the flex)

12 (left) With all parts correctly fitted double check all work and fit plug to cable end

13 (right) A further continuity check of the motor circuit proved OK. The motor used in this machine is the same as that shown in the previous stripdown. Access to it is by removing the four crosshead screws in each corner of the inner plastic housing. This allows the housing to be removed giving access to the motor unit

Refitting the unit is a reversal of the stripdown procedure. Functional testing should be carried out using an RCB-protected circuit

CYCLONE/VORTEX CLEANER STRIPDOWN

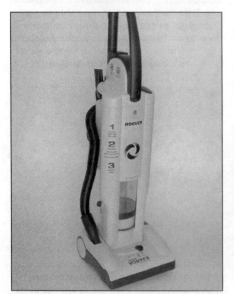

The following stripdown sequence of a vortex/cyclone appliance has been included to highlight the mechanical similarities between both earlier uprights and cylinder models, whilst at the same time showing some of the components unique to this range of machines. The model shown was picked at random from an ever-increasing range of 'bagless' vortex/cyclone models now being produced by most manufacturers. The appliance was working correctly and was not faulty. It was dismantled purely for this photographic sequence. However, as with any servicing, repair or inspection the appliance was thoroughly electrically and functionally tested prior to use.

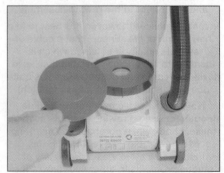

1 In accordance with standard practice before any service, repair or inspection the appliance was isolated prior to commencing the stripdown procedure

2 Removing the dirt container is easy, simply slide the securing catch to the left and this lowers the support base

3 This thin foam pad fits between the support base and the container to create a snug fit between the components and reduce noise

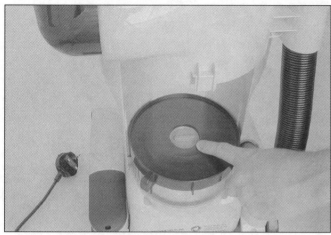

4 Removing the thin foam pad revealed a securing latch at the centre of the support base

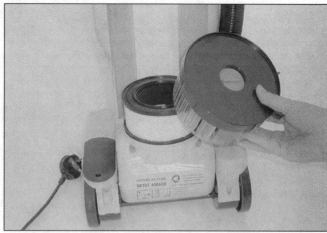

5 Turning the latch anticlockwise allows the support base and filter cover to be removed in one piece. A locating notch on the body of the cleaner and a corresponding recess in the cover are there to ensure it is refitted correctly. Note: The latch is not a screw thread it only needs to be turned slightly to unlock it

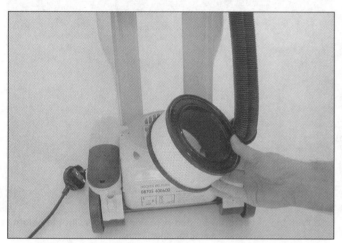

6 The large circular filter can now simply be lifted free

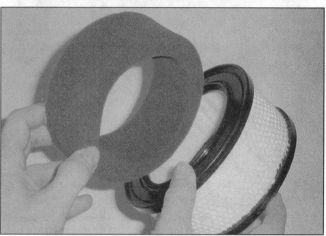

7 The large filter has a removable foam inner and both parts are washable. The manufacturer states that unless damaged they never need replacing. Note: When the filters have been washed (as per the manufacturers instructions) they must be allowed to fully dry before they are refitted

8 At the top of the dirt container compartment are two seals and a coarse plastic filter for trapping larger particles

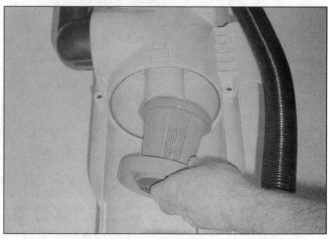

9 The coarse filter is a tolerance (push on pull off) fit. Note: Twisting the unit slightly helps removal

10 The top lefthand side of the main body has a removable top (simple pull off - push fit)

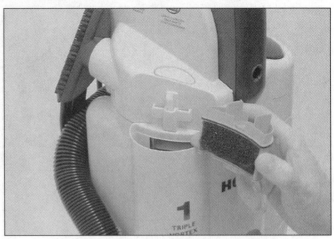

11 Beneath the cover is a slide-in motor exhaust filter

12 To gain access to the brush, drive belt and motor you need to remove the cleaning head top cover. Start by removing the two screws at the rear

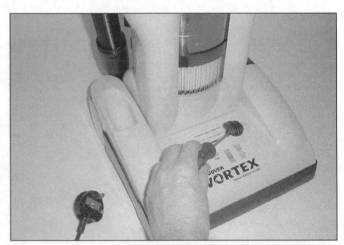

13 With the aid of a flat-bladed screwdriver gently lift the height selector knob free.

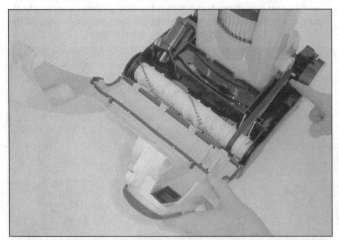

14 With the rear screws removed the top cover can be pivoted forward and lifted free from position. The brushroll, belt and drive pulley are then accessible. Note: re-fit by locating the front lugs of the cover into the furniture guard rubber moulding and then lowering the cover back into position

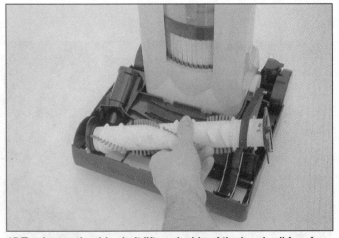

15 To change the drive belt lift each side of the brushroll free from their retaining slots. Note: When refitting the brushroll locate the belt on the motor drive pulley first and then stretch the belt and brushroll into position

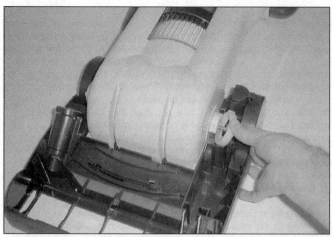

16 To gain access to the motor you first need to separate the cleaning head from the main body of the cleaner. Remove the main body by easing the white plasic support bearing on either side of the main body sideways (they do not need to be removed). Note: the bearings can be left in this position ready for reassembly

17 The body of the cleaner containing the motor can be lifted clear of the head leaving the white plastic support bearings in place

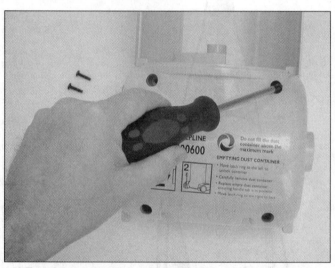

18 To gain access to the motor remove the four screws holding the two halves of the sealed motor casing together

19 The appliance is powered by a series wound through flow motor with integral TOC (see Motors chapter for details) and is housed in a semi-sealed container. Once the casing is opened the motor can be lifted out of position for inspection, repair or replacement. When running the motor draws air in through the cleaning head via hose, cyclone system and filtration medium. The now clean air goes on to cool the motor and is then vented via the exhaust filter

Re-assembly was a reversal of the stripdown procedure.

In accordance with normal practice, a double check of all parts was made prior to re-assembly, ensuring correct positoning of all parts and wiring prior to functional testing on an RCD-protected circuit. If in doubt as to the electrical safety of the product have the appliance PAT tested by a competent person, refer to Chapter 2.

Bagless filtration systems

This method of extracting the dirt particles from the air flow is a relatively new introduction to domestic vacuum cleaners and is used in both upright and cylinder models. However, large industrial versions of this type of extraction process have been around for quite sometime and are used to 'clean' a wide range of both fluids and gases. The real innovation occurred when the large industrial process was made small enough to fit into a domestic cleaning appliance. This allowed a range of vacuum cleaners designed around this 'new' system to operate without the use of the disposable paper bag. Removing the disposable bag from the air flow in this way greatly improves the overall efficiency and reduces the need to continually purchase and fit replacement bags. There are various names for this 'new' process, the most popular ones being cyclone and vortex. No matter what the name they all work by making the airflow through the cleaner rotate at high speed in a specially designed chamber. The faster the column of air can be made to rotate the greater are the centrifical 'G' forces upon the dirt particles. It is this centrifical 'G' force that separates the dust and dirt from the airflow with the resulting residue collecting in a removable container/chamber ready for disposal. All vacuum cleaners work by creating a fast moving airflow that picks up and carries with it the dirt and dust particles. Although the correct combination of disposable bags and filters work well, their efficiency drops as the pores within them block and reduces the airflow through the system. The cyclone/vortex systems do not suffer from this continual reduction in airflow as it remains constant. However, a vacuum cleaner cyclone/vortex system cannot work alone and fixed filtration cartridges are placed at the exhaust point of the airflow from the product. Exhaust filtration ensures that the air that is returned to the room is free from even the smallest dust particles. Although a single cyclone/vortex unit works very well, two or three sequential cyclone chambers designed to work in series can now be found. Such systems have the ability to recycle a percentage of the air back through the last two chambers, effectively cleaning the already cleaned airflow. It is possible for the best filtration systems to return air back into the room that is cleaner than it was when it entered the cleaner! See the following sections on filtration. Although an exhaust filter is used the air reaching it from an efficient cyclone/vortex system is already very clean, which means that the filters can last quite sometime. Some models require renewal of the exhaust filter at around yearly intervals. Others have cleanable filters and some systems employing double or triple cyclone/vortex chambers state that they will never need filter renewal! Check your appliance manufacturers instruction booklet for details. The construction of the cyclone/vortex chamber means that there is little in the way of routine maintenance required. However, for the system to work at its best there must be no air leaks. Ensure the removable dirt container is fitted correctly and ensure that all the seals are in good order. Renew any that show signs of damage or wear.

Ultra fine filtration

The advent of double-wall bags has greatly improved the filtration standards of disposable bags by reducing the recirculation of very fine dust that single-wall bags allow through. The use of double-wall bags creates a micro-filtration effect, which is both beneficial to the appliance and the household environment in general. To keep such a system operating efficiently, change disposable bags and secondary filters regularly.

Sub Micron filtration

In recent years a new means of ultra fine filtration has been utilised and is based on electrostatically charged filter materials, which are capable of filtration down to sub micron levels with minimal resistance to the airflow. This filter medium is often referred to as HEPA filtration from the company that pioneered this technology. The use of this type of filter medium does not mean that mechanical filtration (disposable bag or cyclone/vortex systems) are not required – on the contrary in most instances it is a combination of mechanical and electrostatic filtration that is used in modern machines.

The accompanying theoretical diagram shows six methods of filtration combined in one appliance, all of which are used to remove dirt from the airflow and prevent unseen (micro) dust particles being vented from the appliance. The process is as follows.
1 The airflow ducting and hoses are fully sealed to prevent leakage. **Note:** *Ensure these seals are in good order to maintain both cleaning efficiency and to prevent escape of dust particles.*
2 This is the inner layer of a two-layer paper disposable bag. This first level of filtration filters out the bulk of the debris and particles down to about 100 microns.
3 This is the outer layer of the disposable bag and filters particles down to around 1 micron. *1 micron is 1/25000th of an inch.

4 This particular example is a through flow system (see over page for details) and therefore requires a pre-motor filter. This serves two purposes. **A.** to further filter the airflow and **B.** to protect the motor from sucking dirt should the bag split or be incorrectly fitted which would allow dirt to bypass the first two stages.
5 This is a carbon filter used primarily to help remove odours from the airflow.
6 This is the last filter in this system before the air is returned into the room. In this example this final filter is of the electrostatically charged type, often referred to as an 'S' class filter and can filter down to the sub micro level which is good news for allergy sufferers (as low as .05 of a micron). Filters are used in all vacuum cleaners – ensure that they are checked regularly and renewed with the correct replacement, which matches the original manufacturers specifications.
Note: *Watch out for poor quality alternatives.*

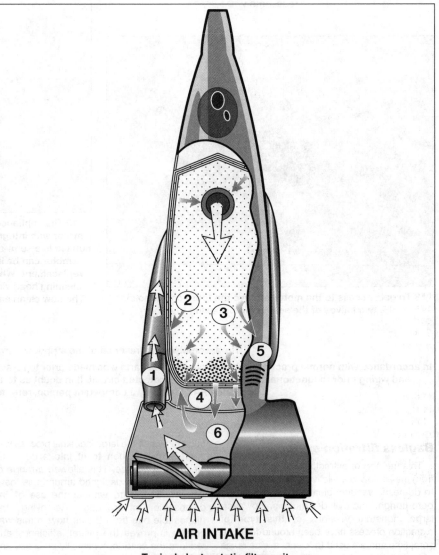

AIR INTAKE

Typical electrostatic filter unit

Chapter 31
Rechargeable batteries Ni-cad, NiMH and Li-Ion

Many appliances normally powered by a mains electrical supply can now be obtained in cordless form. This means they are independent of the mains supply and powered by batteries housed within the unit. Greater flexibility of use has been given to a wide variety of equipment ranging from electric shavers to electric drills and hedge cutters. Small items, such as electric razors, may be powered by ordinary dry cell batteries because their power consumption is low and operational time relatively short. However, once dry cell batteries are run down, they need to be replaced. On larger appliances which are used for longer periods and for carrying out much more strenuous work, the need to renew batteries at short intervals would not only be expensive but extremely wasteful in terms of materials used in their production. Many appliances now overcome this problem by using rechargeable batteries. There are currently three popular types of rechargeable battery, Nicad (Nickel Cadmium), NiMH (Nickel Metal Hydride) and Li-Ion (Lithium-Ion). They can all be found in one of two versions:

1 Permanently fixed batteries. These are located within the main body of the appliance or as a detachable pack. Charging is by a special charger unit designed purely for a particular appliance.

2 Removable batteries. These resemble dry cell batteries but the main difference is that they are rechargeable. A specially designed charger unit is required for these types of cells. As the size of the batteries match those of dry cells, they can be used in place of them in most instances. On some items such as clocks, door bells, etc., it is unwise to use rechargeable batteries. If in any doubt, consult the manufacturer of the item, but as a rule of thumb, items where a dry cell battery would last more than six weeks do not suit rechargeable batteries.

The cost of rechargeable batteries is much higher than the equivalent dry cell when first purchased, but what has to be taken into account is that between 500 and 1000 (or more) recharges are possible if care is taken in their use. This figure relates to both nicad

and li-ion batteries as NiMH batteries last about a third less at around 350 to 700 recharges.

Another advantage of rechargeable batteries is that as they are used, they provide a near constant voltage with a sharp cut-off when expired, unlike their dry cell counterparts where voltage drops continuously during use.

However, there are a few drawbacks:

1 When they run down, it can take several hours to recharge the batteries before they can be re-used.

2 Potentially harmful chemicals such as cadmium may be used in the batteries' construction and great care must be taken when disposing of used batteries or any equipment that contains batteries. Efforts are at present being made to reduce the amount of these harmful materials and although the lithium and metal hydride batteries are a step forward, all batteries must be handled with care and disposed of correctly.

3 If short circuits occur within the circuit, heat will be generated that could result in fire or possible explosion of the battery or pack. Do not short them out or allow a quick discharge of these batteries. Care must be taken to ensure all connections are secure in order to avoid overheating.

Nicad battery packs are still the most popular choice for manufacturers of cordless power tools. Each cell of a rechargeable battery pack holds 1.2V and therefore 10 cells are used to provide a 12V power pack, 15 cells 18V etc. The capacity of battery packs is quoted as amps/hour often abbreviated to Ahr. The best nicad packs offer around a 2Ahr maximum. However, the new NiMH packs offer higher Ahr ratings without the use of the toxic cadmium used in the nicad packs. In the coming years it is likely that more environmentally friendly NiMH batteries will be improved and become more widely used in the larger equipment. The requirement to store more power for longer periods in ever-smaller packs is set to continue for the foreseeable future and will result in an even wider range of battery technology being developed.

Note: *You should not underestimate the potential for environmental damage that such small items can cause. Please ensure that any nicad batteries, packs or equipment with fixed batteries are disposed of correctly and safely. Contact your local council/waste disposal authority for the nearest facility for recycling and safe disposal.*

Do's and Don'ts

Use only the charger unit supplied with the appliance and no other as it will have been matched to the capacity of the batteries within the appliance. For removable batteries, use an approved charger unit and follow the instructions. When charging nickel cadmium batteries, ensure this is carried out in a dry, well-ventilated room. Do not attempt to recharge ordinary dry cells with a charger unit, since to do so would be extremely dangerous.

Do not use a car battery charger. These are for use only with lead acid batteries and totally unsuitable for ni-cads.

Do not mix battery types.

Do not leave them on charge for longer than required. See the instructions that accompany your charger and the information on 'memory' problems later in this chapter.

Do not allow direct short circuit.

Do not incinerate batteries or appliances containing them.

Do not under any circumstances attempt to gain access to a li-ion battery pack, as they are the most volatile of all batteries.

Make sure that when disposing of worn out or damaged cells, this is done correctly and safely and away from children, pets and water.

When renewing fixed Nicad batteries, make sure the correct replacement is obtained and renew all the batteries, not just the suspect one. If soldered into position, fix only to the tags – do not solder to the battery casing as this will cause internal damage and may block safety vents. Batteries have three classifications: CF – contact free; HH – head contacts only; and HB – contacts made at head and base. Ensure that all connections and positions of both batteries and wiring are as original.

Double AA rechargeable NiMH batteries and plug in charger unit

Nicad batteries/packs can handle high electrical loads and are therefore ideal for applications such as cordless power tools

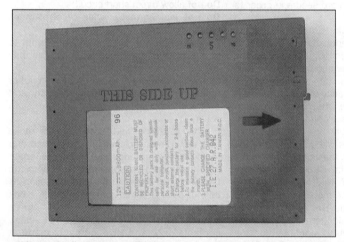

Although NiMH batteries/packs have a shorter life cycle they do have a greater capacity (around 30%). They are ideal for portable electronic equipment such as CD players, tape recorders etc.

14.4V power tool power pack and charger unit

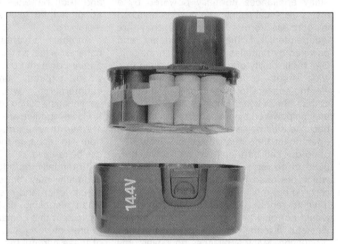

Internal view of power tool power pack showing 12 individual 1.2V nicad cells connected in series to provide a total of 14.4V. Note the black plastic cylinders to the left, they are spacers where additional batteries would be placed to produce a higher voltage pack for other models in the range

Li-Ion batteries/packs are equal to if not better than nicad and NiMH batteries. They are also much lighter and have greater capacity (twice as much or more). All this and half the weight as well. The down side is that they are much more expensive (about twice the price) and are therefore normally only found in specialist applications such as laptop computers and other equipment where power and weight are more important than cost

Battery memory

It has been reported that rechargeable nicad batteries can form a memory. That is to say, if recharged before being completely exhausted, a false discharge level is created and the battery will only discharge down to that point when used, thus reducing the operation time of the appliance. Manufacturers' tests have been unable to duplicate this effect and the manufacturers are, therefore, doubtful about the phenomenon. However, many that use rechargeable equipment believes it does occur and that once created it cannot be removed. In most instances the problem lies not in a mysterious 'memory phenomenon' but with poor battery care combined with incorrect charging techniques. The technical term for the 'memory effect' is voltage depression. There are two main causes for this:

1 Removing the battery or pack from the charger before it has fully charged and using it to power the equipment.

2 Leaving the battery, pack or equipment on charge after it has reached full charge.

Both actions result in reducing the effectiveness and life span of the battery or pack. This is caused not by a mysterious 'memory' developing but to the growth of crystals within chemicals of the cells of the battery due in part 1 but even more so to part 2. In severe cases the crystals may grow large enough to puncture the internal membrane of the cell and render it useless.

To avoid the possibility of such reduction in battery life it would be wise only to recharge from the run down state (but not fully run down) thus avoiding the chance of memory build-up. Also do not leave the batteries, pack or equipment on charge for longer than is required to provide a full charge.

Note: *Some equipment may be designed to provide a long term 'trickle' charge to the equipment battery pack or have an auto shut off system. Check with the manufacturers instructions to see if the appliance has this feature. If not follow the recommendations mentioned in this chapter to avoid problems.*

As mentioned earlier, do not discharge the batteries or pack quickly, as this is dangerous and can cause damage. Some packs contain internal fuses as protection and they are not replaceable, so a new pack would be required. Do not open sealed battery packs. To discharge safely, run the equipment until most of the remaining charge is spent, whereupon a full charge cycle can be carried out, thus avoiding any possibility of memory build-up.

Note: *The charging process will inevitably result in the batteries/pack getting warm (50°–60°C). However, the batteries/pack should not get 'very hot'. If they do it would indicate that they have been left on charge too long. Excessive heat damages the cells and assists in crystal growth within the chemicals of the battery.*

Chapter 32
DIY power tools

There is an ever-increasing range of labour-saving equipment available for use in the home, capable of tackling the wide variety of work that is now taken on by the homeowner. Tools that were once used in workshops and factories are now quite commonplace around the home. Electric drills, routers, grinders, saws, planes, etc. are now produced to meet the demand from the rapidly increasing army of DIY enthusiasts. The diversity and range available is vast. They are all based on an electric motor taking the place of manual effort. Each has a powerful motor for direct drive or reduction via a gearbox or electronic control and can be found in mains or battery powered versions in most instances.

Many of the faults encountered with power tools of this nature are common to all appliances that use electric motors. At the heart of these tools there is a brush motor (see *Electric Motors*) and when mains powered, a supply cable is also present. These are the two areas where most faults occur, misuse and neglect accounting for a large proportion of them. It must be stressed that these types of appliances are extremely powerful, and therefore great care must be taken when using them. Each piece of equipment has a limit to its capabilities, so a sound understanding of its function and operation will be of enormous benefit to the user and for the equipment itself.

Faults on this type of equipment relate closely to those already covered in previous sections, eg poor commutation, brush wear, motor bearing wear, flex faults, etc., therefore references to other sections will be made to avoid undue repetition in this chapter. The most relevant sections will be *A General Safety Guide, Basics, Cables and Cable Faults, Electric Motors* and *Electrical Circuit Testing*. A thorough understanding of all sections will help in tracing many faults because individual and specific faults cannot all be covered due to the vast range of tools available. Photo sequences are used to highlight various problems that might be encountered.

The aim of this section of the book is not just to help in the repair of faulty equipment, but to encourage regular maintenance, avoiding unnecessary faults occurring. It is also designed to promote the safe use of both electricity and equipment in the hope that injury caused by ignorance will be avoided. To this end a guide to safety follows which should be read in conjunction with the instructions that accompany the equipment when bought. Remember, if borrowing or lending equipment, make sure that you understand the correct use and limitations of the product and that you have the correct safety wear. When lending, ensure the borrower understands fully how to use the equipment safely.

Jigsaw

Plane

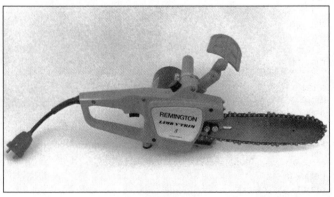

Chain saw

Personal safety

The use of an RCD is highly recommended when using mains powered tools because it affords an extra degree of electrical protection. For outdoor work it is a MUST. Problems with water, cable damage, etc., can happen at any time so it is wise to be prepared. Common sense is, of course, your best protection. Stop, think and plan the work in hand – no amount of electronic gadgetry can take the place of sound common sense. **Before every use always inspect the mains cable, electrical connectors, extension lead and the appliances casing for damage and wear and tear. It is also good practice to do this when you have finished using it. Do not** use any mains powered tools outdoors unless it is in good condition and complete.

Eye protection is often ignored. Around one-third of eye injuries to adults are caused by using equipment without eye protection. The price of protection is cheap, eyesight is priceless. All-round goggles should be worn especially when using drills, grinders, routers, etc.

There is also hidden danger associated with power tools that cut, drill, grind and saw etc. – dust. The larger particles created by your work activities are often all too obvious, it is the fine particles of less than 10 microns that pass easily through our in-built filter system, the nose, and on into the lungs and can present problems. Whenever the work activity creates dust **always** wear a mask suitable for the work in hand. Many single layered masks can only trap particles larger than 10 microns and therefore allow the fine but still harmful dust through. Wood, chipboard (especially MDF), brick, concrete or any other material can all pose a fine dust health hazard. Ensure you wear a mask with a multi-layered construction capable of filtering out the large and fine particles. Also ensure that it is adjusted to fit correctly. In addition to the correct masks and filters, whenever possible keep the work place well ventilated.

Do not use mains-powered equipment in damp or wet conditions, even with an RCD in use.

It is advisable to fit a resilient plug to all mains powered portable equipment.

Do not change drill bits, cutters or attachments without first isolating (unplugging) the appliance; do not rely on the on/off switch only. The changing of drill bits, cutters and attachments on equipment such as drills, routers, and saws often require a fixing tool (Allen key, chuck key, spanner, etc.). **Always** ensure that these are removed before the equipment is used. **Always double check.** Remember, when tightening the 'chuck' of a drill with a chuck key, do so at all three positions and not just one.

Basic safety equipment includes goggles, mask and ear protectors or plugs

Do not use drills or attachments that are too large or not suited to the drill. Each drill has a maximum bit (shaft) size which should not be exceeded. If a speed control is available, use it correctly. The smaller the drill, the faster the speed can be, larger drill bits require slower speeds. The hammer action if fitted should be used only when drilling masonry.

Hold the drill securely and do not overstress it. Remember, if a drill or attachment jams, the body of the drill will try to rotate and if it is not held securely, the torque produced could cause injury. If the drill has an additional grip handle (often removable) then use it.

Do not cover the air vents on the body of the appliance with hands or other items and try to prevent excess dust or dirt entering them. With many jobs, dust will be produced so the wearing of a mask with a suitable filter would provide suitable protection. Many attachments allow for vacuum dust extraction and the use of such equipment is not only healthier for the user but considerably cuts down on the mess.

Do not leave equipment plugged in and unattended even if switched off. Always store equipment safely and tidily when not in use. Never carry any appliance by its mains lead as this will cause excessive wear and damage. When the job in hand is finished, allow the motor and attachments to come to rest before putting the appliance down otherwise damage to property or personal injury could result.

Ensure that safety covers and guards are working correctly. Appliances with cracked cases or missing parts should not be used until repaired. Make sure that any items to be drilled, cut or ground, etc. are securely anchored. Keep your area free from clutter and keep children and pets at a safe distance.

If a fault or problem does occur, switch off immediately and unplug the appliance.

Care must be exercised in garages and workshops where fuel vapour may collect. The use of power tools in these areas can ignite the mixture by the normal spark/arcing of the motor brushes. Ventilate these areas before power tool use and do not use in places where gases and vapours may be present.

An RCD is essential

Additional safety for power saws

There are several types of power saws, all requiring great care and vigilance when in use. Two styles in particular call for extreme caution when used because they are subject to an undesirable characteristic known as kickback. As the term implies, kickback occurs when an obstacle or poorly secured work piece jams the saw – usually momentarily. The inertia can easily pull the equipment free from the hands even when held securely. The sort of injury that can result if kickback is uncontrolled can be very dangerous so take every precaution to prevent it happening.

Both circular and chain saws are prone to kickback if used incorrectly. Read the instruction manual thoroughly before using this kind of equipment. It is also essential that protective clothing be worn.

Circular saws - hand-held

Ensure that all safety guards are in good order and functioning correctly. The correct blade for the job in hand should be fitted and checked for a secure fit and that it runs true (is not buckled) with no teeth missing from it. The item to be cut should be firmly clamped to prevent any movement. Take a firm grip of the appliance and adopt a solid, well-balanced posture, making sure there are no obstacles to trip over. Ensure that cables or any other items are well clear of the blade before switching on. After switching on, allow the blade to reach full speed before starting the cut. Do not force the cut or you will move off line and this is how kickback can happen. Take it slowly and concentrate. When the cut is finished, switch off and allow the blade to stop before removing it from the work piece or putting down the appliance. Remember to remove the plug between use and keep other people at a safe distance.

Chain saws

The possibility of receiving a kickback from a chain saw is greater than that from a circular saw, therefore every precaution should be taken to avoid it. Chain saws are not suitable for general woodwork. Their main function is felling trees and cutting branches into logs. As this is obviously outdoor work, all the previously mentioned safety rules should be followed along with a few extra ones. Protection should include goggles, gloves, ear defenders and stout footwear. To control kickback, a firm grip with both hands at all times is essential. As with the circular saw, the work piece must be held securely and if lopping branches from trees, do not make cuts on underside of branches as they will close as the cut is made and trap the saw resulting in kick-back or damage to the equipment. A well-balanced stance on firm ground must be taken before cutting commences, and on no account should the saw be used above waist height. Check the on/off switch is working correctly and the cable is safe. Allow the saw to reach full speed before starting the cut. Keep other people and pets at a safe distance, although it

is wise to have someone at hand in case something goes wrong. When the cut is finished let the saw stop completely before putting it down and don't forget to unplug it between use.

One type of saw that isn't prone to kickback is the reciprocating saw. This saw produces a double action sawing movement via a gearbox. An action similar to hand sawing is generated but without the manual effort. It is much easier and safer to use though safety precautions must be taken to secure the work piece. The saw must be held firmly and again, cables and other items should be clear of the cutting area. Do not use a reciprocating saw above shoulder height. Obtain a safe working position and firm stance before using and adjust your position according to the work which is to be carried out. The reciprocating saw is a much more adaptable saw which has provision for attaching different types of blades for cutting wood, thermal building blocks, pipe work, plastics and laminates, etc.

Before using any appliance check the mains lead along its whole length for any damage and verify that the on/off switch works correctly and is not sticking. Remember also that tidy work areas are safer work areas. Do not use power tools in cluttered conditions.

Power tool motor

The motors that are used in power tools are very similar to those used in vacuum cleaners

and mixers. Appliances with electronic variable-speed control functions also operate in the same way. One exception is the gearbox-type speed control (usually with only two available speeds). These act in a purely mechanical way by changing the drive gearing, similar to a car gearbox.

The most common cause of motor failure is misuse of the equipment as listed below:
1 Making the equipment (drill, router, jigsaw etc.) work too hard for too long.
2 Applying too much pressure when cutting or drilling.
3 Not allowing the drill or cutter(s) to work at their correct pace/speed.
4 Using drill bits, cutters or blades that are simply too large for that particular piece of equipment.
5 Blocking of air vents during use.
6 Not cleaning the equipment after use.

All of the above faults result in varying degrees of motor overload and ultimately overheating. This inevitably leads to failure of the field, armature, bearings or drive gearing. An interesting point to note is that with care and attention they are all avoidable. Although the following pages relate to specific problems and repairs, prevention is always better (also safer and cheaper) than cure.

A list of other typical fault symptoms follows and should be used in conjunction with the photo sequences in this chapter and motor information in *Electric Motors, Vacuum Cleaners* and *Mixers* sections.

Fault finding- power tools

1. Symptom: Won't work at all

Possible cause	Action
a. Faulty plug or socket	See *Plugs and Sockets*
b. Fault in flex	See *Cables and Cable Faults* and *Electrical Circuit Testing* Renew as required
c. Internal wiring open circuit	Check continuity. See *Electrical Circuit Testing*. This also applies to charging unit on battery versions

Note: *Many charging units are sealed and, as such, non-repairable. Check that all other tests prove OK and renew if suspect*

d. Motor brush worn/sticking	See *Photo sequence, Electric Motors* and *Electrical Circuit Testing*
e. Faulty on/off switch	See *Electrical Circuit Testing*
f. Open circuit TOC or overheat protective device in motor (if fitted)	Check for continuity. See *Temperature control and Thermostats* and *Electrical Circuit Testing*
g. Fault in electronic speed control unit (if applicable)	Double-check all other items thoroughly. If found to be OK, obtain replacement control and retest
h. Low charge	Recharge and retest

2. Symptom: Motor runs slowly or is sluggish

a. Carbon brushes worn or sticking in slides	Check length of brushes and for free movement within holders. Mark brush position prior to removal to ensure they are refitted the same way around. Renew both springs and brushes if worn. Check commutator for wear or damage. See *Photo sequence*.
b. Faulty commutator or armature windings	Inspect commutator for signs of excessive wear, overheating, loose segments, short circuited windings or catching on field coil when rotated. See Photo sequence. If faulty, renew armature and brushes.

Note: *Not all makes allow for individual part replacement. In some instances a complete motor only is obtainable*

2. Symptom: Motor runs slowly or is sluggish (CONTINUED)

c. Worn armature bearings

Check armature for sideways movement. This movement allows the armature to be pulled onto the field coil when motor runs. See *Photo sequence*

d. Loose or defective field coil catching on armature

Check field coil securing screws or clips. Reposition and retighten if possible

e. Gearbox or chuck drive bearing faults

Inspect gearbox and drive for bearing wear. Renew parts or lubricate as required

f. Open circuit TOC or overheat protective device in motor (if fitted)

Check for continuity. See *Temperature Control* and *Thermostats and Electrical Circuit Testing*

g. Insufficient charge on nicad batteries or ageing batteries (battery versions only)

Recharge for correct length of time. Check Symptom 1C relating to adaptor. If these and all other checks prove OK, renew **all** batteries with correct rechargeable replacements

3. Symptom: Excessive noise

a. Dirt or debris on motor or cooling fan

Strip and clean motor and inner casing

b. Motor bearings worn

Check for worn armature shaft/loose bearing. Check sideways movement and free running of bearing

c. Gearbox wear/lubrication

Check gear teeth and bearings. Lubricate as required

d. Main driveshaft bearing

Check for worn shaft or loose bearing. Renew as required

4. Symptom: Body gets excessively hot

a. Vent holes blocked or covered during use

Check correct positioning of hands during use. If OK, check vents internally. Clean as required

b. Battery short-circuited (battery versions)

If this happens, correct short circuits and renew batteries as they will have been damaged

c. Motor short-circuited overheated

Check for overheated or short-circuited coil or armature

5. Symptom: Intermittent operation

a. Poor internal connection to battery, motor or switch

Check continuity and all joints and wiring

b. Check mains lead for wear or intermittent open circuit

See *Cables and Cable Faults* and *Electrical Circuit Testing*

c. Sticking motor brush

Remove, clean or renew as required. See *Photo sequence*

All of the above checks and tests are to be carried out with the appliances isolated – switch OFF and plug OUT, unless otherwise stated as in the case of functional testing to verify correct or incorrect operation. When carrying out a functional test, make sure all cables and wiring have been fitted back into their correct positions. Any parts renewed must be identical to the original specification. Quote model and serial numbers when obtaining spare parts.

The hot air gun is similar in operation to a hairdryer although the heat output is much higher. Keep all such equipment away from children and only use them for the specific tasks they are designed for. *Note: If old lead-based paints are to be removed it is essential to wear a protective mask to avoid breathing the fumes and dust. This also applies to others in the vicinity. If in doubt it may be better to use solvent-based paint removers to prevent the possibility of inhaling lead-laden fumes or dust*

STRIPDOWN OF HEATGUN

This heat gun had fault symptom 1. The fuse in the plug was checked and found to be OK. The following photo sequence details the next steps in the fault finding process

1 Ensure the appliance is isolated

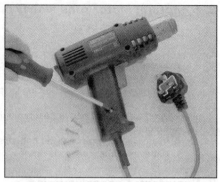

2 Remove the casing securing screws

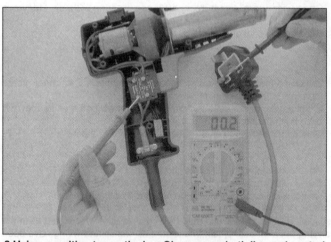

3 Using a multimeter on the low Ohms range both live and neutral connections from the plug pins to the double pole trigger switch were tested for continuity. Both tests indicated that the cable and connections up to the switch were OK

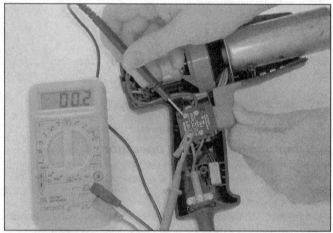

4 The trigger operates a double pole on/off switch. The neutral was tested for correct switching in both positions. It should be closed circuit (low Ohms reading) when pressed (as shown) and open circuit when released

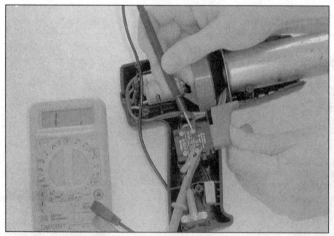

5 The test in sequence 4 was repeated on the live side of the double pole switch. This indicated that the switch was open circuit in both positions (no Ohms reading/continuity could be obtained when the trigger was pressed)

6 A replacement switch was fitted and the appliance was cleaned prior to re-assembly

Note: Re-assembly is a reversal of the stripdown procedure ensuring all parts are refitted correctly. It is normal practice to double check all parts prior to refitting the casing, ensuring correct positioning of all parts and wiring prior to functional testing on an RCD-protected circuit. If in doubt as to the electrical safety of the product have the appliance PAT tested by a competent person - refer to Chapter 2

Power tool typical faults

Power Drills

The electric drill is the most popular power tool and most if not all DIY enthusiasts possess one (or more). They are produced in an extremely wide range of mains and battery powered versions. The power for cutting is supplied by a series wound brush motor and is therefore prone to the problems described earlier in this chapter. Reference should also be made to other relevant sections of the book especially Chapters 7, 8, 9 and 11. The ingress of dust into the motor and gear system is a common cause of problems. Ensure that the appliance is thoroughly cleaned after each use. Another potential cause of damage to the motor and gearbox is the use of incorrect drills or attachments. It is essential to use the correct drill to suit material. Make sure you select both the correct type and size of drill for the material. Worn, damaged or blunt drills result in poor cutting performance. This inevitably leads to more pressure being applied by the user, which in turn over heats the motor and drive gear. Selecting the correct drill size and type not only helps protect the motor and drive gear but also results in a better finish with quicker results. Many attachments can be purchased for power drills. However, due to the multitude of speed and power variations now available not all power drills are capable of accepting them, check the appliance or the attachments manual for details as to the suitability.

Power Grinder

Power grinders are becoming more popular with DIY enthusiasts (and DIY car mechanics). They are available in mains and battery powered versions. The power for cutting is once again supplied by a series wound brush motor and is therefore prone to the problems described earlier in this chapter. Reference should also be made to other relevant sections of the book especially Chapters 7, 8, 9 and 11. Although protected the ingress of dust into the motor and gear system can be the cause of problems. Ensure the appliance is thoroughly cleaned after each use. Another potential cause of damage to the motor and gearbox is the use of incorrect cutting discs or attachments. It is essential to use the correct disc to suit material. Ensure you select both the correct type and size of disc for the material. Incorrect, worn or damaged discs result in poor cutting performance and vibration. Such faults have serious safety implications DO NOT USE incorrect damaged discs, refer to your user manual to help select the correct disc size and type for your equipment and material. Failure to select and use the correct disc is unsafe and will eventually lead to more pressure being applied during use, which in turn overheats the motor and drive gear. Selecting the correct disc size and type not only promotes safety it helps protect the motor and drive gear and results in a better finish with quicker results.

Jigsaws

The jigsaw is an extremely versatile power tool and as a result has become very popular with the DIY enthusiast. It can be found in both mains and battery powered versions. The power for cutting is supplied by a series wound brush motor and is therefore prone to the problems described earlier in this chapter. Reference should also be made to other relevant sections of the book especially Chapters 7, 8, 9 and 11. Due to the motors close proximity to the material being cut – ingress of dust into the motor and gear system is a common cause of problems. Ensure the appliance is thoroughly cleaned after each use. Another potential cause of damage to the motor and gearbox is the use of incorrect or worn blades. It is essential to use the correct blade for the type of material being cut. Ensure you select both the correct type and size of blade for the material being worked on. Worn, damaged or blunt blades result in poor cutting performance. This inevitably leads to more pressure being applied by the user which in turn over heats the motor and drive gear. Selecting the correct blade size and type not only helps protect the motor and drive gear it also gives the correct finished edge to the work.

This internal view of a mains powered electric drill shows clearly the large brush gear motor and gearbox drive

Removing five securing screws on this cordless power screwdriver enabled the casing to split. The small but powerful motor, simple gear system and battery packs can easily be seen. The transformer on the far right denotes that a separate charger is not used as it is mounted internally

STRIP DOWN OF NEW STYLE CORDLESS DRILL + CHARGER AND BATTERY PACK

This cordless drill abruptly stopped working after only a short period of use. It had been working well up to the point of failure and the battery had been fully charged before use

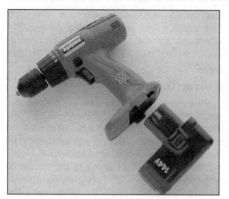

1 Remove the battery pack

2 For 'chuck' removal details refer to the photo sequence *Removing a 'Chuck'*

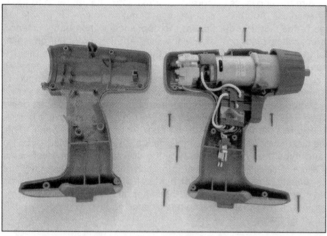

3 Removing eight securing screws allowed the casing to be split

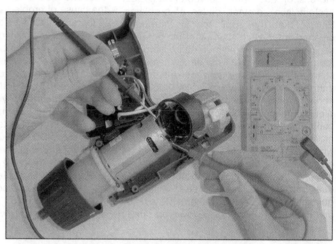

4 It was decided to test the motor for continuity. This was done by placing a probe on each motor terminal and selecting the Ohms range on the test meter. This should have shown a resistance reading (continuity) but unfortunately it did not. Selecting higher Ohms ranges gave the same open circuit result. The cause is probably a sticking carbon brush but unfortunately in this instance the motor is a sealed unit

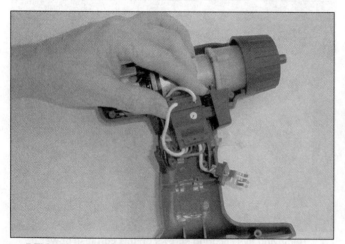

5 This particular drill has a variable speed control and motor reversal mechanism built into the trigger switch unit. If the motor test in sequence 4 had proved to be OK then this would have been the next item to check

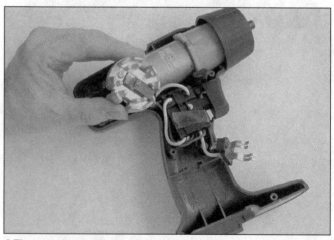

6 The speed control circuit operates in conjunction with this Triac which is connected to the large metal 'heat sink' to keep it cool when in use

Re-assembly was a reversal of the stripdown procedure

This cordless drill has an adjustable torque feature. The torque system works by pressing a series of ball bearings onto a disc with a series of recesses housed within the drive gearbox. The external black selector ring has a series of raised sections, which presses onto the ball bearings by means of a spring-loaded mechanism. Depending on the setting selected, the raised sections exert a degree of pressure on the ball bearings resting on the recessed disc and create drive through to the chuck. The ball and disc drive will 'slip' as the bit and the chuck encounter resistance equal to the torque setting selected by the user. The highest setting effectively locks the disc into a direct drive that will not slip

The following stripdown shows the accessible components of a torque drive

1 Removing the chuck (see photo sequence *Removing a 'Chuck'*) exposed two securing screws

2 With both screws removed the torque selector ring can be carefully removed

3 With the selector ring removed the torque selector mechanism can be carefully eased from its position. This item is made up of several small individual components. Make a note of the position of all the parts prior to removing it. Remove it by gripping the whole of the unit and sliding it free whilst at the same time keeping all the pieces together.

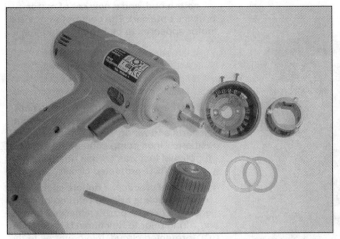

4 Removing the two large slip rings exposed the ball bearings (two in each hole). Note: *These items are not fixed, take care not to dislodge/lose them.*

5 To assist selection and prevent wear the raised sections of the selector ring were cleaned and re-lubricated

Re-assembly was a reversal of the stripdown procedure

MAINS POWERED DRILL PROBLEM

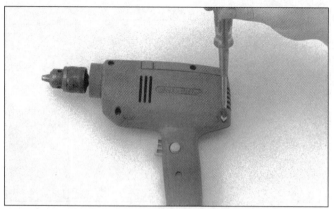

1 This drill had Symptoms 3 and 5. The removal of five screws allowed the casing to be split thus giving good access to all parts. Ensure a note is made of the position of all parts and correct wiring routes

2 A check of the front bearing was made. Whilst firmly holding the unit, grip the chuck and check for excessive movement signifying bearing or shaft wear.

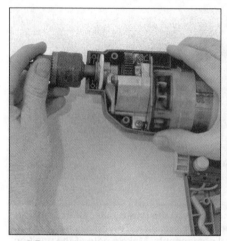

3 By rotating the chuck, a check was made of the gears within the (in this case) open gearbox. Look for excessive wear, damaged teeth and lack of lubrication

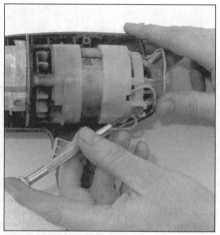

4 The motor brushes were removed for inspection with the aid of a small screwdriver

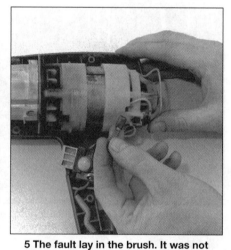

5 The fault lay in the brush. It was not moving freely in the holder thus causing an intermittent fault and poor commutation. The brush slides were cleaned using a cotton bud, and a new set of motor brushes obtained. The commutator of the motor appeared to be in good condition in this instance

6 Before refitting the outer cover, a final double check was made to make certain all parts and wiring were in their original positions. Upon completion of the repair, a functional test was carried out using an RCD-protected circuit

As is normal practice, a double check of all parts was made prior to refitting casing, ensuring correct positioning of all parts and wiring prior to functional testing on an RCD-protected circuit. If in doubt as to the electrical safety of the product, have the appliance PAT tested by a competent person, refer to Chapter 2

REMOVING A 'CHUCK' BOTH KEYED AND KEYLESS

1 Ensure that the drill is unplugged (if battery powered remove the battery pack and turn the chuck to fully open the jaws)

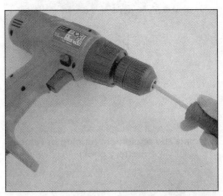

2 On most models with reverse action this will expose a 'set' screw in the base of the jaws recess. The head of the screw will differ from make to make, from normal slotted type (like the one in this sequence) to TORX and Allen headed versions. Note: *Most single direction drills do not use a 'set' screw as the normally right-hand thread will keep the chuck fitting tightened during use*

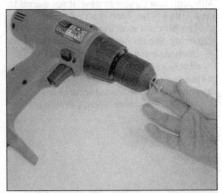

3 The 'set' screw (if fitted) on models with reverse action will normally be left-hand threaded and will therefore need to be turned in a clockwise direction to remove it

4 With the set screw removed or if the chuck does not have a securing (set) screw, insert and securely tighten a large Allen key into the chuck. With a block of wood or mallet (*not* a metal hammer) strike the protruding arm of the Allen key in an anti-clockwise direction to 'shock' the chuck free from the normally right-hand threaded drive shaft. Several sharp blows may be required, as 'Loctite' or a similar fixative may have been used on the threads during manufacture to secure the chuck to the drive shaft. If 'Loctite' or a similar fixative was used, ensure it is renewed when you refit the existing or replacement chuck. Note: *Eye protection must be worn when carrying out the removal and refitting procedure*

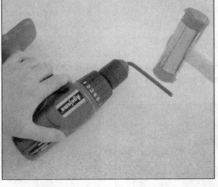

5 When the threads release, continue to turn the chuck anti-clockwise to fully remove it from the shaft

6 Key type chuck can also be removed using these steps. This single direction hammer drill did not have a 'set' screw. However it did have a shaft locking button that could have been pressed to help the removal process

7 Once the threads are freed the chuck was removed by continuing to turn the chuck anticlockwise

Refitting is a simple reversal of the stripdown procedure. In accordance with normal practice, a double check of all parts was made prior to use ensuring correct positioning of all parts prior to functional testing on an RCD-protected circuit. If in doubt as to the electrical safety of the product have the appliance PAT tested by a competent person, refer to Chapter 2

Ensure eye protection is worn when tightening the chuck using the large Allen key method (this time in a clockwise direction). If a set screw was found and removed in step 3 ensure that it is refitted and securely tightened (in an anti-clockwise direction)

STRIP DOWN OF JIGSAW

Although this jigsaw is new, it appeared to be a little noisier than it should have been. The product was investigated out of curiosity. We do not recommend that you dismantle a new product as this will inevitably invalidate your guarantee. Faults within the guarantee period should always be referred to the manufacturer or retailer where the goods were purchased

1 Isolate the equipment (unplug or remove battery pack)

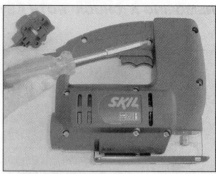

2 Remove the casing securing screws. In this instance they were a combination TORX 20 and slot

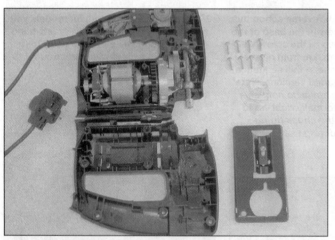

3 With the casing screws and bottom plate removed the casing can be eased apart to expose the internal components

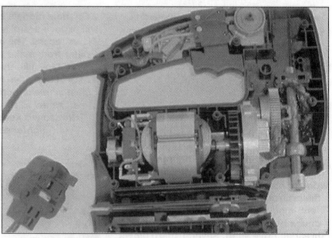

4 It can be seen from this close up that the lubrication (grease) had settled in the casing recess. This left the drive gears dry

5 The grease in the casing recess was re-distributed around the gear system

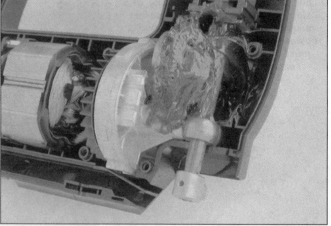

6 Re-distributing the grease should improve both the running and the life of the gear system in this instance. Note: *Settling can also occur in older equipment. Ensure that the lubricant is uniform and do not allow dust or dirt to contaminate the lubricant. Renew old or contaminated lubricant after thoroughly cleaning all the components and the casing*

Re-assembly was a reversal of the stripdown procedure. In accordance with normal practice, a double check of all parts was made prior to refitting casing, ensuring correct positioning of all parts and wiring prior to functional testing on an RCD-protected circuit. If in doubt as to the electrical safety of the product have the appliance PAT tested by a competent person. Refer to Chapter 2.

STRIP DOWN OF GRINDER

This angle grinder had been subjected to a lot of use and very little if any maintenance had been carried out. Finally it simply stopped working mid way through an important job

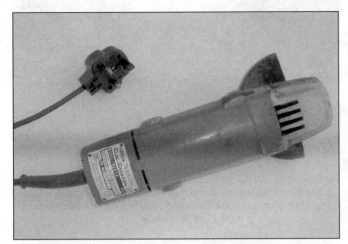

1 Isolate the equipment (or remove battery pack if cordless)

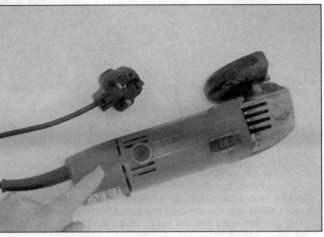

2 The on/off slide to the right of the picture operates a switch at the bottom of the unit via a connecting rod

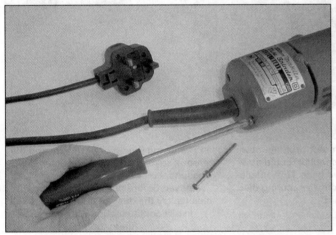

3 To gain access the two base screws were removed

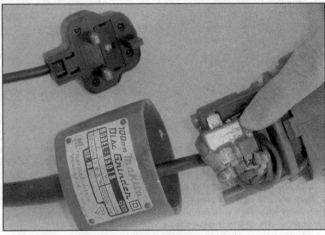

4 Removing the cover allowed access to the mains input terminals and the on/off switch

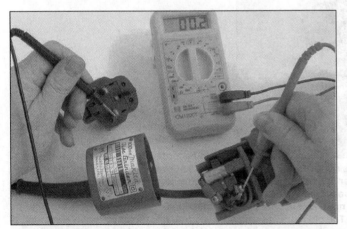

5 The neutral connection from the mains plug to the on/off switch was checked for continuity and found to be OK (low resistance therefore continuity). The live connection was also checked for continuity and found to be OK (low resistance therefore continuity)

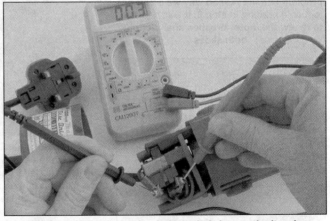

6 The next step was to check the switch for continuity when switched to the on position. Again this test proved to be OK on both live and neutral connections (the switch has double pole operation)

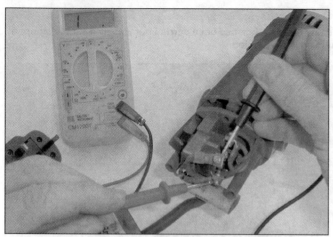

7 Testing from the output side of the double pole on/off switch should give a reading through the motor circuit. In this instance no reading was obtained on any of the Ohms ranges. This indicated that the motor was open circuit

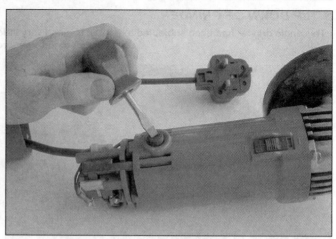

8 The next step was to check the motor brushes. On this model you simply unscrew the insulated securing cap on each side of the appliance

9 With the cap removed, the brush with its return spring can be removed. Take care to note the orientation of the brush as if they are to be refitted it is essential that they are the correct way round and put back into their original side. In this instance one of the brushes was found to be both worn and sticking within its slide preventing power being supplied to the armature. This was the cause of the problem and the reason why we could not obtain a reading in step 8. It was decided to renew the motor brushes after cleaning both slides

10 With the original motor problem now corrected, further inspection could now take place to the drive gear. This entails removing the three screws securing disc guard

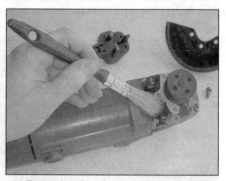

11 Removing the disc guard exposed the gearbox securing screws. However, it was essential that the accumulated dirt be removed before proceeding. Failure to clean away the dust and dirt would result in dirt contaminating the gearbox lubrication

12 When the exterior of the gearbox is clean the four screws can be removed

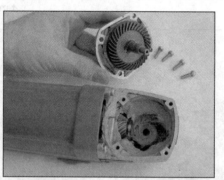

13 With the screws removed the front cover and bevel gear can be removed in one piece. It can be seen that the lubricant has churned and is no longer in contact with the drive gears. The old lubricant was removed, the casing and gears cleaned and new lubricant applied prior to re-assembly

Re-assembly was a reversal of the stripdown procedure

In accordance with normal practice, a double check of all parts was made prior to refitting casing, ensuring correct positioning of all parts and wiring prior to functional testing on an RCD-protected circuit. If in doubt as to the electrical safety of the product have the appliance PAT tested by a competent person, refer to Chapter 2

Chapter 33
Garden power tools

This section of the book deals specifically with gardening equipment but due to the similarities in construction of electrical products it is closely related to the previous section on power tools which, in some areas of operation, overlap (some power tools having attachments for garden work). The use of electrically powered machinery will obviously require the highest degree of safety observance as highlighted throughout this book. In this and many other aspects, DIY power tools and garden power tools are alike.

To avoid undue repetition, the preceding section on DIY power tools should be read in conjunction with this section and applied as necessary. Reference to other sections is also essential to obtain a better understanding of the equipment before use, maintenance or repair. The relevant sections are: *A General Safety Guide, Basics, Cables and Cable Faults, Electric Motors, Vacuum Cleaners, Power Tools* and *Electrical Circuit Testing*. As in the main power tool section, a brush gear motor is used to power the equipment whether it is mower, trimmer or weeder, etc.

Both mains and battery (rechargeable) versions are available, again similar to DIY power tools. The similarity with vacuum cleaner motors was noted in the previous section and this also applies to the garden equipment as can be seen from the photo sequence of the hover mower and garden vacuum. The motors have more than a passing resemblance to the cylinder cleaner and dirty fan motors featured in the *Motors and Vacuum Cleaner* Chapters. Due to the many similarities, the need for detailed explanations of motor operation are deemed unnecessary although photographs and details of common faults and maintenance requirements are given. The latter are most important for items used outdoors in harsh conditions and often stored for long periods

between uses. Remember that prevention is better than cure and cleaning and sensible storage will help reduce the possibility of serious faults. If a fault should occur during use, switch off the equipment immediately and remove the plug from the mains supply. If an extension lead is being used ensure that it is unplugged from the mains supply first. **DO NOT** attempt to inspect the equipment until it is completely isolated.

When purchasing equipment, make sure that it is suitable for the task. Overtaxing an item that is not suited for the job in hand causes all sorts of problems and will often lead to personal injury. Remember that choosing the right equipment is important. Also, repair and maintenance cannot make equipment work satisfactorily if the conditions are totally unsuitable, so seek the advice of experts before buying.

Read the instruction book thoroughly and make sure you fully understand the capabilities and restrictions of your product (if possible before buying and certainly before use).

When cleaning, inspecting or repairing equipment, always make sure that it is first isolated – switch OFF and plug OUT

Safety for garden power tools

Before every use always inspect the mains cable, electrical connectors, extension lead and the appliance casing for damage and wear and tear. It is also good practice to do this when you have finished using it.

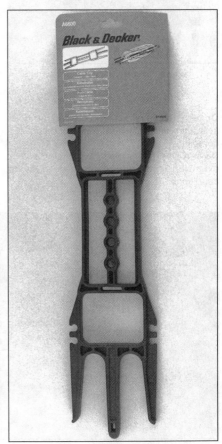

Store cables neatly to prevent problems

Use the correct extension lead and connector

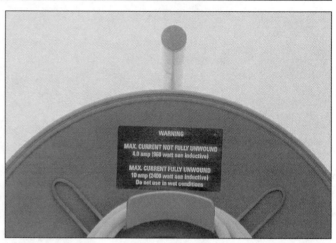

As this label states great care must be taken when using coiled extension cables

Keep air vents clear of debris

Ensure the item is isolated and clean the equipment after each use. Do not store equipment unless it is clean

Check the area to be mown for debris (stones, twigs, toys, etc.) as they may not only damage the mower but may cause personal injury.

Do not lift or move a mower of any description if the blades or cylinder is still rotating. Always switch off and unplug first.

With hedge trimmers, do not tackle branches that are too thick for your particular cutting head. Always make sure the cable is safely positioned before commencing cutting. Drape the flex over your shoulder and down your back but remember to allow enough flex so that movement is not impeded.

Always allow the motor to reach full speed before starting to cut and do not over-reach.

Remember that safety applies not only to you but also to others. Keep this under consideration at all times. Do not be distracted when using equipment, but be aware of any possible danger areas (pavements, borders, clotheslines, etc.) and take measures to avoid them.

Do not use any mains powered outdoor appliance unless it is in good condition and complete.

Do not use mains powered equipment or extension leads in wet grass or in damp conditions.

Always wear sturdy footwear when using a lawn mower, and wear goggles and gloves when using a hedge trimmer or nylon strimmer.

Take extra care when mowing on uneven terrain. Never mow up steep slopes and do not pull hover mowers towards you.

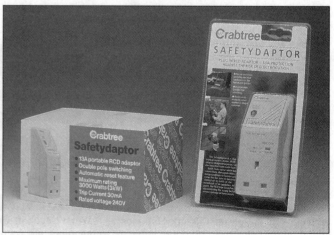

Always use equipment on an RCD-protected circuit or an RCD adaptor.

This cylinder mower switch unit has an overload switch (TOC) that requires manual resetting should it trip

The positioning of the switch can vary with different models. Not all electric mowers are fitted with an overload protection

Note: *Tripping of the TOC can be for any number of reasons, ie use in unsuitable conditions, continual use over a long period of time, jamming, etc. When tripping occurs, unplug the equipment and take a little time to assess the cause of the problem. The motor could overheat if the equipment is used over a long period of time in unsuitable conditions. If the motor does overheat, allow a short time for cooling before resetting the button. If jamming is the cause, investigate and remove any debris, then check to see if any damage has been caused to any parts. REMEMBER this must only be done when the equipment is fully isolated*

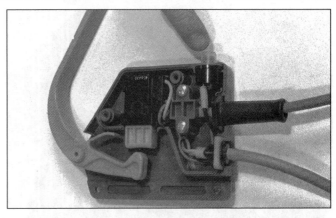

Common Problems

Electrical problems on this range of equipment relate closely to those already covered in previous sections, eg poor commutation, brush wear, motor bearing wear, flex faults, etc., therefore references to other sections will be made to avoid undue repetition in this Chapter. The most relevant sections will *be A General Safety Guide, Basics, Cables and Cable Faults, Electric Motors* and *Electrical Circuit Testing*. A thorough understanding of all sections will help in tracing many faults, as individual and specific faults cannot all be covered due to the vast range of tools available. The following photo sequences are used to highlight various problems that might be encountered.

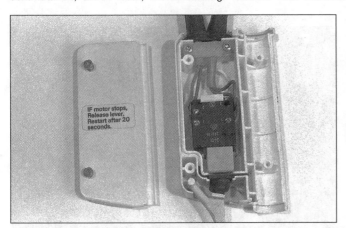

Switches and cable faults are the most common. It can be seen from these two photos of typical mowers that checking and renewal is similar to other equipment such as vacuum cleaners. It is essential that all parts are refitted correctly and any suspect parts renewed before further use

HOVER MOWER REPAIR

1 This hover mower had little or no maintenance. Although it worked, it produced poor results and was very noisy. The air intake vents were badly blocked by grass cuttings. In addition to repair, thorough cleaning of the whole machine was needed

2 By removing four screws from the corners, the top cover can be taken off. This exposed an inner cover that was a push fit only

3 With the cover removed, clear access is gained to the motor. This also requires a thorough cleaning. Note the strong similarity between this motor and the cylinder motor shown in the vacuum section. Note also the poor state the wiring was in due to poor positioning from a repair after a previous fault. This was corrected prior to tracing the original fault

4 The exposed motor was carefully but thoroughly cleaned and inspected for faults and loose connections caused by vibration

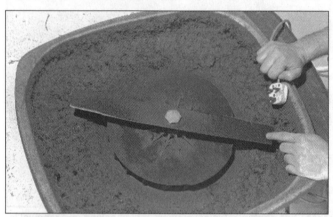

5 With the mower upturned, the cause of the vibration was found. The cutting blade was badly damaged (due to careless use)

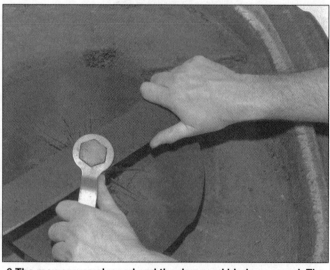

6 The mower was cleaned and the damaged blade removed. The motor bearings were checked for excessive movement Luckily, all was OK

7 A new type of safety blade was fitted. Note: *Out of balance blades create vibration so it is advisable to check all electrical connections as they may have been loosened by the vibration*

Re-assembly was a reversal of the stripdown procedure

In accordance with normal practice, a double check of all parts was made prior to refitting the casing, ensuring correct positioning of all parts and wiring prior to functional testing on an RCD-protected circuit. If in doubt as to the electrical safety of the product have the appliance PAT tested by a competent person refer to Chapter 2

The hover action is a reversal of the vacuum cleaner system. It is the expelled air that is used to create lift. Blocking of the airflow reduces lift, which in turn results in more effort being needed to manoeuvre the mower due to drag. The reduced airflow will also cause the motor to overheat. As with the cylinder vacuum cleaner motor, internal faults usually require a complete motor. A little care and attention however can help reduce motor failure

CYLINDER MOWER TYPICAL FAULT

This mower regularly tripped the overload TOC even on short periods of use. A thorough stripdown was carried out to identify the cause

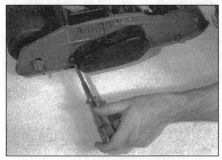

1 With the equipment isolated as usual, the screw securing the plastic belt cover was removed

2 With cover removed, the belt could be eased off the pulley

3 To remove the large drive pulley the cylinder was jammed and the pulley turned to unscrew it from the shaft. Note: *Do not hold the cutting cylinder with hands. The rear/drive pulley securing bolt was removed using a socket and ratchet. The pulley was then pulled from the shaft*

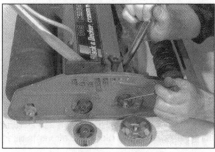

4 With both pulleys removed, the cylinder bearing securing clip could be eased out of position by lifting the spring-steel points with a small screwdriver

5 Removal of the clip allowed the bearing spacer and spring washer to be removed. The position of each item was noted and laid out in order to ensure correct refitting. In this instance a new bearing was required due to wear

6 All the screws securing the side panel were removed and a note made of their correct positions as well as laying them out tidily

7 Slackening the cutting plate adjustment nut allowed the motor and end frame to be removed. Care was taken to make a note of items before removal, especially the spring washer to the base of the adjusting rod, and the filter/grille cover

8 Once removed, two problem areas became apparent. Motor air filters were blocked and a solid build-up of grass had formed on the cylinder shaft to the rear of the bearing. This acted as a brake and combined with poor cooling of the motor, resulted in overload

A thorough cleaning of all internal parts of the motor compartment was carried out. Reassembly was a direct reversal of the stripdown procedure taking care that all parts were refitted into their original positions. A similar but more simple stripdown was carried out on the other side where a further build up of debris was found. As stated earlier, new cylinder bearings were required

Re-assembly was a reversal of the stripdown procedure

In accordance with normal practice, a double check of all parts was made prior to refitting the casing, ensuring correct positioning of all parts and wiring prior to functional testing on an RCD-protected circuit. If in doubt as to the electrical safety of the product have the appliance PAT tested by a competent person refer to Chapter 2

Spool type strimmers

Bladeless strimmers are an extremely popular power tool with professional, amateur and reluctant gardeners alike. The electrically powered versions (as opposed to petrol driven) are produced in a wide range of mains and battery powered models. The power for cutting is supplied by a series wound brush motor and is therefore prone to the problems described earlier in this Chapter.

Reference should also be made to other relevant sections of the book especially Chapters 7, 8, 9 and 11. Cutting is achieved by rotating a short length of nylon filament at high speed. The filament is housed in a spool that is fixed directly to the motor shaft without gearing to take advantage of the series wound brush motor's high speed rotation. When used correctly this is a very effective means of cutting around trees, areas of grass and light vegetation.

To avoid problems and for the strimmer to work effectively, only the end of the filament should be used. If not, the cutting action will not be effective and there is an increased chance of small items such as stones being propelled at high speed from the head of the tool by the filament (always wear eye protection when using a strimmer, goggles not just prescription spectacles). Incorrect use will also result in excessive filament wear and the need to renew the length of cutting filament more often. However, even when used correctly the filament will need to be extended as normal wear and tear occurs. There are four ways in which the cutting filament can be extended.

1 On early versions a nut at the centre of the spool holder was slackened and a length of filament pulled out and trimmed to length by a small cutting blade on the edge of the protective disc.

2 A bump feed system that released a length of filament each time the spring loaded end cap of the spool holder was pushed against a hard surface.

3 A trigger/button system that advances a length of filament each time the trigger/button is pressed.

4 An automatic system that advances the correct amount of filament required by means of a centrifugal sensing mechanism. Most problems are caused by operator error and misuse and are therefore avoidable. Ensure the strimmer is cleaned after each use as dust and plant debris can block the air vents used to cool the motor. Always wear eye and hand protection when using this type of appliance, wear goggles not just prescription spectacles and keep onlookers and pets at a safe distance (at least 15m).

Do not use a mains powered strimmer in damp or wet conditions.

Fixed line strimmers

Fixed line strimmers are similar in both appearance and drive systems to the spool type strimmers described previously. However a semi rigid length of plastic is used in place of the spool containing a coil of cutting line. There are various versions of this type of system on the market and most are designed only to accept the manufacturers own shape/size of cutting line. **Note:** *This type of system can also be found within some garden vacuums to finely cut and shred the debris to further increase waste bag capacity. Do not attempt to fit non-standard cutting lines to these appliances.*

For general service, repairs and safety refer to the previous section Spool type strimmers.

STRIMMER TYPICAL FAULT

1 The fault with this strimmer was purely mechanical. The spool holder that houses the nylon line had shattered

2 A new part was obtained prior to stripdown

3 With the equipment isolated, removing the nut and nylon spool allowed the outer spool holder to be unscrewed from the armature shaft (LH thread in this instance)

4 The spool holder in this case was easily unscrewed from the shaft. This may not always happen, as often the holder will simply turn the armature shaft. Further stripdown would be needed so that the armature could be held and the holder unscrewed. Further checks were made on the motor. Removing ten screws allowed a complete stripdown

5 Debris was found within the motor casing, especially around the motor brushes and field coil. This could have led to problems of poor commutation or overheating. All parts are carefully but thoroughly cleaned

6 The motor brushes were checked for wear and freedom of movement. Each brush was marked to ensure correct position and orientation when refitted. The existing brushes were refitted after cleaning of brushes and holders

7 Checks on both bearings proved OK. The bottom bearing is a sealed ball race type and the top is a sleeve bearing. Though the ball race could not be lubricated, a little light oiling to the top sleeve bearing was applied. DO NOT use an excessive amount, and remove any surplus to avoid the build up of debris or brush contamination

Re-assembly was a reversal of the stripdown procedure

In accordance with normal practice, a double check of all parts was made prior to refitting the casing, ensuring correct positioning of all parts and wiring prior to functional testing on an RCD-protected circuit. If in doubt as to the electrical safety of the product have the appliance PAT tested by a competent person refer to Chapter 2

MODERN DUAL LINE STRIMMER AND LAWN EDGER

This strimmer combines both strimming and lawn edging in one appliance. The curved design and roller allows the unit to be used vertically for strimming or rotated for lawn edging. A double action trigger system on the handle allows switching in both positions. In addition to these features the unit also has dual line cutting with an automatic line feed spool. The following stripdown sequence has been included to highlight the similarities between the early and late versions of this type of product

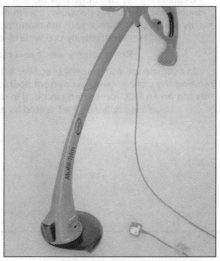

1 Ensure the appliance is isolated

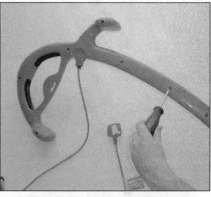

2 The handle on this model is firmly clipped together when first assembled. In order for the stipdown to proceed the two handle sections need to be separated. Slackening or removing the top two screws nearest the joint

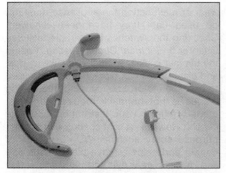

3 With the two screws removed or slackened the two sections can be eased apart

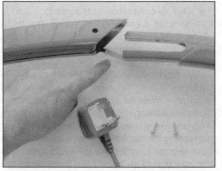

4 Within the handle joint the motor supply cable has a protective sleeve which is an essential part of the electrical safety of this class 2 double insulated product. Ensure that it is in good order and that it is refitted correctly

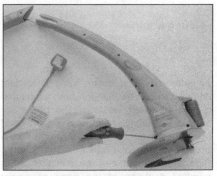

5 Remove the remaining screws from the lower section of the handle

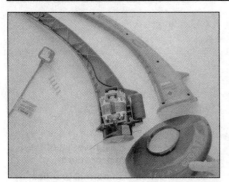

6 Removing the casing screws allows the guard cover to be easily removed and the lower casing to be split. Note: *The guard cover has a twist and lock type fitting and can be refitted after the two casings are screwed back together. To do this, line up the two arrows, one on the guard and the other on the casing and twist the guard to lock it into position*

7 After marking and removing the supply wires the motor and spool assembly simply lifts out of position. The top end of the armature has a slot to assist spool support removal

8 To remove the spool insert a large flat bladed screwdriver in the slot in the top end of the armature and turn the spool housing anticlockwise as it has a normal right-hand thread fitting. Note the spacer washer seen here at the centre of the shaft. Ensure that it is refitted correctly.

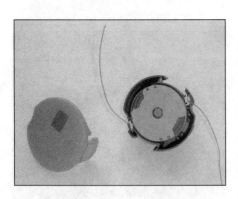

9 Depressing the two large lugs on either side of the spool cover allows access to the double line spool. It is possible to wind new line onto the spool but this must be done neatly and in accordance with the manufacturers instructions to avoid problems such as snagging. Alternatively pre-wound spools can be obtained and easily fitted

Re-assembly was a reversal of the stripdown procedure

In accordance with normal practice, a double check of all parts was made prior to refitting the casing, ensuring correct positioning of all parts and wiring prior to functional testing on an RCD-protected circuit. If in doubt as to the electrical safety of the product have the appliance PAT tested by a competent person refer to Chapter 2

Hedge trimmer

An extremely useful labour saving device that once again can be found in both mains and battery powered versions. The power for cutting is again supplied by a series wound brush motor and is therefore prone to the problems described earlier in this chapter. Reference should also be made to other relevant sections of the book especially Chapters 7, 8, 9 and 11.

Cutting is achieved by turning the high-speed rotation of the motor into a reciprocating action by means of a gearbox. There are two cutting blades – one fixed and the other is connected to the gearbox and is free to slide back and forth over the fixed blade. This results in a very effective cutting action. There are many shapes and sizes of blade but each work on the same principle. Both physical and electrical safety is paramount with this type of equipment and great care must be taken to avoid cable and personal damage. Modern hedge trimmers incorporate a two-handed safety feature preventing the appliance from working unless both support handles are being gripped. This ensures that both hands are away from the cutting area at all times.

The system works by having two switches, one in each handle and both must be closed for the motor to run. It is essential that both of these switches are in good order and are working correctly. If they show any signs of wear or malfunction the appliance must not be used until they have been renewed. Checking the switches is a simple task see Chapter 5 *Electrical Circuit Testing*. Ensure the trimmer is cleaned after each use as dust and plant debris can block the air vents used to cool the motor. Lubrication of the cutting blades is not normally required for most models (check your instruction book for details). However, a light coating with a multi-purpose spray such as WD-40 will be of benefit and helps remove plant debris and sap. Always wear eye and hand protection when using this type of appliance, wear goggles not just prescription spectacles and keep onlookers and pets at a safe distance (at least 15m – 50ft).

Do not use a mains powered hedge trimmer on a damp or wet hedge.

HEDGE TRIMMER

This hedge trimmer was being used when it stopped without warning. Thinking that it may simply be due to overheating during use the appliance was left unplugged to cool down. Unfortunately overheating was not the problem. Next the fuse was checked for continuity and once again this proved not to be at fault. The following sequence details what happened next

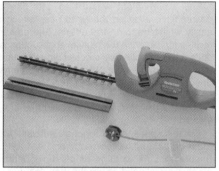

1 Ensure the appliance is isolated

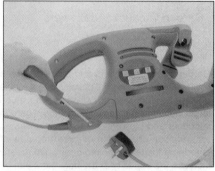

2 Removing this single screw will allow the cable access cover to be removed

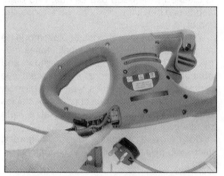

3 With the cover removed the mains lead terminal block connector is visible

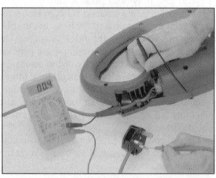

4 The neutral connection from the mains plug to the on/off switch was checked for continuity and found to be OK (low resistance therefore continuity)

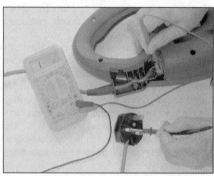

5 The test in step 4 was repeated this time on the live cable connection. This should also have given the same reading but in this instance no reading was obtained on any of the Ohms ranges. The fuse in the plug had been checked for continuity prior to beginning the repair therefore this open circuit indicated that the fault lay somewhere along the length of the live supply of the mains cable. The correct type and length of mains lead would be required to correct this fault

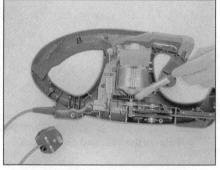

6 Removing the casing securing screws allowed access to the main compartment for cleaning

7 This is the double action switch safety system. It requires both the handle trigger and the front grip lever to be pressed simultaneously for the metal rod to operate the main on/off switch below

8 Lifting this card cover allows examination of the commutator and motor brushes. In this instance both are in good condition. Note: *It is essential that covers such as that shown here are refitted in exactly the same position as they form part of the overall electrical safety of an appliance*

Re-assembly was a reversal of the stripdown procedure

In accordance with normal practice, a double check of all parts was made prior to refitting the casing, ensuring correct positioning of all parts and wiring prior to functional testing on an RCD-protected circuit. If in doubt as to the electrical safety of the product have the appliance PAT tested by a competent person refer to Chapter 2

Garden Vacuum and Blowers

Garden vacuum cleaners and blowers are the larger and more powerful cousins of the mains powered indoor vacuum cleaner. With much larger suction tubes and special tools garden vacuums and blowers are specially designed for outdoor use and most are capable of shredding the leaf litter into a mulch to greatly increase the capacity of the bag. Most can be used as either vacuums or blowers. The blower feature can be used instead of raking debris from border edges, paths and patios. Converting the appliance to blow use differs from model to model, refer to your instruction book for specific details.

The vacuum pick up system is similar to the dirty fan vacuum cleaner shown in Chapter 30. However, in this instance the fan and fan chamber are relatively damage resistant when used to pick up light garden waste such as leaves and small branches. The suction fan is especially damage resistant and is also designed to shred items in the air flow before propelling the residue on into the waste bag.

The woven cloth waste bag acts like a coarse filter, allowing the air to pass through easily whilst trapping the debris. The power required to produce the high level of suction is once again supplied by a series wound brush motor and is therefore prone to the problems described earlier in this chapter. Reference should also be made to other relevant sections of the book especially Chapters 7, 8, 9 and 11.

For the appliance to function efficiently it must be assembled correctly and securely. Ensure that fixing clips or plastic locating notches are aligned as per the manufacturer's instruction booklet. Failure to observe these basic requirements can result in ineffective pickup and may also pose a safety hazard. Most problems are caused by operator error and misuse and are therefore avoidable. Some models have interlock switches to prevent the motor from running if the pick up tubes are not fitted correctly. If the appliance fails to run at all check the pick up tube fitting. If fitted correctly refer to the fault finding sequence in the DIY power tools chapter and Chapter 5 *Electrical Circuit Testing* to check the switch(es).

Other common problems relate to fan damage and blockages. If the motor runs but pick up is poor, the most likely cause is a blockage. The appliance must be fully isolated before you investigate the problem. Check both the inlet tubes and outlet to the bag and clear any blockages preferably with a stick. If the inlet and outlet tubes are clear the problem may be in the fan chamber and this may require a careful stripdown of the unit, see photo sequence. Abnormal vibration of the unit during use signifies possible fan damage and you must stop using the unit immediately. Continuing to use an appliance with a damaged fan (or blockage) can be dangerous and lead to further damage to the motor. To maintain peak performance, empty the waste bag regularly. Ensure the appliance is cleaned after each use as dust and plant debris can block the air vents used to cool the motor.

When using the appliance in blow mode be aware that objects such as small stones may be thrown at speed by the airflow and constitute a safety hazard. Always wear eye protection when using this type of appliance, wear goggles not just prescription spectacles and keep onlookers and pets at a safe distance (at least 15m-50ft).

Do not use a mains powered garden vacuum/blower in damp or wet conditions.

This garden vacuum/blower had been used for a full season and during its last use several large stones had been accidentally picked up. Although it appeared that no damage had occurred it was thought wise to check the fan and chamber prior to storage. The following photo sequence gives details of the stripdown and inspection of the appliance. Although the fan and chamber was found to be OK a blockage and a potential electrical problem were found and corrected

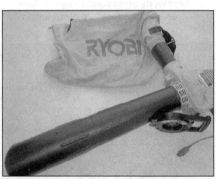

1 Ensure the appliance is isolated

2 Remove the inlet and outlet tubes

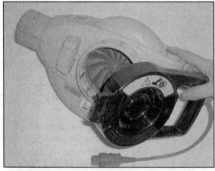

3 When the inlet tube is removed or the unit is to be used for blowing this spring-loaded safety plate snaps into position to prevent access to the vacuum fan and shredder chamber

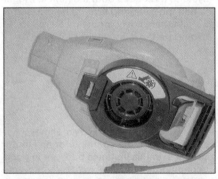

4 Ensure guards like this are in perfect working order

5 Remove the casing securing screws. In this instance they were a TORX and slotted drive combination

6 Removing nine securing screws then allowed the casing to be split exposing the internal components

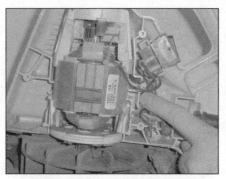

7 Although this product had never previously been stripped down this wire was not in its correct position and had been trapped between the two mouldings. This had caused damage to the outer insulation. This was repaired and the wire correctly fitted into the recess provided. This is an unusual fault and had obviously occurred during manufacture yet proves that nothing should be taken for granted. Ensure that all components and wiring are fitted correctly prior to assembly

8 Housed within a moulding recess is this small suppression unit

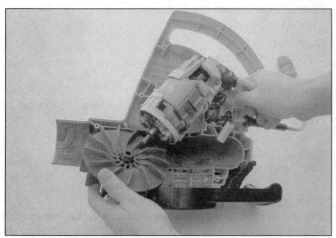

9 The double sided fan and shredder simply screws onto the motor shaft. To remove the fan, grip the exposed top end of the armature with pliers or suitable grips and turn the fan. In this instance the fan and shaft are left-hand threaded and therefore the fan needed to be turned clockwise to remove it. Note the spacing washer at the centre of the shaft, this goes between the fan and the motor end frame. Ensure it is in place when you fit a new fan or refit the old one. Check the fan closely for damaged blades or cracks renew if damaged

10 The opposing housing had quite a build-up of debris at the top end of the fan chamber outlet. This was removed and the appliance was cleaned prior to re-assembly

Re-assembly was a reversal of the stripdown procedure

In accordance with normal practice, a double check of all parts was made prior to refitting casing, ensuring correct positioning of all parts and wiring prior to functional testing on an RCD-protected circuit. If in doubt as to the electrical safety of the product have the appliance PAT tested by a competent person refer to Chapter 2

Glossary

Amp
Short for ampere. Electrical unit used to measure the flow of electricity through a circuit or appliance.

Armature
Wire-wound centre of brush motor.

Bi-metal
Two different metals which have been laminated together. When heated the strip bends in a known direction.

Boss
Protection around entry point.

Burn-out
Overheated part or item.

Cable
Conductors covered with a protective semi-rigid insulating sheath, used to wire up the individual circuits on a wiring system.

Centrifugal
Force that increases with rotation causing movement away from its centre.

Circuit
Any complete path for an electric current, allowing it to pass along a 'live' conductor to where it is needed and then to return to its source along a 'neutral' conductor.

Closed circuit
A normal circuit that allows power to pass through.

Coaxial
Cable specifically for the transmission of RF (radio frequency).

Commutator
Copper segment on motor armature.

Conductor
The metallic current-carrying 'cores' within cable or flex.

Consumer Unit
Unit governing the supply of electricity to all circuits and containing a main on/off switch and fuses or circuit breakers protecting the circuits emanating from it.

Contact
Point at which switch makes contact.

Continuity
Electrical path with no break.

Component
Individual parts of the machine, ie heater, relay, motor are all components.

Early
Machine not currently on the market.

Earthing
The linking of exposed metal parts on earthed appliances to a known external earth point for safety. Earth conductors sheathed in green/yellow striped PVC; earth terminals are marked E.

Energize
(Energise)
To supply power to.

Energized
(Energised)
Having power supplied to.

ELCB
Earth leakage circuit breaker – see RCCB.

Flowchart
Method of following complicated steps in a logical fashion.

Functional test
To test machine for normal operation.

Fuse
Failsafe device to sever supply voltage if fault occurs. See also MCB.

Governor
Device to regulate speed.

Harness
Electrical wiring within a machine.

Hertz
Periodic cycle of one second, ie cycles per second.

'Hunting'
Oscillating.

Insulation
Material used to insulate a device or a region.

Isolate
To disconnect from the electricity supply and water supply, etc.

Kick-back
Adverse reaction of equipment to jamming or misuse.

Laminations
Joined metal parts of stator.

Late
Current machine on market.

Leap-frog
Logical approach to electrical fault finding (see Chapter 5).

Live
Supply current carrying conductor.

Make
1. Manufacturer's name.
2. When a switch makes contact it is said to 'make'.

Miniature Circuit Breaker – (MCB)
A device used instead of fuses to isolate a circuit if fault/overload occurs.

Neutral
Return current carrying conductor.

Open-circuit
Circuit that is broken, ie will not let any power through.

Oxidization
Chemical reaction with oxygen to form oxide.

Pyrometer
Test instrument used to calibrate iron thermostats.

RCCB
Residual current circuit breaker (also known as RCD, residual current device).

Reciprocating
Mechanical action of backwards and forwards movement.

Rotor
Central part of an induction motor.

Schematic diagram
Theoretical diagram.

Seal
Piece of pre-shaped rubber that usually fits into a purpose built groove, therefore creating a watertight seal.

Sealant
Rubber substance used for ensuring watertight joints.

Shell
Outer of machine.

Spades
Connection on wires or components.

Stat
Thermostat.

Stator
Electrical winding on induction motor.

Stroboscopic
System used to synchronise speed.

Swarf
Material removed during machining or thread cutting.

Terminal block
A method of connecting wires together safely.

TOC
Thermal overload cutout. At a pre-set temperature, the TOC will break electrical circuit to whatever it is attached, ie prevents motors, etc. overheating.

Thyristor
Electronic switching device.

Triac
Electronic switching device.

Volt
Unit of electrical pressure (potential) difference. In most British homes the mains voltage is 240V.

Watt
Unit of power consumed by an appliance or circuit, the product of the mains voltage and the current drawn (in amps). 1000W = 1 kilowatt (kW).

Acknowledgements

I would like to offer my thanks to the companies and individuals listed below for their invaluable help given when compiling the various sections of this book:

Airflo Industries plc (Chapter 30)

Backer Electrical Co. Ltd
(Chapters 13, 18 & 22)

Crabtree Electrical Industries Ltd
(Chapters 2, 9 & 33)

Diamond H Controls Ltd
(Chapter 19)

Ebac Limited (Chapter 17)

Ever Ready Ltd (Chapter 31)

Labgear Cablevision Ltd
(Chapter 29)

M.K. Electric Ltd (Chapter 9)

Oracstar Ltd (Chapter 19)

Path Group plc (Chapter 29)

Wash-Vac Services (King & Robertson Ltd)
(Chapter 30)

David Shimmin for loan of some appliances featured in various sections. Andrew Morland for much of the photographic work. Martin Coltman and Paul Tanswell for the illustrations and diagrams.

Thanks also to Miles Hardware Limited of Yeovil, Somerset and Jerry's Electrical of Wincanton, Somerset for the loan of appliances used in the cover shots.